KUNH8

The Artistry of the English Watch

'The weight of these valuables exceeded three hundred and fifty pounds avoirdupois; and in this estimate I have not included one hundred and ninety-seven superb gold watches; three of the number being worth each five hundred dollars, if one. Many of them were very old, and as time-keepers valueless; the works having suffered, more or less, from corrosion — but all were richly jewelled and in cases of great worth'.

The Gold Bug
Edgar Allan Poe
(1843)

THE  Artistry OF THE ENGLISH WATCH

Cedric Jagger

DAVID & CHARLES
Newton Abbot   London

CHARLES E. TUTTLE COMPANY: PUBLISHERS
Rutland,   Vermont

ILLUSTRATION CREDITS

The Royal Collection: Plates 28 and 29 are reproduced by gracious permission of Her Majesty The Queen.

The British Museum: Plates 15, 18, 19, 21, 22, 25, 34 (part), 38, 53 (part), 56, 58, 60 (part), 69.
   Colour plates 3, 4, 9, 13, 14, 15.

The Victoria & Albert Museum: Plates 10, 11, 12, 27 (part).

The National Maritime Museum: Plates 3, 13 (part).

The Museum of London: Plate 4.

The Ashmolean Museum, Oxford: Plate 2.

The Museum of the History of Science, Oxford: Plates 23, 24, 64, 82, 86.

The Clockmakers' Company Collection: Plates 1, 13 (part), 26, 27 (part), 30, 31, 32, 33, 34 (part), 35 (part), 37 (part), 39, 40 (part), 49 (part), 52, 54 (part), 57, 60 (part), 61 (part), 68 (part), 70 (part), 71, 72, 73, 77, 78, 79 (part), 81.
   Colour plates 1 (part), 2 (part), 5, 6, 8.

Sotheby's: Plates 16, 35 (part), 37 (part), 40 (part), 41, 46 (part), 47, 48, 59, 61 (part), 63, 65, 66, 67, 83 (part).
   Colour plates 10 (part), 11 (part), 12 (part).

Christie's: Plates 17, 55, 74.
   Colour plates 10 (part), 11 (part).

Phillips: Plate 42.
   Colour Plate 10 (part).

Asprey's: Plate 76.
   Colour Plate 16.

The Antique Connoisseur: Plate 85 (part).

East Anglian Daily Times: Plate 85 (part).

J.-C. Sabrier: Colour Plate 12 (part).

Objects in private ownership are not individually credited.

British Library Cataloguing in Publication Data

Jagger, Cedric
   The artistry of the English watch.
   1.   Clock and watch making —— England
   —— History
   2.   Decoration and ornament —— England
   —— History
   I.   Title
   681.1'14   TS543.97

   ISBN 0-7153-8935-1

First published in Great Britain by David & Charles, 1988
First published in United States by Charles E. Tuttle Co Inc, 1988

Typeset by ABM Typographics Limited, Hull
Printed in Great Britain
by Butler & Tanner Limited, Frome and London
for David & Charles Publishers plc
Brunel House   Newton Abbot   Devon
Colour origination by Columbia Offset (UK) Ltd

ISBN 0-8048-7022-5 (United States)
Library of Congress Catalog Card No. 87-51206

Published by the Charles E. Tuttle Co Inc
of Rutland, Vermont & Tokyo, Japan
with editorial offices at
Suido 1-chome, 2-6, Bunkyo-ku, Tokyo, Japan

Preface and Acknowledgements

Forty years ago, a book such as this would have been regarded as a heresy. The writers of the seminal works on antiquarian horology — great pioneers like the Brittens and G. H. Baillie, who were active mainly in the years between 1890 and 1950 — believed passionately in looking at the subject as a total package, that is to say, considering history, decoration and mechanism together and in relation to one another. Starting from a basis of what had been known about old clocks and watches during the nineteenth century — some of that being either fundamentally wrong or based on speculative or unsubstantiated hearsay — it was natural that they should wish to grasp the nettle firmly, and in so doing set proper foundations for what was virtually a new field of study.

They could not possibly have foreseen how popular it was to become in the decades that followed. Advances in knowledge since World War II, together with the formation of learned bodies like the Antiquarian Horological Society in Britain, and comparable organisations in a number of other countries, not to mention the international perspectives adopted by such 'household name' collectors as the late Courtenay Ilbert, have opened up the entire subject in a way that, even within living memory, would have seemed quite incredible. Traditionally, the British have excelled at the mechanics of time measurement, so that there used always to be a bias in that direction; but now other aspects of the subject are being re-examined to see what extra knowledge they can contribute to the sum total already set down. Hence, what might once have been regarded as wholly peripheral, even if not trivial — the place of the English watch within the whole broad spectrum of the decorative arts — can now be regarded as legitimate and worthy of investigation.

It is always difficult to express adequately the thanks due to the many individuals and institutions who, in a variety of ways, contribute to a book of this kind. If, by some mischance, anybody has been omitted, let me express my unreserved apologies.

First, then, I should like to thank Her Majesty The Queen for graciously permitting me to reproduce two fine seventeenth-century watches from the Royal Collection.

Next, I offer formal acknowledgements and thanks to the following learned bodies and institutions for permission to reproduce objects from their respective collections:

The Trustees of the British Museum, the Victoria & Albert Museum and the National Maritime Museum
The Museum of London
The Museum of the History of Science, Oxford
The Ashmolean Museum, Oxford
The Worshipful Company of Clockmakers of the City of London

I have greatly benefited from the encouragement, advice and practical help of a handful of my museum contemporaries, to whom I would like to pay special tribute. At the British Museum, my young friend David Thompson far exceeded the call of duty in not only scouring that institution's enormous collection of watches for certain categories in which I was particularly interested, but also then helped me in the choice of those to be illustrated and, finally, directed the photography to my entire satisfaction. Meanwhile, my old friend Hugh Tait, whose enormous experience and encyclopedic knowledge of so many classes of artifacts are legendary, applied himself to the subject of English porcelain watch-cases, with fascinating results that will be found elsewhere in these pages. At the Victoria & Albert Museum, Dr Richard Edgcumbe is generally recognised to have the most up-to-date specialised knowledge of gold chasing, embodying embossed or *repoussé* work, to be found in this country; he answered all my questions most generously, and was unstinting in putting his considerable knowledge at my disposal. Finally, Beresford Hutchinson, another old friend — this time at the National Maritime Museum — searched willingly for information on my behalf, as well as pointing out aspects of one important object that would otherwise not have occurred to me. It is good to have such friends.

I come now to the not inconsiderable number of individuals and institutions who have supplied me with information, loaned photographs — or taken them specially for me — and, in a whole variety of other ways, helped with the compilation of this work. I know that they will understand that space does not permit my detailing their individual contributions, but this in no way reduces my dependence upon and indebtedness to them. I freely acknowledge this, and ask them all to accept my best thanks.

Charles Allix (Malcolm Gardner), A. M. Baldwin, Revd J. D. Bickersteth, Geoffrey Crabtree, C. R. Croft, Dr H. Crott (Crott & Schmelzer), J. Duly (N. E. C. Redford), *East Anglian Daily Times,* Dr Norbert Enders, Jeremy Evans (British Museum), Richard Garnier (Christie's), A. B. Grant (*The Antique Connoisseur*), Christopher Greenwood (Phillips, Son & Neale), Mrs Julia Harland (Lord Chamberlain's Office), John Heller, Rodney Law, Brian Loomes, Tina Millar (Sotheby's), Godfrey New Photographics, Louis J. Pigott, Jean-Claude Sabrier, M. P. Sampson (Asprey's), G. C. Spencer.

When all is said and done, however, my greatest debt has to be to my wife, Chris, with whom it is always such fun to work, and upon whom I rely so greatly to ensure that the end-product is both intelligible and inviting by the time it eventually reaches the publisher. It would make my task immensely more difficult were it not for her skills and versatility, freely applied at every stage, so that any tribute I can pay seems inadequate; suffice it, then, for me simply to say a heartfelt 'thank you'.

Contents

To Chris,
With My Love

1 Background To A Beginning

PLATE 1: In the centre, the canister-shaped timekeeper from which watches are said to have evolved; German, second quarter of the sixteenth century. Flanking this object, German watches from the last quarter of that century.

The word 'artistry', in its dictionary definition, means 'artistic workmanship, quality'; and this book is essentially concerned with the *appearance* of the English watch over the centuries, and hardly at all with its mechanism, save for those instances where the one influences the other. In the majority of cases, the appearance of the watch relies, to a greater or lesser extent, upon some manifestation of the decorative arts; and the range and quality of their application will be particularly germane in the pages that follow.

The indigenous English watchmaker seems to have emerged in the decade or so immediately before 1600, and for the first twenty-five years was a very scarce artisan indeed. The imported watch — brought from elsewhere in continental Europe — had been well-known to the monied few in Britain for a considerable time, however, so that when it eventually reached the stage of native manufacture, it was already quite highly developed. It may be relevant just to outline the sequence of events that preceded its appearance, including those crucial mechanical developments without which it could not have been entertained at all.

As can be easily envisaged, the watch had to result from the gradual miniaturisation of the medieval mechanical clock — that great iron machine which, so it seems, had its origins in the need to regulate the offices and disciplines of the monastic regime. Yet there were certain essential technological advances inherent in this miniaturisation, as well as in procuring that special characteristic of the watch, portability. The most important was the discovery of an efficient new source of power: you cannot carry a mechanism that is driven by a weight acting under the force of gravity.

This new power source eventually emerged as the thin ribbon of spring steel which, when coiled upon itself provides, in its efforts to straighten itself out again, enough energy to drive the watch movement. Whether indeed those earliest springs were of steel must be open to some doubt, since it would have been very difficult, at the time, to make such a spring that did not tend constantly to break under tension. It seems more likely that they were fashioned from beaten brass, but none has survived to tell the tale, so far as is known.

The earliest reference to this invention yet discovered is contained in a letter of 1482 from an Italian engineer called Comino da Pontevico, who writes of 'a ribbon of tempered steel fastened in a brass barrel around which is wound a gut line . . . [that] has to pull the fusee'. This extract, in fact, encapsulates two separate inventions, one of which — the fusee — ought logically to have followed from the invention of the mainspring, rather than simultaneously with it. The fusee is an elegant and surprisingly sophisticated solution to a problem that is peculiar to springs, and could not have been encountered previously, when the conventional power source was a falling weight. The latter, acting under the force of gravity, exerts a 'pull' upon the mechanism that is virtually constant, from the point of being fully wound up to fully run down; and this constant, rather than variable, motive power is an essential ingredient for accurate time measurement. The coiled spring, on the other hand, exerts most power when fully wound, the effect waning substantially as the spring runs out. The fusee — a variable pulley taking the form of a spirally grooved cone — simply ironed out this unevenness; but it seems unlikely that it could have been designed before a successful spring had been made and tried out, for not until then would the problem have been recognised for what it was. Hence, it is likely that the spring appeared some years before Comino da Pontevico wrote of it. In any event, a further reference, from 1493, makes it abundantly clear that, by that time anyway, the spring-driven timekeeper was a fact of life.

The Italians seem, on present knowledge, to have master-minded both of these fundamental innovations, but then they must have faded from the picture. Peter Henlein of Nürnberg (Nuremberg), who lived from 1480 to 1542, is credited with making timepieces which 'in any position and without any weights, both indicate and strike for 40 hours even when they are carried on the breast or in the purse'. This was written in 1511; and the earliest spring-driven clock with fusee that survives, which was made by Jacob the Czech for Sigismund I, King of Poland, is dated 1525. The only other record of an artisan active in this field at such an early date relates to one Caspar Werner, who was a contemporary of Henlein; but it is to the latter that most historians turn, and especially to his recorded capability to make 'the small watchworks which he was one of the first to make in the form of the musk-balls at that time in use'. Indeed, Nürnberg town records reveal a payment to him of fifteen florins for a gilt musk-apple with a watch, in 1524.

It is worth mentioning that the Germans also devised their own means of evening out the pull of the mainspring, calling the device a stackfreed. This involved a snail-like cam, around the edge of which ran a roller pivoted on the end of a strong curved spring, and so arranged that, when the mainspring was fully wound, the device provided a brake upon it. As this gradually ran down, it resulted in converting the braking effect into one of assistance. However, the degree of compensation afforded by the stackfreed was a very rough one by comparison with that of the fusee, and it lasted only a relatively short time, whereas the fusee has survived into the present century, and has been universally acknowledged. The stackfreed, incidentally, was never used outside Germany, so far as is known.

The other European country to contribute to the heritage of the watchmaker's craft, was France. The first recorded French watchmaker, Julien Coudray, worked in what was to become the first centre of French watchmaking, at Blois. He was paid 200 gold crowns, in 1518, for two fine daggers with 'horologes' in their hilts, for the king, Francis I. It is possible that these were only sun-dials, but by 1532 the estate of Florismond Robertet, who had been treasurer to three French kings, contained no fewer than twelve watches, which are described in some detail and about which there can be no mistake. Of the five other watchmakers recorded as working at Blois during the first half of the sixteenth century, two were designated 'horlogers du roi'.

One other component of the great medieval clock needed adaptation to fit it for use in a watch. The escapement — that part of a mechanical timekeeper which can be heard to tick — allows the power of the mainspring to 'escape' at a rate commensurate with the passage of time and, in most clocks, uses a swinging pendulum as its regulator. The first iron clocks pre-dated the application of this device, which did not occur until the seventeenth century. Instead they used a 'foliot', which was a bar swinging in a horizontal plane, its speed of rotation, first in one direction and then in the opposite, regulated by weights that were movable either side of the central pivot. As translated into watches, this became the 'dumb-bell' balance, a tiny bar shaped exactly as its name implies, the regulation now being achieved by judicious intervention of a hog's bristle. It was not long, however, before the advantages of a solid-rimmed wheel prevailed, superseding the dumb-bell.

So, the watch became a mechanical reality; but what did it look like? Two different design approaches have now to be pursued, one deriving from German influences, and one from the French, and both having a detectable effect upon the earliest native English practice.

The earliest German manifestation of the small port-able timekeeper took the form of a drum-shaped device — perhaps a small clock rather than yet a true watch, but undoubtedly a direct predecessor. This simply told the time, without any frills; and it seems to have appeared before 1550. After that time, almost all German watches had striking or alarm facilities, sometimes both, and it therefore became necessary to pierce the case around the edge and the bottom, to permit the sound of the bell to be heard. Such piercing, incorporated naturally into the decoration of the case, became a distinguishing feature of the German usage.

Another individual characteristic of German design was the employment of the twenty-four-hour dial. This took the form of an outer ring, running from I to XII, and an inner ring showing 13–24; the cover, not yet fitted with glass to permit the time to be read, had also to be pierced sufficiently to allow the position of the hand to be detected. The Gothic character of German script typically represented the figure '2' as 'z' and the dial-centre was likely to be decorated with an engraved star or rose; finally, it was customary to provide the dial with touch-pins, one located at each hour with a larger, distinguishing one, at twelve, to enable the time to be ascertained in the dark. In those days, even the provision of light was a major undertaking, and certainly more troublesome than the mere throwing of a switch.

Following upon the emergence of its small drum-shaped progenitor, the German watch started to develop in shape as well as detail: the earliest might seem to have derived directly from its forerunner, having simply been squashed in the process, although still retaining the flat top, bottom and sides, or 'band' as it is more properly called. By about 1575, this profile was becoming softened, with the covers becoming domed and the band curved, rather like the old-fashioned lady's powder compact, to which it has been compared. By around 1600, this last feature had become completely convex. While these progressions from the original drum-shaped timekeepers were taking place, however, another parallel development emerged: from 1575 onwards, watchcases of octagonal and elongated octagonal shape started to come into use, although not replacing the circular varieties. Throughout, of course, decoration has to take account of the piercing for functional reasons, which has already been mentioned. Oval cases for German watches were very uncommon before 1600.

The development of the early French watch is, sadly, by no means as clear cut as is that of its German counterpart. The earliest surviving example is spherical, dated 1551, and the work of Jacques de la Garde. It is now in the Louvre. Another watch by this maker, of the same form but dated 1552, is in the National Maritime

PLATE 2: Spherical watch, unsigned, but probably German, of mid-sixteenth-century date.

PLATE 3: Another spherical watch, signed Jacques de la Garde and dated 1552. More refined decoration bespeaks its French origin.

Museum, although there may be grounds for believing that this example originally formed part of an armillary sphere, and was never intended to be used on its own. Nevertheless, this maker, established at the famous watchmaking centre at Blois prior to 1551, was 'horloger du roi' 1578–80, and died before 1583. His son, Jean, was also a watchmaker of renown, working from 1578, and dying without issue in 1621. There is a watch by him in the British Museum. Naturally the survival of watches in this singular shape evokes thoughts of Peter Henlein, and it seems likely that the spherical watch in the Ashmolean Museum at Oxford is of German origin, if only because of its pierced arabesque decoration, as opposed to the mostly engraved ornament upon the French examples; yet the connection, if there is such, remains unclear.

With the exception of the two spherical watches by Jacques de la Garde, and perhaps another four or five isolated examples from subsequent decades, no French watches survive that pre-date 1590; furthermore, they are nearly all oval, and none resembles in the least the German styles that were then current. From 1590, how-

ever, the situation improves with the survival of a number of specimens, both round and oval, but with flat bands and only slightly domed covers that are engraved with scenery, figures and foliage patterns. There is also to be found at this time the elongated octagon case, but without the piercing that accompanies the German version. As a general rule, then, any surfaces that were pierced and chiselled in German watches, were engraved in their French equivalents.

When the scene was set for the English watch to make its debut, perhaps a little before the year 1600, there already existed at least two strong design influences deriving from elsewhere in Europe, which could not fail to have an effect upon it, more especially since so many of the early craftsmen working in England had their origins outside that country. In the ensuing chapters, an attempt will be made to see how these foreign influences affected the native product and, more particularly, how it set the seal of its own individuality upon such cosmopolitan foundations.

2 Sources of Inspiration

PLATE 4: A six-sided emerald hollowed to receive a watch. Probably part of an Elizabethan jeweller's stock-in-trade, this object comes from the Cheapside Hoard, recovered during excavations in 1912.

In the preceding brief résumé of the mechanical origins of the watch, no account has been taken of any decorative features it may have possessed, nor any mention made that all surviving examples of these very early timepieces are of gilt-metal. Yet it is clear both from royal inventories and other contemporary documentation, that exceptional skill and much expense was lavished upon such articles. One inventory of the jewellery and other precious objects belonging to Elizabeth I lists no fewer than twenty-four of them, a typical one being described as 'one clocke of golde wrought like deyses and paunses' which was 'garnished' with diamonds, rubies, emeralds and pearls, finishing with 'a pendant acorne'. A list of gifts proffered to the Queen in 1572 includes 'one armlett or shakell of golde, all over fairely garnishedd with rubyes and dyamondes, haveing in the closeing thereof a clocke'. Horological history has a knack of repeating itself, so that it is by no means beyond the realms of possibility that this was an early precursor of the wristwatch.

At that time, however, watches were customarily worn suspended from the waist-belt or around the neck, being often enclosed in a small bag or purse. While, in these locations, they must have received much more of a jolting than they would have done in a waistcoat pocket — and that would certainly not have improved their already erratic timekeeping — they would have been far more readily visible; so some kind of decoration would have been expected of them, being worn almost as if for personal adornment.

In purely practical terms, it is inconceivable — even in the reign of Elizabeth I — that any one craftsman could first have made a watch with all its mechanical complexities, and immediately followed this with the manufacture and lavish ornamentation of its case, created from precious metals and literally encrusted with gemstones. The most that could have been expected of him would have been the simplest case of base metal.

Such considerations beg a number of questions, which can be only partially answered in the light of existing knowledge. These include 'What sort of craftsman made watchcases?' and 'Where did he obtain the inspiration for his designs?' Not knowing the answers to such questions for certain only reinforces one's sense of loss, in that not a single example comparable with those so mouthwateringly described in contemporary documentation, appears to have survived, save for the tiny glimpse afforded by the watch shown in Plate 4.

So what do we know about the conditions of craftsmen in those far-off days? There is some evidence pointing to a properly structured division of labour to be found in the work of Hans Sachs. The excessively long German title of his book in 1568 may be abbreviated to read: *Descriptions of all the professions on earth . . . of all Arts, Crafts and Trades, from the highest to the lowest . . .* but it is probably better known for the 106 illustrations by Jost Amman. These include a famous depiction of a clockmaker's shop of the time, with what is unquestionably a mechanical clock in the foreground of the picture, even though the accompanying verse deals entirely with hourglasses.

In any event, as watch- and clockcases became ever more elaborate, and with the second half of the sixteenth century seeing the introduction of rock crystal and hard stones, as well as the more general use of precious metals accompanied by the emergence of engraving as a highly specialised technique, it can be reasonably supposed that guild rules would have specified that only certain craftsmen, such as goldsmiths, jewellers and lapidaries, could work upon them. Any such work with pretensions to real quality would have been contracted out by the watchmaker. It is also a reasonable supposition that engravers could have worked for a number of different watchmakers, thus accounting for the occurrence of watchcases, which appear to be by the same hand, containing movements signed by different horologists. This phenomenon did not finally disappear until the third quarter of the seventeenth century. What is even more curious, however, is that virtually identical engraved watch dials can, on occasion, be found on watches that not only have different makers but different nationalities, notably English and French. This means either that there was a trade between the two countries in such things, or that English and French engravers used the same pattern books as their design source.

That the second of these suppositions is correct must seem the more likely since, although there is a long and splendid tradition of the use of pattern books by the continental engraver, there is no similar tradition in Britain. Indeed, no surviving example of an English engraver's pattern book has been recorded before the closing years of the seventeenth century; yet engravers were not automatically also creative artists, and they needed help with the composition of their work. Being craftsmen, they disliked repetition, so that engravers of gun mounts are known to have kept rubbings of their designs as 'file copies' for future reference, in order that they could vary their output. Other types of engravers probably did exactly the same.

The progenitor of the engraver's pattern book — only very much earlier in time — may well have been the guides provided for the manuscript illuminator. Designs for the engraver, as such, first appeared towards the end of the fifteenth century and, initially, were just compositions of ornament unrelated to any particular objects; in other words, the engraver had then to modify and adapt them to his own special requirements. The first designs intended for specific articles appeared fifty years later, but watch- and clockcases were not included; nevertheless, these were also capable of adaptation.

Designs specifically aimed at the watch- and clockcase engraver did not emerge until around the middle of the sixteenth century. They arrived at a particularly interesting time in the history of ornament, too, when there were several conflicting design 'streams' competing for attention in what art historians describe as the mannerist style. The earliest decoration found on clock- and watchcases is variously called Mauresque or, more usually, arabesque, and is represented by the familiarly complex arrangements of scrolling and interlacing foliage, tendrils and suchlike, which covered the entire surface of an object and which seem to have had their origins in the Moorish culture. There was also, however, the exactly contemporary 'school' of ornament pioneered by Giovanni Battista Rosso at Fontainebleau in the 1530s. Called either 'strapwork' or 'rollwork', this is described as a deliberate distortion by Italian Renaissance artists, of classical sources of decoration; yet its equally complex designs of interwoven straps and thongs were enormously popular in Elizabethan England.

Finally, there was the 'stream' usually called 'grotesque'. Not unlike arabesque in its small, loosely connected motifs, it also included human figures, sphinxes, monkeys, and the like, all living elements hitherto unknown in such a context. A writer in 1612 described the grotesque style as 'an unnatural or unorderly composition, for delight's sake, of men, beasts, birds, fishes, flowers etc, without (as we say) Rime or Reason'. Yet this style of ornamentation, too, was based upon good classical foundations, deriving directly from that found on the walls of certain Roman buildings that had remained buried for centuries.

By the mid-sixteenth century, when engravers' pattern books first embraced the needs of the watch- and clockcase decorator, the Germans already held sway as the masters of the arabesque. Even so, not only German pattern books, but French ones also, were used all over Europe. Three artists stand out above all others as possessing the most fertile imaginations, when it came to creating such designs: these were Virgil Solis of Nürnberg, Balthasar Sylvius — who was a Flemish engraver, his surname being a Latin version of Bosch — and Peter Flötner, an influential German designer who worked in Nürnberg from 1522 onwards but who was probably trained in Augsburg. Virgil Solis is credited with the production of some six hundred ornamental and figurative prints from his workshop, an indication of the demand for such material at that time.

The type of ornament purveyed by artists such as these remained in vogue for some fifty years, so slowly did fashions change in those days. The only concession to change, in horological engraving, was the introduction of allegorical figures to meet the special perspective needs of vertical clockcases. Some of this work was of the very highest quality.

There were other designers at work apart from the Germans, however. The French artist Etienne Delaune was a most prolific producer of ornamental prints. Born at Orléans in 1518, he started his professional career as an engraver of medals, and it is said that he was helped by none other than Benvenuto Cellini. He spent much of his working life in Strasbourg, together with his son Jean; eventually he died there, but biographical sources disagree about the date, some favouring 1583 and others

PLATE 5: Designs by Etienne Delaune, capable of adaptation for decorating the backs of watchcases.

PLATE 6: Antoine de Jacquard was the first designer to produce compositions specifically for the horologist. Here he shows his ideas for dials, and engraved bands of watchcases.

1595, while yet another gives both! Delaune is said to have produced more than a thousand engravings, and although none of these was specifically directed to use on watchcases, his arrangements of minute figures and scrollwork set against a black ground were fashionable throughout western Europe until the middle of the seventeenth century. Casemakers, in the event, contributed something of their own to Delaune's compositions by substituting a ground of delicate foliage and flowers for his simple hatched surfaces.

Delaune's style was copied copiously by other engravers, the most important to the horologists of the day being a Dutchman, and another French artist. Abraham van der Hecken (otherwise Hecke or Heckius), working in Amsterdam, engraved a set of ornaments for goldsmiths and jewellers in 1634, but his work remains exceedingly rare. Antoine de Jacquard, of Poitiers, variously described as 'Arquebusier, Fourbisseur and Orfèvre' although, surprisingly, never as 'Horloger', was nevertheless the first engraver to produce designs specifically aimed at the watchmaker; and he also introduced the formalised foliage background. There exist a number of small vignettes incorporating figures and grotesque ornaments that are signed with the initials 'ADIF', and it is generally assumed that these stand for 'Antoine de Jacquard fecit'.

During this era, it seems probable that many truly creative craftsmen, such as those already described, not only designed for others but also engraved some work themselves, and this might well account for the splendid quality of so many early seventeenth-century watchcases. If this is indeed so, no means of identification, nor even of attribution, has yet been discovered.

Throughout both the sixteenth and seventeenth centuries, much more flamboyant decorative procedures were available than the simple engraving of pre-ordained designs on naked metal surfaces. There was, for instance, much use of enamelling upon gold, as well as the employment of rock crystal and hardstone. These must have been the work of jewellers and lapidaries, yet several engravers towards the end of the sixteenth century left designs for enamelled cases. Among these were Jacques Hurtu, a French artist working during the early years of the seventeenth century, and Jean Toutin. The latter worked at Châteaudun from 1618 to 1640, both as engraver and miniature painter in enamels. He is generally credited with the discovery of the art of enamel portraiture about 1630, while, during 1618 and 1619, he published two sets, each of seven engraved designs, for the use of goldsmiths. The design fashion set by artists such

COLOUR PLATE 1: Shagreen outer cases in black, green and white, all from the eighteenth century. One of the black examples has gilt *piqué* decoration, while the white version in the centre — this colour is hardly ever seen in the context of watchcases — is further enriched with silver mounts. The glazed version is a third, protective, case for use with high-relief *repoussé* outer cases.

COLOUR PLATE 2: Silver is relatively uncommon on watch movements. These examples date from the mid-seventeenth to the late-eighteenth centuries. The specimen at the top, signed 'Ellicott', has a glazed cock table centred with a garnet endstone in a silver setting; and only the slide plate is also in silver, the cock being conventionally of gilt-metal.

as these was for fine foliate patterns on a black enamel
ground which entirely covered the watchcase.

The trend towards strongly conventional floral ornament prevailing during the early years of the seventeenth
century was eventually to give way to a much more
naturalistic treatment, both in engraved and enamelled
work. The outstanding designer during this stage was
Jacques Vauquer. Born in Blois in 1621, he came of a
family of watchmakers, and it seems likely that, as well as
publishing patterns for ornamental purposes, he also
decorated watchcases himself. His work can be compared with his near-contemporary Antoine de Jacquard,
whose earlier designs had included arrangements of the
flower, fruit and foliage of the strawberry, while
Vauquer's more baroque compositions extended to the
rose, carnation and daisy. Vauquer made special provision, in his patterns, for the watch cock, and he was one
of the very few designers to do so. He is also known to
have engraved several plates of flowers and foliage from
his own designs, for a *Livre des Fleurs propres pour
orfèvres et graveurs.*

Vauquer died in 1686. One of his brothers, Robert,
was an enameller; other significant artists at this time
included Isaac Gribelin, and Henri and Jean Toutin of
Châteaudun. Jean Toutin, representing the Blois
'school', has already been mentioned. Henri Toutin, his
son, was born at Châteaudun in 1645, subsequently
moved to Blois and, by 1676, was working as an enameller in Paris.

No mention has yet been made of Johannes Heel, of
Nürnberg, a versatile artist active during the first half of
the seventeenth century. He was not only both enameller

and engraver, but also a designer of very baroque
creations for watchcases; and his small-scale works give
an impression of greater opulence while simulating a
higher relief, than do those of his precursors.

The next motif to fire the imagination of decorators
was the Dutch tulip; it appeared in all sorts of unlikely
guises, including that of the pillars separating the plates
that constitute the main frame of the watch movement
itself. It would be difficult to find a more intimate
example of art encroaching upon mechanics. In the more
conventional arena, despite the popularity of enamelled
work, patterns for engravers were still needed. It is surprising, therefore, that only one such book entitled *Livre
de Taille d'Espargne,* which was published by Michael
Wernle in Nürnberg in 1650, contains any hint of the
enormously complicated arrangements of tulips, fritil-
laries and daffodils that are so characteristic of Edward
East and his contemporaries. Although Wernle was an
orfèvre and, therefore, probably decorated watchcases
himself, there is no evidence whatsoever that his book
enjoyed any real circulation in Britain.

Several references have already been made to the
baroque elements detectable in the work of such as
Jacques Vauquer and Johannes Heel, but this
mainstream movement in decorative art, in practice,
came very late to England. Characterised by its insistence
upon the symmetrical arrangement of the design features, which resulted in every composition, whatever the
medium, appearing to be made up of elements that are all
most scrupulously balanced one against another, the
baroque style, like the mannerist, had its roots in Italy
where it was fully developed by about 1620, only event-

PLATE 8: Vauquer's designs for watch cocks.

ually reaching England by way of Holland and France. The time was not ripe for its emergence there until the Restoration of Charles II in 1660 who, in John Evelyn's words, 'brought in a politer way of living which passed to luxury and intolerable expense'. This must have been partly due to the influence of the Royalists, who had assimilated continental habits and attitudes while in exile; and indeed, the new fashion might well have been contained within Court circles, had it not been for the Great Fire of London in 1666. The only event of modern times in England to bear comparison with that total destruction of 10,000 houses with all their contents, was the *blitzkreig* on the same city during World War II; that also had repercussions upon the arts with which we are not concerned here.

Many of those dispossessed by the fire replaced their losses with furniture and other household articles in the latest style, starting a fashion that quickly spread from the capital into the provinces. The effects were remarkably wide-ranging, the main influence coming from Holland in the shape of floral marquetry, turned legs on furniture, chairs with caned seats, silver embossed with garlands of flowers, and many other outlets too numerous to list. French influence did not begin to make itself felt until the beginning of the William and Mary period, around 1688, when the influx of Huguenot craftsmen, who became refugees following the revocation of the Edict of Nantes in 1685, brought with them their own fashions and styles. These included the elaborate use of gilt gesso, and furniture features among which were side-tables with pillar legs, scrolled stretchers and pendant aprons, chairs with cabriole legs and elegantly carved splats, and other style-setting influences, such as the increased popularity of looking glasses. Inevitably, all these major upheavals in the decorative arts were bound to react upon even their smallest manifestations.

Reverting to watch decoration, some interesting developments started to occur towards the end of the seventeenth century, following upon a fashion led by Jean Berain at the Court of Louis XIV. This resulted in a number of watchcase designers producing patterns of strapwork intermingled with acanthus leaves; foremost among these designers was Simon Gribelin, of the Blois watchmaking family. Born in the town in 1661, he came to England with his father, who was also a watchcase maker, in 1680, but failed to make any real impression for another twenty years. Indeed, he was remarkably unsuccessful — or perhaps just unlucky — in other spheres, for he also undertook portraits as well as making copies of the work of some of the great masters. Not until 1697 did he at last receive the recognition he deserved, with the production of the first English engravers' pattern book ever to be published. Entitled *Book of Ornaments useful to Jewellers, Watchmakers and all other Artists,* and with a

London imprint, the book even included many patterns for watch cocks. Sadly, however, such an endless profusion of different designs were available by that time, that it is clear that their makers no longer relied upon pattern books to guide them.

The early eighteenth century is remarkable principally for the appearance of three French pattern books, all produced by Parisian goldsmiths whose names were Pierre Bourdon, Jean Bourguet, and a certain Briceau. The last-named included designs appropriate to the dial-centres of contemporary French watches, but otherwise nothing very striking resulted. By the end of the first quarter of this century, however, the emphasis was turning towards embossed work — that is to say, *repoussé* — which cannot be rendered very effectively as flat designs although a few goldsmiths, like van der Cruycen, did try to incorporate them.

There are no sudden and irrevocable changes of direction in the decorative arts and there is always overlap as between one style and the next; yet, in very approximate terms, the decline in the taste for engraved decoration and the rise in the fashion for embossed work corresponded with the decline in the popularity of the essentially symmetrical baroque and the rise in the wholly

asymmetrical rococo. Some authorities find it difficult to differentiate between the baroque and the rococo, regarding the latter simply as the last phase of the former; and indeed some celebrated craftsmen and designers were influential and active in both. For present purposes, it is sufficient to consider baroque as epitomised by expansive curvaceous forms that, even so, possess a solemn, sometimes pompous and square-set grandeur. Rococo, on the other hand, with its freely handled S-shaped curves, harmonious combinations of naturalistic motifs like sprigs of flowers, unrepresentational effects symbolising such things as splashing water, and the overall appearance of being delicately poised rather than firmly based, has an essential lightness and elegance which gave it much individuality. This may be partly because it made its first impact in the decorative rather than in the fine arts. Indeed, arguably its most important manifestations are in schemes of interior decoration where it also embraced chinoiserie as well as other exotic motifs.

The art of modelling metal with hammer and steel tools, properly called chased or *repoussé* work, had already arrived in London as the influence of rococo started to take hold, and some of the finest watchcases in the world had resulted from it. Chambers's *Cyclopaedia* (1728) noted 'with what Beauty and Justness . . . the Artist in this Kind will represent Foliages, Grotesques, Animals, Histories, etc'. Yet the overlap effect between one style and its successor produced watchcases by the great London gold chasers such as Augustin Heckel, G. M. Moser and John Valentine Haidt, which still retained, in the late 1730s, the symmetrical cartouche that had dominated such artifacts throughout almost the whole of the previous two decades.

So, too, when neoclassicism replaced the rococo, London chasers were slow to catch up. Essentially a reaction to its predecessor, this new style was dignified, restrained — as opposed to the exuberance of what had gone before — and rather cold, being characterised by the use of geometrical designs and the sparing utilisation of Greek and Roman architectural ornament, coupled with a preference for flat and linear, rather than highly modelled effects. It had begun to emerge in the 1750s, becoming well-established across Europe during the succeeding twenty years.

The best summary of the subject-matter that inspired the watchcase chasers throughout this period of more than half a century, is to be found in Dr Richard Edgecumbe's very useful essay, *Gold Chasing,* which was included in the splendid catalogue of the exhibition mounted by the Victoria & Albert Museum in London, during 1984, and entitled 'Rococo — Art and Design in Hogarth's England'.

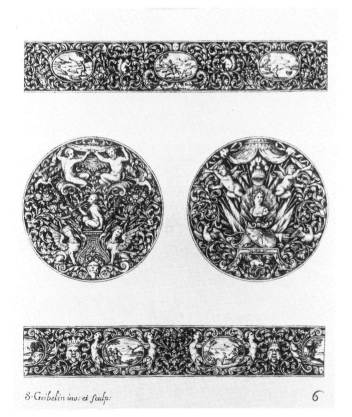

PLATE 9: Simon Gribelin's designs — here, for case backs and bands — heralded the end of seventeenth-century designers' influence.

He writes:

> While the scroll and shellwork of the London chasers became heavily indebted to Meissonier and the French rococo, the figure scenes within the cartouches on boxes and watch cases remained predominantly classical, as they had been in the 1720s and 1730s. Biblical scenes are not uncommon, but *fêtes galantes, Commedia dell'Arte* scenes and chinoiserie are rare. Almost any print of a classical scene might be borrowed and sometimes adapted by the chaser. Scenes were taken not only from such celebrated books as the Earl of Shaftesbury's *Characteristicks* but from prints by, or after, Italian and Flemish masters and a wide range of French masters from Vouet to Boucher and Gravelot.

Dr Edgcumbe goes on to discuss the status of the gold chaser during this period, from which there can be no doubt that such people were to reach the peak of achievement, both as artists and craftsmen, by comparison with any other type of watch decorator throughout the entire history of such activity in England. More than twenty chasers have been identified by signed work, thus acquiring the standing, not to mention the prosperity, of artists. Henry Manly appears in local rate books with the title of 'Esq', Augustin Heckel generated sufficient means to be able to retire to Richmond, while the great G. M. Moser was 'followed to his grave in grand funeral pomp by all the capital artists'; so reported *Gentleman's Magazine* in 1783.

George Michael Moser had been an influential figure in obtaining proper recognition for artist-chasers. Born in Schaffhausen in 1704, he seems to have come to London in the 1720s, working at first for a coppersmith; yet, at his death, no less a figure than Sir Joshua Reynolds had described him as 'the Father of the present Race of Artists'. After becoming a leading light in the St Martin's Lane Academy, his influence almost certainly led to chasing being included in all subsequent proposals for academies. Thus, in 1753, proposals for such included thirteen painters, three sculptors, one chaser, two engravers and two architects to form the professorial body. Two years later, *Plan of an Academy* produced by a committee of which Moser was a member, included chasing as one of the 'Performances in which Art and Genius,

PLATES 10–12 (*from top*): Three designs for watchcases by G. M. Moser. It is noticeable that only one of these — Plate 11 — has a cartouche in the baroque style to border the figure scene, which is itself based upon a depiction of a wedding by Gravelot. Architecture, the subject of Moser's drawing in Plate 10, inspired other designers including Augustin Heckel; and both this example and that of Plate 12, with its *putti* carrying a basket of flowers, are enclosed within cartouches in the rococo manner.

Elegance of Fancy, and Accuracy of Workmanship are confessedly united'.

In 1765, Moser was named as a director in the Charter of Incorporation of the Society of Artists, and he became the first Keeper of the Royal Academy in 1768. Among his other accomplishments he had been drawing-master to George III, for whom he had engraved his first Great Seal; and the versatility he himself exhibited throughout his career was mirrored in many of his contemporaries. Moser was enameller, drawing-master, designer and almost certainly modeller as well as chaser. His apprentice George Parbury, to whom he had taught chasing, was also a modeller in wax, as well as making models for coins and medals. Jean-Nicholas Wieland and Richard Morton Paye were both wax modellers and chasers, and Paye subsequently became a painter and engraver. Dr Edgcumbe quotes a number of other examples of similar versatility among artists who were initially trained as gold chasers, to underline the accomplishment as well as the standing of such artist-craftsmen in mid-eighteenth-century London.

Moser was not the only artist in his family. His nephew Joseph was equally if differently versatile, being artist — he exhibited at the Royal Academy during the period 1774–82 — author of political pamphlets, drama and fiction and, unlikely combination though it may seem, the magistrate for Westminster. His daughter Mary became a distinguished flower-painter, and a foundation member of the Royal Academy, contributing to its exhibitions until 1802. Similarly, Augustin Heckel, born in Augsburg c1690, was the son of the goldsmith Michael Heckel (died 1722), and the cousin of Christopher Heckel, a gold chaser working in the Covent Garden area of London, who benefited under his will.

The exhibition of rococo in England mentioned above also included a number of pen and ink drawings of designs for watchcases, by several of the best artists, including Moser himself, Hubert François Gravelot (1699–1773), and Augustin Heckel, as well as prints from suites of ornamental plates by Peter Glazier (active 1748–52) and Jacob Bonneau (active 1741, died 1786), this last after William Delacour (active 1740, died 1767). Delacour's *Eighth Book of Ornaments,* consisting of a title page and six plates, embraces designs for some forty-six articles, mostly jewellery and snuff boxes, but five are for watchcases. Glazier's plate is one of only two recorded as surviving, from a suite of unknown title published in 1748, and shows two watchcases and an element for a chatelaine, out of a total of nine items, five being designs of uncertain purpose. Delacour's and Glazier's suites of plates are the only English pattern books to show rococo gold chasers' work, but other pattern books of the time include *A Book of Jewellers Work Design'd by Thomas Flach in London,* consisting of a title page and five plates, which appeared in 1736; *A Book of Ornaments useful for Jewellers, Drawn and Invented by Christian Taute, London,* probably 1750; and *A New Book of Designs for Jewellers Work,* by Sebastian Henry Dinglinger, engraved by J. Brooke, 1751.

Another interesting feature is reminiscent of the age of engraved decoration, when records of work done were maintained in the form of rubbings. Gold chasers, by contrast, kept plaster casts of their work, and there are existing examples. Ismael Parbury owned more than four hundred such casts when he died in 1746; and a lot of thirty watchcase casts after his own work fetched 13s 6d. After Moser's death in 1783, more than seven hundred casts were dispersed. Such casts were not only invaluable as records of work done, but they could be, and often were, exhibited; and it seems likely that they were also shown to prospective clients as a yardstick of the artist's capabilities.

Thus far, some relationship has been readily detectable between the art factor in English watches, and the styles prevailing in the fine arts and architecture for which terms like mannerist, baroque, rococo and neoclassical are conventionally employed. During the last quarter of the eighteenth century, however, a variety of new influences affected the situation, unbalancing it in the process.

First, three entirely different revolutions can be said to have taken place. The French Revolution had a profound effect upon the horology of that country. The advent of the Industrial Revolution in Britain was to have a cumulative effect upon British horology. Arguably the most significant, however, was the revolution in time measuring technology brought about by innovations connected with precision performance. This completely changed the design emphasis so far as watches and chronometers were concerned, so that function became all-important and decoration, relegated to a very secondary place and degenerating in the process, was eventually to be phased out altogether.

Clocks, though, which were not subjected to these same influences since they were already as precise, in time measuring terms, as they were ever likely to be, were not affected in the same way. Many of them, of course, were also to be regarded as pieces of furniture and, therefore, susceptible to the architectural ethos. Thus, when egyptiennerie attracted the attention and enthusiasm of the neoclassical designers, in just the same way as rococo artists had been attracted to chinoiserie, the makers of clockcases eagerly followed suit, the impetus deriving variously from Nelson's excitements at the Battle of the

Nile, in 1798, to Belzoni's archaeological discoveries in the Temple of Abu-Simbel and his penetration of the second Great Pyramid during 1817 to 1820.

Later, while the fine arts were passing through those stages usually called romanticism and realism, some decorators of watches, in the provinces, were combining both styles into a kind of folk art, primitive but, in its least crude forms, remarkably appealing. This trend showed itself especially during the declining years of underpainted horn watchcases, and on movements, where new technical developments were gradually encroaching more and more into those areas previously considered susceptible to embellishment. With the gradual erosion of the traditional full-plate movement, culminating eventually in one where almost all the mechanical elements were individually located rather than grouped under one 'umbrella', the process was complete.

Whether or not they were aware of it at the time, the great pioneers of chronometry provided a mighty thrust towards the eventual objective of the purely functional, wholly undecorated watch. Chronometers are 'free-sprung'; regulation is not carried out by adjustment of the balance spring, which anyway takes the form of a helix rather than a spiral, so that any need for a slide plate and regulator dial instantly disappeared. The heartbeat of the chronometer — the detent escapement — needs to spread itself far more within the mechanism than did the age-old verge or yet the cylinder escapement, which superseded without ever actually replacing it.

The last vestiges of decoration, certainly on movements, died out everywhere around 1900 and it is tempting to think that the innovation of the Kew Trials sounded its death-knell. Kew Observatory, in the Old Deer Park at Richmond in Surrey, had been built for George III, who was keenly interested in practical horology. In 1885, performance certificates for timekeepers, based on tests carried out at Kew, were introduced, and transferred in 1912 to the National Physical Laboratory at Teddington. A Kew 'A' Certificate must certainly have added a premium to the purchase price of any watch. Such certificates were judged so important that it was customary to inscribe a suitable legend on the movement, even going so far as to quote the marks gained, if these were exceptionally good. London 'makers to the trade' often supplied readymade Kew-tested movements to provincial retailers, who then had their own names engraved upon them, doubtless with much wholly spurious pride. Such was not, however, the sort of environment in which the decorated movement could reasonably be expected to survive — and it did not.

NATIONAL PHYSICAL LABORATORY

REPORT

TEST OF A GOLD KEYLESS HALF HUNTER WATCH

A gold keyless half-hunter watch no 25701 was submitted by Usher and Cole to the Class A test at the Kew Observatory over the period July 17 to August 30 1886 and as a result of the test a Class A Kew Certificate was issued for the watch.

The following information is abstracted from the records of the test:-

Average daily rate: gaining 2.2 second
Average difference of daily rate: + 0.6 second
Average difference of daily rate for 1° Fah: 0.10 second
Difference of daily rate between vertical and horizontal positions: - 3.6 seconds
Difference of daily rate between pendant up and pendant right: - 5.9 seconds
Difference of daily rate between pendant up and pendant left: - 6.4 seconds
Difference of daily rate between dial up and dial down: + 5.6 seconds
Difference between extremes of daily rate: 12.5 seconds

Marks awarded

In respect of consistency of rate		27.2
" " " " " " with change of position		28.0
" " " temperature compensation		13.5
Total marks		68.7

Note: It should be understood that the results given in this Report do not necessarily represent the present performance of the watch.

22 February 1978
Issued 8 September 1886
Register No 1
KO Register No 726

S. R. Swavey.

PLATE 13 (*left*): The departure of decoration from the movement is nowhere more graphically illustrated than on the last two of John Harrison's prototype marine timekeepers, known as H4 and H5. The first, dated 1759, is covered with a tracery of ornament while the second, only eleven years later, is plain apart from some symmetrical treatment of the balance bridge.

PLATE 14: A Kew-tested watch movement with its 'pedigree'. Although manufactured by the famous London firm of Usher & Cole, it bears the name 'W. B. Pidduck, Manchester'. With premises at 1, St Ann's Place in that city, and listed as 'Watchmaker and Jeweller', Mr Pidduck was simply a retailer, whose private residence was at Macclesfield, some eighteen miles to the south.

3 The Formative Years

In his indispensable book *The Early Clockmakers of Great Britain* (1981) Brian Loomes has listed, with as much biographical detail as records have so far revealed to him, everyone he could find who was associated with the horological craft before the year 1700. These associations were often of the most tenuous and indeed, in some cases, require a considerable feat of the imagination to make the necessary connection; yet this was quite deliberate since information, in these early years, is so sparse that it is necessary to cast the net as wide as possible. It is very much better to start with too much information, which can be refined as and when more specific data is accumulated, than to risk missing altogether somebody who may subsequently turn out to have been of the first importance to the history of the craft.

Despite the obvious limitations, some useful trends can be derived from this book to illustrate the growth rate of the craft in its formative years. For this purpose, a count was made of all entries with a first date — even if that was only the date of birth — that preceded 1600. The total of all such entries was 174, which divided into chronological segments as follows:

Fourteenth-century entries:　8
Fifteenth-century entries:　22
Sixteenth-century entries:　144

Mr Loomes must have had to accept the sheer physical impossibility of tapping every conceivable source of information for a work such as his; but in the words of the pollsters, his 'sample' must still be big enough to be representative of the 'universe'. There is no disguising the positive explosion of interest in horology that occurred in Britain during the sixteenth century.

This survey, small though it may be, also revealed other characteristics that are probably typical. There is no impression of cohesion in the craft, save for the number of those included who are shown as 'keepers' of church or town clocks. Very many of the names of all those involved are clearly not British, and references to watchmaking as a separate activity do not even start to appear until almost the end of the period concerned.

Perhaps all of this was predictable, yet it does illustrate the difficulty in assessing who, among the craftsmen listed in books like this, were the truly influential figures when the foundations of English watchmaking were being laid.

For present purposes, a twofold approach seems appropriate. Looking, for a moment, through the wrong end of the telescope, who might be expected to have employed the best watchmakers all those centuries ago? Secondly, what are the finest surviving artifacts of this type, and who made them?

There can be little doubt about the answer to the first part of the above proposition; it must be the English Court. The instruments of time measurement, both large and small, have always held a great fascination for English kings and queens, and inevitably they would have employed the very best practitioners available. For surviving artifacts — and they are by no means numerous — it is necessary to turn to the big museums, for very few such objects remain in private hands.

The first really eminent native-born British craftsman in this field was Bartholomew Newsam. He succeeded Nicholas Urseau as royal clockmaker — to Elizabeth I — in 1590; and whereas his predecessor does not seem to have made watches, Newsam certainly did. There survives a large striking watch marked B + N in the Metropolitan Museum of Art in New York, which can reasonably be attributed to him. Apart from that, his will, dated 5 January 1586, included such items as a jewel with a watch in it, and a watch-clock in a purse, among other horological items. Newsam's working life, certainly from 1573, seems to have been spent in accommodation in 'Stronde Way' — that thoroughfare in Central London known to this day as the Strand, and still as fashionable an address as can be found thereabouts — and he was indeed a man of substance. He is thought to have died about 1593.

The craftsman who followed Newsam also made watches. Randolph Bull was appointed Clockmaker-in-Ordinary to Elizabeth I in a document dated 31 July 1591, and continued in office until the Queen's death in 1603. He then formally vacated his employment, but was immediately reinstated jointly with his son Emmanuel, and worked for James I, on the same terms as before, save that henceforth he not only maintained existing clocks but also supplied new ones. In 1612 there is documentary evidence that he supplied a watch to the Earl of Salisbury 'which was trimed with silver' and cost £8; and there survives, in the British Museum, another of his watches which is dated 1590. He died in 1617.

These are the only two craftsmen in royal employ before 1600 who can be shown to have made watches.

Nouwen, strangely, was appointed overseer — or executor — of the will of another eminent watchmaker, Nicholas Vallin: this was proved only in 1608, although Vallin had died in 1603. By no means a prolific maker — for either these early craftsmen had a low output, or the survival rate has been excessively small — two of Vallin's watches passed through a London salesroom a few years ago. Born about 1565, Vallin had come originally from Brussels, marrying a Dutch girl in London in 1590, and afterwards living in Blackfriars. He and his father, John Vallin, who was also a practising clockmaker (although there is no evidence that he made any watches), both died during the same year. The only other English watch from this exceedingly early period to pass through auctioneers' hands of recent times was one by Charles Whitwel, for whom speculative dates of 1593–1606 have been quoted. Very little is known about him; Brian Loomes hazards that he may have been the one of that name claimed as a brother-in-law in his will, by the eminent maker Robert Grinkin.

PLATE 15: Dial view of the early English watch by Jacques Bulcke, c1600.

There were others in the business, however, as can be demonstrated by surviving examples of their work, even if they are exceedingly few and far between. The British Museum houses a watch by J(acques) Bulck(e), who was active in London in the 1590s although credibly said to have been of French origin. The Victoria & Albert Museum has an English watch of the same period — or at least one must suppose so since, although the original movement has been replaced, the case bears the arms, granted in 1592, of Stephens, of Essex. The Royal Museum of Scotland owns a truly magnificent watch signed *Hieronymus Hamilthon Scotus Me Fecit 1595,* proving that watchmakers were also at work north of the border by that time. Finally, the Clockmakers' Company Collection possesses a somewhat altered watch by Michael Nouwen, who is recorded as working in London as early as 1582.

PLATE 16: Dial views of two watches by Nicholas Vallin, who died in 1603. Both covers of the larger watch are decorated with profiles of Roman Emperors while, inside, the smaller has the crest of the Woodward family, of Avon Bassett,. Co Warwick, while the larger is engraved with the figure of Christ surrounded by the instruments of the Passion.

PLATE 17: Early English watch by Charles Whitwel, sold in London in 1986.

Mention of Michael Nouwen calls to mind that other maker from this same period, François Nawe — or any variety of alternative spellings, including Nouwen. Indeed, Brian Loomes states that he was believed to have been born in Brabant and was a relative of Michael. However that may be, he came to London about 1580 and, sadly, died of the plague together with some of his children in 1593. Even so, he left behind several watches, of which two found their way into the famous Webster Collection, which was dispersed in 1954. They are as interesting for their dissimilarities as for the features they share in common, suggesting a slight difference in their dates of manufacture. One is simply signed 'Françoy Nawe' whereas the other has a fine signature in a scroll reserve encompassing more than half the circumference of the plate, which reads 'François Nawe at Londen'. Conversely, the two oval cases both have engraved emblematic figures as central features, and make use of such devices as laurel and other garlands and canopies, not necessarily in identical localities but indicating like sources for such ornament. Both have the English feature of an engraved border around the back plate of the movement, but the otherwise rather Netherlandish appearance of both watches was underlined by yet a third watch from the same collection, by Ghijlis van Ghelle.

The decade immediately following the year 1600 did not, in practice, see any great increase in the number of watchmakers at work, but there is now some impression of consolidation. Reverting to the British Museum, one of the very finest early English watches, with a complicated dial, from the first years of the seventeenth century, must be the one signed 'H Roberts'. It is tempting to identify this maker with the Hugh Roberts who was apprenticed to Solomon Bouguet in 1657 — indeed, Baillie says as much — but the watch in question is clearly very much earlier than this. The splendid dial has both solar and lunar indications, including the age, phase and aspect of the latter; the chapter ring is divided into two periods of twelve hours — but not in the German manner — and there are symbols for the zodiac. Inside the dial cover there is a fine blazon of arms, said to be those of the family of Gurney, of West Basham, in Norfolk, although Fox-Davies casts doubt upon the authority for their use.

PLATE 18: Dial view of the magnificent watch by H. Roberts, c1600
PLATE 19: The movement of the H. Roberts watch.

PLATE 20: Dial view of a watch by Nicholas Vallin, virtually identical with the previous one.

The attribution of such an early date to the Roberts watch can be disputed; in fact, it is usually described merely as 'early seventeenth century', which can be taken to mean that nobody is quite certain about it. The really outstanding feature of this watch, however, is without doubt its dial, complex and superbly executed; the remarkable thing is that, though this might well be thought unique, another virtually identical example does exist, on a watch by Nicholas Vallin. Since Vallin died in 1603, it does not seem too unreasonable to place the Roberts watch within that particular decade.

Another splendid watch in the same collection is by Isaac Symmes. Round like the Roberts watch, it has something of the same quality and feel, without the same elaboration. Symmes was said to have been of French origin but new research has shown that he was well and truly English. There is a watch by him in the Pierpoint Morgan Collection housed in the Metropolitan Museum of Art in New York, which gives his locality as 'Aldgette' — that

PLATE 23: Watch by John Tiese At London, c1610.

PLATE 21: Watch by Isaac Symmes, dial view with cover open, early seventeenth century.

PLATE 22: Movement of the Symmes watch, showing engraved border.

PLATE 24: Movement of the Tiese watch, again with engraved border.
PLATE 25: Oval watch by Randolph Bull, dated 1590.

is, Aldgate, one of the four original gates to the City of London — and his active dates are generally given as c1600–20; but he was also one of the original petitioners, in 1622, against the intrusion of foreign workmen into the City which eventually led to the formation of the Clockmakers' Company in the decade that followed.

Arguably just eligible for inclusion in this first decade of seventeenth-century English craftsmen's work, is a watch in the Museum of the History of Science, at Oxford. Signed by 'John Tiese At London', this watch-maker's active life is usually attributed to a slightly later period, c1610–20; yet this particular example has several features that might tend to place it just that much earlier, such as the engraved border to the back plate, the signature within a reserve and the use of touch-pins on the dial. The nature of the dial engraving, too, suggests that it belongs to a period before this settled down into a much more stylised form.

So, what conclusions are to be drawn from a consideration of these and other surviving examples of watches made in England — but not necessarily by native-born craftsmen — in the decades either side of 1600? It is clear that they were subject to both French and German influences and, indeed, there are examples in which features from both national styles rub shoulders. There is, for instance, in the Ashmolean Museum in Oxford, a fine watch by Randolph Bull that has a typically German pierced and rounded case, while the movement shows clear signs of the French mode in its mechanical features; yet the back plate has a decorated border, suggesting English influence, and the signature is contained within a cartouche, a typically early touch. The dial retains the German form of 24-hour display but without depicting the '2' as 'z'; and there are no touch-pins. By contrast, the watch by the same maker in the British Museum, although unfortunately incomplete, already shows more English influence in its oval case and in the decorative border around the edge of the back plate of the movement. The engraved gilt dial has a simple I–XII chapter circle, which has been used as a device to divide the decoration between a conventional foliate centre and, without, a formalised radiating design suggestive of the folds of a cushion, upon which the dial rests. It is difficult to attribute this design to any national style.

Similar comparisons are possible with two watches by Michael Nouwen. The one in the Metropolitan Museum of Art in New York has a pierced and engraved circular case in the German manner, while the movement has the English decorated border to the back plate although much of the mechanical layout is French in style, save for the German S-shaped cock and foliot balance. The example in the Clockmakers' Company Collection would appear to have had a similar case, although the front cover has been altered; the dial, however, has a raised chapter circle on which the numerals appear as gold on blue enamel. The dial-centre is engraved with rabbits and foliage and the outer zone has simply a foliate design. Both watches share a feature in the maker's signature, which is engraved in a circle concentric with the edge of the back plate. The enclosing of the signature within some kind of shaped reserve may have originated on the Continent but it did not last long in English usage and was probably found restrictive by makers who were not notably backward in promoting their handiwork.

Germanstyle pierced cases on Englishmade watches are not common, nevertheless. Early editions of Britten illustrate a large oval alarm watch by Richard Crayle of London, which seems unlikely to post-date 1610, and there is the splendid octagonal watch by Hieronymus Hamilthon mentioned earlier, which yet has Germanic dial characteristics in the 24-hour display, the Gothic 'z' for '2', and touch-pins. A second watch by Richard Crayle, which was in the Webster Collection, had progressed to a rock crystal octagonal case, but retained all the German dial features, which were lacking in the previous example by this maker.

Reference has already been made to two watches by Nicholas Vallin, sold in London in 1985. One of these —

the larger by far, at 81mm overall, by comparison with the more normal second at 53mm — had devastatingly effective decoration inside the front cover, consisting of engraved depictions of the Instruments of the Passion, a Crucifix and a seated figure of Christ. Religious overtones are surprisingly uncommon in the context of watch decoration; but there is in the Clockmakers' Company Collection, an early oval watchcase — no trace of the dial or movement remains — which has the Nativity on its front cover, and the Crucifixion on the back, both scenes very well executed.

Finally, there is the watch by Jacques Bulck(e) in the British Museum. The name sounds French and this maker is believed to have worked in Paris; yet the mixture is much as before. The case could not be more Germanic, being round and pierced; the twelve 'windows' giving views of the hour numerals are delicately executed; but the dial has a simple I–XII display against an otherwise overall-engraved dial-plate which, in the centre, incorporates two figures. However, it also has touch-pins.

It seems clear, therefore, that when the watch started to appear as a homemade product in England, makers chose to adapt the styles that might have been most familiar to them — possibly because of their own antecedents — yet, at the same time, felt under no constraint to follow slavishly in the footsteps of those fellow-countrymen who had preceded them. Presumably they selected from the gamut of contemporary usage those characteristics that most appealed to them, or which they thought most appropriate, or which the customer demanded. The purchaser of an expensive watch must have exerted some control over its creation in those days, even if the extent of this is unknown; and it is feasible that his or her nationality and taste had a considerable effect upon the finished product. What is certain is that we shall never know precisely how these factors interrelated, in any of the splendid objects being reviewed in these pages.

COLOUR PLATE 3: At its best, tortoiseshell inlaid with silver and — extremely rarely — gold can produce a sumptuous effect. The central gold example is on a watch by Peter Garon and it is interesting that another example by this same maker is in a virtually identical outer case, the serial numbers of the movements being 153 and 163 respectively. The seemingly scratched decoration of the case at lower left, from a watch by Samuel Macham, is open to several interpretations; while the effect looks original, there appear to be slight traces of silver in some of the grooves. The arms of the Ithell family adorn the case of a watch by Charles Gretton; and the makers of the other watches, moving clockwise from the upper right, are John Harris, Markwick, Joseph Kenton and (upper left) Thomas Tompion.

4 Fashions in English Watches — The Main Trends

PLATE 26: Comparisons in the work of father and son, both called Robert Grinkin. On the left, the big watch with alarm facility dates from c1625 and is Grinkin senior's work. The other watch, from more than a decade later, must be by the son. Both watches display, inside their covers, different versions of the commonly-found motif consisting of two leafy branches formed into an oval reserve. Robert Grinkin the father died in 1626 and his son in 1661.

COLOUR PLATE 4: Underpainted horn outer cases enjoyed a popularity extending over at least half a century and offered a great opportunity for the unknown folk artist; never great works of art, they are, nevertheless, very charming. The most common versions — centre left and right — feature fern patterns, sometimes with insects and also some attempt to simulate tortoiseshell, usually not very successfully. The early examples often enclose the main motif within an oval reserve (top), and homely countryside scenes abound. Biblical overtones (centre) are uncommon.

During the last thirty years or so museums, auctioneers and specialist dealers have brought to a fine art the accurate describing of old watches, but it is both revealing and instructive to read contemporary accounts of them, where these can be discovered. One invaluable source is the 'Lost and Found' columns in the media of the day, where it is common to turn up notices in the style of the following:

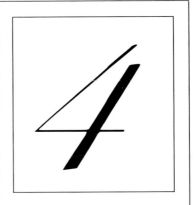

> Lost on the 13th instant a Gold Watch enamelled, the outside case seal-skin studded with gold; in the backside of it was the History of St. Paul's Conversion, with small character *Saul, Saul, quid me persequeris?* And on the dial part was the stoning of Stephen, with Lanskip round about; and in the inside of the back, a Damask Rose exactly enamelled, the Key fastened with a black ribon. Whoever gives notice of it to Mr. William Crayle, a Watchmaker at the Black Boy in the Strand, near the Savoy, shall have 3l. reward.
>
> (*London Gazette*, 13–17 July, 1676)

Although three pounds sterling was a great deal of money at the end of the seventeenth century, it probably represented even then only a fraction of the cost of such a beautifully endowed watch, when new. Redolent of its time, even to the Miltonian 'Lanskip' for 'landscape', it has not been necessary to mention a single mechanical characteristic in order to describe it down to the last detail, despite the notice having been almost certainly compiled by Crayle, himself a watchmaker. Notices of this kind also make clear the fact that watches were built in those days to last, not just for years but for generations. To give one typical example, in 1755 a lost watch is described as 'oval and striking', both characteristics of a century earlier; and it is commonplace to find watches advertised as 'very large and old' or just 'very old'. It can even be argued, perhaps, that the decorative elements of the English watch had developed rather more rapidly than the mechanical ones, contributing greatly to their popularity in their own times as well as to their appreciation by connoisseurs in succeeding ones.

In the pages that follow, therefore, the purpose is to outline the main trends affecting the appearance of the typical English watch during the period from 1600 to about 1900. It is a sad fact of life that styles and fashions in watches, as in most other artifacts, have no hard-and-fast cutoff points, and the overlap between one practice and the succeeding one can be anything up to half a century, especially if the time-lag between London and pro-vincial usage is taken into account. This is more particularly noticeable on the watch movement, where old habits — in terms of watch cock decoration — tended to die hard, making it almost impossible, for instance, to distinguish with real certainty between a cock from the last quarter of the eighteenth century and one from the first quarter of the nineteenth, when these specimens have been divorced from their parent movements, as so many have been, for a variety of different reasons that need not really concern us here.

THE SEVENTEENTH CENTURY

This has to be the period when that paradox about function versus decoration manifests itself most clearly. For all but the last quarter of the century, the watch as a timekeeper was unreliable, unpredictable and wholly inaccurate; yet its decoration was wide-ranging, complex and often breathtaking in its brilliance so that, at its best, it could deserve the appellation 'work of art'. The introduction of the balance spring about 1675, however, transformed the performance of watches and, although the decorative momentum that had built up lasted to the end of the century and a little beyond, there were soon signs that the rot was setting in. Whatever wonders the succeeding century might produce — in terms, perhaps, of embossed or enamelled work — nothing could ever be quite the same again.

WATCHCASES   Such was already the development of the watch in continental Europe that, when it emerged in England, several different patterns of case came into use almost simultaneously. There were round cases with deep bands, the latter pierced to allow the sound of the bell to be heard, for many of these early timekeepers had hour-striking or alarm facilities, or both; but the slightly domed lids were usually solid rather than pierced, as in German practice, so that it was necessary to open them in order to read the time. Inevitably there are exceptions, so that the Jacques Bulck(e) watch in the British Museum has its lid pierced with twelve hour-apertures. There were also oval cases, more in the French style, again usually with solid covers but, when required, with pierced bands. Both types of case were in gilt-metal, so far as surviving examples demonstrate; and the ovals exist in a wide range of sizes. The decoration of these early cases could be fairly coarse, also following the German practice as well as contrasting greatly with what followed. Scrolling foliage was commonplace on the band, while the covers sometimes had figure scenes, probably symbolic and usually unidentifiable save for those that were clearly religious in content. Coats of arms or other tokens of ownership frequently adorn the covers.

Early in the century, the Thirty Years War effectively brought to an end any further German influence on English watchmaking, so that what gradually emerged was a mixture of existing French practice together with an evolving native English usage. The oval case, generally with carcase of gilt-metal and sometimes with a decoratively engraved silver strip riveted to its band, was to have a long life, extending well into mid-century. However, another shape — the octagon — came into use from an early date both in its pure and elongated form: if anything, the oblong octagon is more suitable for its purpose than the simple one and is consequently that much more common. It also lent itself particularly well to being made in rock crystal, the surface faceted and with matching cover, which was connected to the carcase by a jointed gilt-metal bezel, this too being often decorated with an innocuous engraved border. Rock crystal, incidentally, is always faceted; the examples of its use in a plain state are all the more noticeable for their rarity.

The ubiquitous oval case, too, was susceptible to construction in rock crystal, but its next manifestation was arguably its most elegant, even if not its most unexpected. Increasingly puritanical trends at home are said to have influenced the creation of what is still called the 'Puritan' watch, which was completely devoid of decoration. This can be found in oval form, or in the closely related 'egg' shape which is peculiar to English usage; but there are also round versions. Most usually, the metal employed was silver, but one or two gold examples exist. Such cases continued in fashion presumably until the Restoration, and there is indeed a specimen in the British Museum by John Midnall, the original ownership of which is credibly attributed to the Lord Protector himself.

In view of the foregoing it must seem all the more astonishing that, virtually simultaneously, there was an outpouring of creative craftsmanship in the production of what are now called 'form' watches. These are more common in the French and Swiss versions. The English never aspired to some of the more far-fetched manifestations, such as birds and dogs, a 'form' watch being the method of disguising the very nature of the object so as, presumably, all the more to astound the onlooker. Perhaps the commonest European variation was the cruciform watch, also hardly known in English practice; the six-pointed star form, however, which was also

liberally embellished with biblical scenes, exists in a magnificent version by David Ramsay, in the Clockmakers' Company Collection. That same source has a square watch — not quite the so-called 'book' watch favoured by some German makers — by Francis Raynsford, which dates from about the end of the century, showing how long the fashion lasted. Other types include the well known 'tulip' watch; the most usual English version differs from the continental in having a solid cast and chiselled silver case, rather than one of silver-mounted rock crystal. Another type has its case cast to resemble a Tudor rose, a form which might be thought to be so typically English that it comes as some surprise to find versions with continental movements inside them. The cockleshell, usually in silver, came in for use as a watch-case in both seventeenth and eighteenth centuries, and there are examples simulating the pomegranate and the fritillary. In general, the English versions of these splendid creations tend to be less flamboyant and arguably more tasteful than their continental counterparts.

Form watches, in the main, were timepieces only: any attempt to pierce such cases in order simply to hear a bell would have been totally unacceptable. Nevertheless, there was still a demand for those more sophisticated instruments that struck the hours like a clock or sounded an alarm at a pre-set time, albeit that the timekeeping capability rendered any such extra facilities laughable.

In the second half of the century, therefore, there evolved a style that became typically English and, at its best, as perfect an expression of engraved ornament as can be imagined. At first all-over pierced and engraved with openwork floral decoration — a degree of chiselling, too, was implicit to obtain the best effects — this eventually settled into a slightly less elaborate form in which the centre of the back of the case remained engraved but unpierced, as a kind of boss from which the remainder of the decoration was separated, often by a stylised leaf border. In its finest examples, pivoted keyhole covers — supplied to prevent dust entering the movement by means of the winding holes — are decorated en suite, the effect being almost to camouflage them from view.

Enamelled decoration was used in the sixteenth century and, in the period under discussion, was already a highly developed technique; yet English enamelled watches from this period are rare: it may be a matter of survival, since this medium is very susceptible to damage. Where they have survived in prime condition, however, they are likely to be fabulous. One of the best known is in the Victoria & Albert Museum, in the form of a watch by Edward East. The circular gold case is enamelled on the outside with a pale blue ground and decorated with small

PLATE 27: 'Form' watches are those in cases which are intended to disguise their true purpose. Here, cases have been derived from a pumpkin, a cockleshell, a sea urchin, a Tudor rose, a tulip and a square box. There is also a fluted oval case, not uncommonly encountered, but the 'form' it is intended to simulate remains a matter for speculation. Makers of the associated movements are Edward East, Richard Masterson, Benjamin Hill, William Clay, Sam Aspinwall, Francis Raynsford and Henry Grendon.

flowers in relief, while inside there is a landscape with buildings and figures, in black on a blue ground. Unusually flat for its period, the pendant is formed as a ribbon bow. A similar case encloses a watch by Jacob Cornelius, of London, which was in the Webster Collection; the general style of both is reminiscent of contemporary miniature cases. Yet another example, albeit not quite in such pristine condition, and with movement by Samuel Betts, has its gold case enamelled translucent green with central white daisy and a border in relief of white flowers with pink markings. Inside both case and cover are depictions of scenery, while the dial has a white chapter ring separating an engraved gold outer band from a centre which is enamelled green, with a sunflower and a

border of flowers. All three watches date from the mid-century, and are remarkably rare.

Probably a little later, and arguably the finest English enamel watch dial to survive from this period, is the quite large polychrome floral dial that fronts a movement by Henry Jones. There is a tradition that this watch was handed to his servant John Ashburnham on the scaffold by Charles I; in that case the movement has to be a replacement and, indeed, contemporary documentation describing a fully enamelled watch might make this seem likely. If so, what a supreme marvel the original watch must have been, decoratively speaking.

The foregoing account might easily convey the totally erroneous impression that many seventeenth-century watchcases were decorated; nothing could be further from the truth. Apart from the 'Puritan' phenomenon already described, the end of the century — when the round watchcase had become standard — provides an abundance of plain examples. Indeed, for timepieces only, by contrast with striking and alarm watches, for instance, there was no purpose in piercing the case and, therefore, no need to disguise it decoratively. Only one further development in case-work needs to be described to complete this section.

PLATE 28: Dial views of a remarkable pair of seventeenth-century royal watches; (left) the silver quarter-striking clock-watch with original minute hand, made by Edward East for Charles I and given by him to his servant Thomas Herbert, while (right) the coach watch with both striking and alarm facilities, by David Bouguet, which was much favoured in the early nineteenth century by William IV.

PLATE 29: The superb cases of the two watches above. The coach watch incorporates caryatid-like figures and parrots into its radiating decoration, while Edward East's watch has his oft-employed openwork arrangement of flowers. An early feature, in both cases, is the loose ring through the pendant, rather than the later pivoted bow.

The so-called pair-case — which means housing the watch movement in one case, which is then enclosed within a second, to provide added protection from accidental shocks as well as additional dust exclusion — is usually associated with the standard round-cased watch; but, in fact, it arrived upon the scene much earlier. Many 'Puritan' oval watches still possess matching second cases, sometimes in the same material — usually silver — and sometimes in a different one, such as fish-skin upon a metal carcase. They have latch closures, much like those on contemporary cases housing pocket sundials, but otherwise their purpose was the same. Pair-cases had a very long life, still being fashionable on provincial watches as late as the mid-nineteenth century. This can make plain and unmarked specimens difficult to place in date terms, but it is worth mentioning that seventeenth-century examples invariably have protruding squared-off joints, rather than the rounded-off style that followed in the next century.

That part of the case forming the external attachment is called the pendant. In early watches, the pendant was simply a knob with a loose ring through it; but, later in the century, the 'stirrup' pendant, named because its ring, or 'bow', was so shaped, became universal.

DIALS AND HANDS The all-over-enamelled watch with en suite dial has already been mentioned in the previous section, and also the magnificent floral enamel dial

PLATE 31: Early astronomical watches could be readily adapted to the round or oval shape, and even the small decorative features adjoining the 'windows' were retained. These watches are (left) by Nathaniel Barrow, and (right) by James Nellson. Both date c1660, although the movement of the former has been altered.

PLATE 30: Authentic seventeenth-century white enamel dials are rare, and usually of a creamy hue. This one is to be found on a watch by an unlisted maker, Gulielmus Whatley, dating from c1650.

of a Henry Jones watch which may be all that remains of another such specimen. Enamel dials did exist in the seventeenth century in their own right; with polychrome decoration embracing flowers or figures, they could be very effective allied to a case enriched with some totally different technique. There are even very rare examples of plain white enamel dials with black hour numerals, presaging what was to come later; the actual tint, however, is usually a rich cream rather than pure white and all the more effective for that. They are quite unmistakable.

Nevertheless, any kind of enamel dial of authentic seventeenth-century origin has to be treated as the rare exception. Most watch dials throughout the entire period were made from uncoated metal, upon which the chapter ring of hour divisions, and any desired decoration were obtained by engraving, together with occasional and minimal infilling with wax. This was the period of the single-handed timepiece — both clocks and watches — and a minute hand on a watch that pre-dates 1675 must, of necessity, be viewed with suspicion, all the more because a handful of authentic specimens have been discovered.

The incorporation of a minute hand on a timepiece whose accuracy barely extended to measuring the hours correctly is a patent absurdity; but no more so than a fashion, from the earliest part of the century, for watches with complicated dials indicating a whole host of solar

PLATE 32: A range of typical seventeenth-century dials. The popular decorative features of these include the central rose on a matted ground, the overall floral arrangement, a figure scene and the small countryside vignette from the magnificent 'pumpkin' watch by Edward East (see Plate 27). Makers of the other watches are Benjamin Hill, William Clay and Henry Mott.

and lunar data, together with zodiac signs and calendrical information. This was an astonishing phenomenon which resulted in some very splendid watches, such as the H. Roberts watch in the British Museum, its dial a virtual twin of that on a watch by Nicholas Vallin. This type of watch showed its functional paces by means of a series of concentric bands, each divided according to its purpose, with appropriate gearing behind the dial. In other versions, shaped apertures cut into the main dial plate allowed discs, engraved with the relevant information and rotating behind them, to bring the data into sight at the proper moment — such was the theory, at any event. What is, perhaps, especially interesting in this last fashion is that identical dials were adapted to suit the round or oval watch, even to the tiny decorative features adjoining the apertures. It was to be a century and a half before comparable astronomical watches would reappear, with the work of such makers as George Margetts.

This, however, is sidestepping the main issue — the everyday workmanlike watch by which to tell the simple time. The earliest English watch dials, both round and oval, seem often to have inclined towards the particular horological culture that inspired them, so that those with leanings towards the French tradition favoured stylised and rather simplistic patterns, while their German equivalents incorporated figures and, now and again, religious themes. The chapter circle could be engraved directly on to the dial plate, or separately on to a ring that was subsequently applied to the dial. In the latter event, some colour was occasionally introduced, or a different metal employed, often silver if the dial plate was gilt.

The 'Puritan' period encompassed a gamut of dial treatments, presumably depending upon the dedication

PLATE 33: The versatility of individual makers is demonstrated by two watches by James Vautrollier. The round 'Puritan' watch has touch-pins at the hours and is devoid of decoration. By contrast, the oval watch is elaborately decorated both as to case and dial, although its silver outer case, which wholly envelops it leaving no aperture through which the watch can be glimpsed, is again wholly plain and in the 'Puritan' style. Note the curving leaf fronds inside the cover of this watch, and embracing the probably later glazed window (cf Plate 26).

PLATE 34: The four most usual versions from the 'transitional dial' period are shown here. The 'sun and moon' and the 'wandering hour' examples both come from watches by Windmills, while the 'six hour' version is by Will Bertram and the 'differential dial' by the Nottingham maker James Banks.

of the watchmaker — or the customer. At its plainest, the hour circle was engraved upon an otherwise absolutely bare dial plate, and the resulting simplicity almost smacks of bigotry and is often far from pleasing. Even so, an outwardly perfectly plain case can well house a dial that is quite elaborately engraved, often with the centre including figures and scenery, and with an applied silver chapter ring. There is a sense of the sardonic in some of these watches — what the eye doesn't see, the heart won't grieve over — for it is even possible to find an absolutely plain oval pair-case which houses within itself quite an ornamental watch.

Around the mid-century, when the fashion for simplicity and plainness was on the wane, engraved dial centres could incorporate figures such as Father Time, complete with scythe, or classical or military personages, with appropriate surroundings. Floral arrangements also became fashionable, such designs as already shown being equally, although infrequently, applicable in polychrome enamels. Finally, the dial-centre could simply be matted with a punch, but leaving the hand to spring from a small central reserve, which might take the form of a flower, left polished for contrast. Throughout the single-hand dial period, the width of the chapter ring varied considerably, often depending upon the other features of the dial — a day-of-the-month band or an alarm-setting disc could easily affect the proportions of the other dial elements, as could also the decoration employed.

The introduction of the balance spring, from about 1675, immediately made it worthwhile, in performance terms, to measure the minutes — and even the seconds — on a watch dial, so that this component had suddenly to confront the greatest changes in its existence up to that time. The concentric hour and minute hands, and a subsidiary seconds dial just above the hour-numeral VI, are so familiar to us and their efficiency seems so obvious that it is difficult to conceive of the design stages that led, eventually, to their universal adoption. Nevertheless, a whole variety of different and transitional dial arrangements preceded that state which, beautiful though they often are, give some indication of the trauma that must have confronted watchmakers and their customers seeking the best solution to this purely technical problem.

Four of these transitional dials will be briefly described. The commonest is the 'sun and moon' watch, in which a semicircular opening is provided in the top half of the dial plate. The curved edge of this is divided into twelve hours, running from VI to VI, with XII at top centre. Behind this aperture rotates, once in twenty-four hours, a disc with images of the sun and moon depicted, one opposite the other, so that only one is ever in view to the observer. As this travels across the opening, it registers the hour against the divided area, while the minutes are measured by a central hand against a minute ring at the outer edge of the dial plate.

The next two versions are rather rarer. The 'six-hour dial' watch has, as its name implies, the dial divided into six hours only, but superimposed over the numerals I to VI are a second series running from 7 to 12. There is an outer minute band, which divides each hour into graduated twenty-minute periods, and the single hand rotates twice each twelve hours. Because the hour divisions are so large — twice as large as on a conventional dial — it becomes possible to calibrate them effectively for minutes also, a device used in France a century later on his large twelve-hour dial 'Souscription' watches, by the great French genius, A. -L. Breguet.

The third transitional form is the 'wandering hour' watch. Somewhat similar in effect to the sun-and-moon dial, this version has no hands at all, but the hour numeral itself is allowed to rotate behind a curved opening that is calibrated for minutes, and as the hour disappears from view at one end of the aperture, the succeeding hour comes into view at the opposite one. It could conceivably be argued that a method by which the hour numeral acts as its own minute hand must be more functional than the conventional two-handed arrangement.

Finally, there is the 'differential dial' watch. This is a rare form, made by only one or two makers — like John Bushman in London and J. Banks in Nottingham — with dials that are so similar in their decoration as to suggest that they originated from the same source. The principle with these watches is a rotating central disc calibrated in hours, and an outer band on the main dial-plate calibrated in minutes. The single hand rotates twelve times as fast as the hour disc, and is thus capable of indicating both hours and minutes simultaneously from the respective scales. The decoration of the dial almost always incorporates a band separating the hour disc from the minute circle, which is *repoussé* with a trophy of arms, leaving blank only a plaque for the maker's name and town at the bottom of the dial. The outer minute circle is divided, on some models, to provide numerals every five minutes, and on others, only every fifteen.

These transitional dials are to be found throughout a period starting about 1680 and running to beyond the turn of the century; yet the usual concentric two-handed arrangement had established itself well before the end of this time, eventually settling down, c1700, to a layout that was to remain in vogue even after enamel dials replaced metal ones. The general arrangement on these was an outer minute ring with Arabic five-minute numerals, inside which was the chapter circle with Roman hour numerals, bordered by yet another ring calibrated with

PLATE 35: Variations upon a theme — the *champlevé* dial of the late seventeenth century. One example has the rare-for-this-period seconds dial above VI; another shows the so-called 'pendulum watch' with its 'bob' appearing in an aperture below VI and is the work of David Lestourgeon; the third, by Andrew Dunlop, permits regulation of the watch from the front, by means of a key on the 'square' which bisects the half-hour ring below XII. On this watch there is an aperture for day of the month above VI.

half-hour graduations. The dial centre usually had some simple embossed or engraved decoration, besides allowing two plaques for the maker's name and town. Such dials are always called *champlevé*, because the numerals are hollowed out from the surface of the metal and in-filled, although with engraver's wax rather than enamel; and the metals commonly found range from silver and gold to gilt-metal.

Overlapping the end of the century, there were one or two short-lived fashions that need to be noted. Several of the best makers — Daniel Quare was one of them — experimented with winding and regulating the watch from the front rather than the back. As Quare's best-quality watches were technically some of the finest to be had, since not only the balance itself but also the escape wheel was run in jewelled bearings, he was probably trying to exclude dust from the mechanism. Anyway, the addition of a winding square near the figure III, and an elliptical aperture below XII to show part of a regulation dial, does very little for the appearance of the watch. A similarly un-attractive development is said to have derived from the application of the pendulum to clocks and the splendid reputation they acquired as a result. Some watchmakers decided to provide a 'mock pendulum' on their watches by transferring the balance from back to front of the movement, cutting an aperture in the dial so that part of it could be seen, and even fixing a 'bob' to one of the arms

— that is, spokes — to heighten the illusion. Inevitably, of course, regulation had also to be carried out from the front, which further cluttered up the appearance. It may be that this was appreciated at the time, for a more popu-lar arrangement, and one still more frequently encoun-tered, is said to have a 'pendulum cock', in its normal position on the movement but cut away to show a 'bob' on the balance. Since the pendulum had no application whatsoever to watches, such devices can only be viewed as the fashion gimmicks of their day, especially as, in one version, the 'bob' appears as a Cupid, complete with bow and arrow.

In the last quarter of the century, quite a wayward artistic influence asserted itself, in the form of dials on

PLATE 36: A so-called 'pendulum' cock on the back of a move-ment by Richard Howe, of Dorchester, early eighteenth cen-tury. The balance has a 'bob' fixed to one of its arms in imita-tion of its namesake. Sometimes, however, a more fanciful 'bob' was installed, one such being Cupid with bow and arrow.

which the hour numerals appeared on shaped plaques — hearts, diamonds, squares and others — these sometimes being set at eccentric angles. Although rare today, these watches are charmingly fanciful as well as unexpected.

Seventeenth-century watch hands present some difficulty when it comes to classification: such elements are fitted only friction-tight, so can easily become lost; while, if of steel, they are brittle and so break if subjected to too much tension when, for example, the fingers are used to set them to the correct time. It is only human nature, in this respect, to adopt the easy way rather than use the key provided for the purpose by the watchmaker. As a result of such occurrences, the hands of an old watch may easily have been replaced several times during its life to date — and who is to say what the original ones looked like?

With these reservations, early single hands were generally of blued-steel with a little simple modelling and some pretence to a 'tail', which, on occasions, stretches back across the rest of the dial in quite a flamboyant manner. When two hands became topical, the first style was called 'tulip' — yet another manifestation of the Dutch influence — and this was followed by 'beetle and poker', which continued in use well into the next century.

MOVEMENTS The technical layout on the back of the watch movement, despite slight changes of treatment, remained fairly standard throughout the first three-quarters of the century. Essentially, there would be a tracery of blued-steel with no discernible decorative content — simply an openwork pattern — which embraced the mainspring setting-up arrangements, and sometimes involved an indicator dial. On the earliest watches there was an engraved border, which ran around the edge of

PLATE 37: Every period had its idiosyncracies — here, two late seventeenth-century makers, Ignatius Huggeford and George Tomlinson, place their chapter numerals on shaped reserves, respectively hearts and diamonds. In one, the dial is centred with four crowns, and in the other with an emblematic rose.

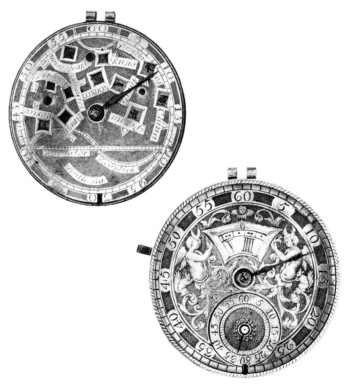

PLATE 38: Two more idiosyncratic dials showing (*top*) world time by countries — apart from 'London', that is — and (*below*) digital hours, foreshadowing the present-day fashion. The makers are John Neale, who patented a 'quadrantal planetarian' watch in 1744; and Edward Appleby, who was active in the 1680s.

PLATE 39: Two late seventeenth-century movements, one signed H(umfrey) Adamson and the other Anna Adamson; despite superficial similarities, there is no evidence that they were even related, although a woman watchmaker is a rarity in the history of the craft.

the plate, either entirely, or with a small gap left for the maker's name; and this purely decorative feature was peculiarly English. The watch cock, at first fairly simple and pinned to the plate by means of a mortice-and-tenon-type arrangement through the neck — the tenon taking the shape of a square post riveted to the plate — eventually settled into a basic outline in which both foot and table were irregular ovals, often of different sizes, pierced and engraved, and separated by a narrow neck pinned as above-mentioned. Very rarely indeed, foot and table have a properly defined edge. Before this type of cock was superseded, however, the method of attaching it to the movement was modified to screwing through the foot, a system that was never subsequently changed again and which, with the use of two or, more usually, three steady-pins to obviate any possibility of lateral movement, could not be bettered.

The introduction of the balance spring brought in its train the possibility of a more refined method of regulating the going of the watch which, hitherto, had depended on the much coarser means of adjusting the initial tension of the mainspring. This, however, required an extra fitting on the back, taking the form of a slide plate, a component whose shape hugged the edge of the main plate and largely surrounded the cock, abutting on to the foot on at least one side. This plate was the subject of decora-

tion en suite with the cock; and it, too, incorporated a small dial, invariably at this period silver, which had rather meaningless graduations intended solely as an indication of the amount of adjustment administered to the balance spring. The shape and decoration of the cock altered dramatically from the double-oval style, the latter becoming much more formalised, while the former allowed the table to become round — thus completely covering the balance wheel — and the foot gradually to splay out, with first a so-called 'wavy edge' that quickly became regular and properly defined, following the outline of the plate.

Between the plates, there were several areas of potential decoration; these included the blued-steel 'gate' on striking watches, one or more mainspring barrels where there was more than one anyway, the verge potence, and so on. The only features really worth special consideration, however, are the pillars that separate the movement plates. Starting as simple round or tapered baluster shapes, some of them vaselike, with perhaps one or more turned 'collars', the best English makers soon showed preferences — East for his tapering pedestals, with or without engraved 'drapes', and solid or hollow, Tompion with his highly individual cocks, and so on. Most makers, even so, were influenced by contemporary decorative taste and settled for the so-called 'tulip' pillar, reflecting Dutch trends; and this style saw the century to a close.

Movement decoration is best understood by reference to pictures, and the reader is referred, both for the seventeenth century and succeeding ones, to relevant illustrations throughout this work, as also to Appendices IV and V.

THE EIGHTEENTH CENTURY

This is the period during which the movement towards precision time measurement gathered momentum, fuelled by the urgent need for a marine timekeeper to help in finding a ship's longitude with predictable accuracy when out of sight of land. An Act of Parliament of 1714 offered a maximum reward of £20,000 to this end, which was eventually won, after some fifty years, by John Harrison, although part-awards were also made to other eminent craftsmen joining in the scheme.

WATCHCASES   One important type of case, its popularity overlapping the turn of the century, had its outer — of pair-cases, that is — covered in tortoiseshell or sometimes leather. After shaping, this extra 'layer' would be attached to its foundation by pinning the two together around the edge, the tails of the pins being bent flat on the inside. Further decoration with pins, usually of silver, in the style called *piqué,* could then be used to cover much of the case back with some abstract symmetrical pattern or, occasionally, with a simple motif such as a crown or a monogram. A more elaborate method was actually to inlay the shell with silver — or, rarely, gold — when it was possible to build up small pictorial features such as birds and flowers, cherubs or even a coat of arms. The earliest such cases still possess that typical seventeenth-century feature, the square joint; and both *piqué* and inlaid decoration on these cases must have had some common sources, since the same designs recur with unerring frequency.

This same principle, of adding an extra layer to the metal carcase of the outer case for decorative purposes, extended — throughout the second half of the century — to materials like shagreen and horn. The first is so attractive in its own right that, in English usage, it is rarely thought necessary further to adorn it with *piqué* or inlaid work; while horn, a versatile material, can be underpainted to resemble tortoiseshell or even to present a charming pictorial theme. Horn outer cases are still to be found during the early part of the nineteenth century.

Popular though these fashions were, there was another which was to sweep the field throughout much of the century — *repoussé* cases. This work, sometimes called chasing or embossing, was highly skilled and, at its best, undoubtedly seen by contemporary eyes as an important art form. It is not surprising, therefore, that such cases were much in demand by those who could afford to pay the highest prices for the best workmanship, with the result that many of the considerable number to survive the ravages of time are of supreme elegance and beauty, and constitute an important part of the nation's heritage.

The art of *repoussé* decoration arrived in England just in time to herald the emergence of the rococo, so that some of the earliest examples still contain elements of baroque design, seen especially in the cartouches that often surround the central motif. In summarising the trends, Dr Richard Edgcumbe of the Victoria & Albert Museum writes:

> Only a small number of London embossed watch cases survive that are associated with hall-marks from 1700–1720. Some have low relief patterns of symmetrically arranged foliage and strapwork in the style of contemporary engravers such as Jean and Claude Berain, Simon Gribelin, Pierre Bourdon, Jean Bourguet and Masson. Classical heads or baskets of flowers appear outside the cartouche at the intermediate cardinal points, while within this border there may only be further ornament or space for an engraved monogram or crest. From about 1720 there are more examples from which to generalise, and figure scenes then become the most common form of decoration although there continue to be examples in the older style.

The sources of design inspiration as well as the method of working are discussed elsewhere in this book, as are also the principal personalities employed in it, including such artists as G. M. Moser and the Heckels.

Repoussé is essentially a means of obtaining a third dimension — depth or relief — and, indeed, a few such cases exhibit a very high relief, so much so that it is almost possible to insert a fingertip behind the principal figures. In such cases — which are anyway extremely rare — examination makes it clear that those areas that are most raised from the background have been made separately, after which they are then attached to the main work. This adds greatly to their fragility so that it was customary to supply a third, glazed, case to protect them both from accidental damage and from rubbing during normal wear, which would, inevitably, have blunted the fine detail. These extra cases invariably take the same form, being merely two shagreen-covered bezels, jointed together and with one fitted with a glass which, when in place, covered the *repoussé* scene.

There was only one drawback to the splendours of embossed watchcases; they were not susceptible to being pierced, to allow the sound of an internal bell to be heard. Furthermore, to add to the existing striking and alarm watches, there were now the comparatively newfangled repeaters, in which depressing the pendant caused the time to the nearest quarter-hour to be sounded. Hence, the earlier style of pierced and engraved pair-cases continued, although now modified to the extent that decoration was confined to the band, the back of the case being simply left as a polished surface. At the same time, the quality of such decoration started to decline, becoming more stylised than heretofore.

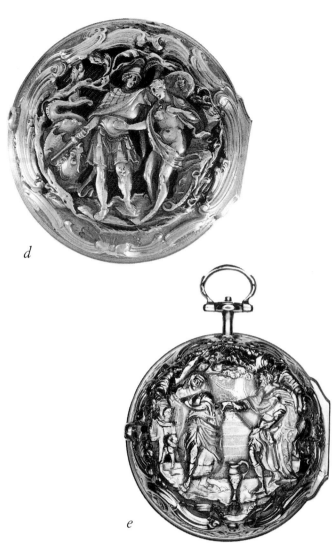

d

a

b

e

c

PLATES 40a,b,c,d,e: Some examples of fine *repoussé* gold outer cases, illustrating just a few of the variety of classical scenes which could be depicted. a) The scene within a rococo border represents Vertumnus and Pomona, and is the work of the great G. M. Moser; the inner case of this watch is hallmarked 1739, and this is the earliest datable example of Moser's use of this asymmetric outline. b) This example, in very high relief, probably represents Esther and Ahasuerus and is signed 'Manly f.'. The watch is by Ellicott and can be dated to 1767. There is a third, glazed, case to protect this masterpiece. c) It is rare to find a *repoussé* case in such remarkably fresh condition; the scene represented is of Alexander and Diogenes, complete with barrel, and the watch, signed Windmills, dates c1720. d) The combination of *repoussé* and cut-out work is most rare; combined with a backing of red silk, the overall effect is opulent indeed. The associated watch is by Thomas Rayment, a London maker who flourished during the middle fifty years of the eighteenth century, while the scene depicted is of Perseus rescuing Andromeda from the sea monster. e) This gold outer case, from a watch by Daniel Grignion, can be dated accurately to 1726. The scene, in high relief, shows Rebecca at the Well and as might be anticipated, there is yet a third glazed case to safeguard this fragile work from undue wear and tear.

The second half of the century saw the emergence of perhaps the most frivolous of English watchcases; it might seem that the watch, as a personal possession, was now here to stay and was just as susceptible as any other such artifact to the flights of fancy that seemed to characterise that period. English enamel watchcases emerged, which are nowadays always described as 'Battersea' although that source only existed from 1753 to 1756. Most of them are far more likely to have originated in the Birmingham and South Staffordshire manufactories, now usually categorised as 'Bilston', which operated from c1740 to the century's end, deteriorating markedly in its later output. Porcelain watchcases of considerable delicacy and charm are believed to have been created by a number of factories, including Chelsea, but the fragile nature of the material has almost certainly affected the survival rate of these, which are nowadays exceedingly rare, although a few specimens do exist.

Towards the end of the century, one or two new developments occurred. Watch pendants continued to have stirrup-shaped 'bows', or rings, until about 1750, after which they became oval. Cases decorated with engine-turning (qv) started to appear about 1770, and this type of mechanical ornament, it was soon discovered, looked very well indeed beneath a covering of translucent enamel. The consular case — which is said, traditionally, to be associated with Napoleon's appointment as First Consul, even if the dates do not actually match up — seems first to have been introduced by the precision watchmakers c1775. Essentially, it is a single

case with a double back, the outer of which is opened for access to the winding and hand-setting squares, while the movement hinges out from the front. Even so, the majority of watchcases, especially in the provinces, remained as they had been for some time — plain gold or silver cases, heavy and robust in the true English tradition and ideally suited to a nation that still mostly worked on the land to earn its living.

DIALS AND HANDS   The *champlevé* metal dial, which had appeared in the previous century eventually to become the standard design for watches with concentric hour and minute hands, continued in use for at least the first half of the one now under consideration, but with subtle changes — half- and quarter-hour markings, for example, were unnecessary for any but single-handed watches, although this does not seem to have been realised until c1740, around which time the best makers started to omit them. The early *champlevé* dials had very prominent five-minute divisions, their Arabic numerals

PLATE 41: Old habits die hard — and the six-hour dial watch survived into the eighteenth century, but now with an enamel dial and a conventional minute hand. This example by Thomas Tompion and George Graham dates from c1712 and its accoutrements are not without interest as well. The short steel fob chain also accommodates a variety of watch keys and a seal; and the roughly heartshaped device encloses a retractable bedhook with which to suspend the watch at night from the drapes of a four-poster bed.

PLATE 42: This watch, by James Swingler, of Holbeach, is hallmarked 1802. On the painted dial, the chapters consist of signs of the zodiac, while the observer with the telescope is said to be watching Halley's Comet, although such an attribution is not consistent with the date of the watch.

PLATE 43: An arcaded minute ring on a watch dial inevitably bespeaks the Dutch practice, and it was universally adopted by English makers on the products they exported to that country, as in this example by Richard Bradshaw. The ship, however, flies a version of the Union flag.

contrasting effectively with the Roman hours; but these gradually assumed less prominence. The design of the *champlevé* dial, even to the proportions of its numerals, transferred most sympathetically to the white enamel dial, when this came into general use around 1720; there are earlier examples. On this new-style dial, which ran alongside before eventually superseding the *champlevé* dial, the last remnants of the earlier usage, the five-minute numerals, were finally phased out altogether by 1800. During the second half of the century, too, the proportions previously favoured for dial numerals changed subtly, making them a great deal slimmer and more elegant, and thereby reducing the density of black on the dial, or at least appearing to do so. In the 1780s, one of the main design changes allowed Arabic hour numerals to be used for the first time, although this style never seemed to gain wide popularity.

A particularly popular fashion in the second half of the eighteenth century, which is usually found on provincial watches, spilled over well into the one that followed. This is the painted dial, in which the centre is occupied by a pictorial scene that could embrace almost any familiar subject from farming and the countryside to naval battles; on some versions, the scene runs around the outside of the chapter ring.

So much for the ordinary watch that told the simple time. The only real departure from the conventional arrangement of concentric hours and minutes, with perhaps subsidiary seconds above VI, had been to indicate this last by means of yet a third hand, springing from the centre to the minute ring which was, of course, already divided into sixty. This arrangement, called 'centre' or 'sweep' seconds, was favoured by George Graham from the 1730s.

One of the side-effects resulting from technological advances, however, was an increasing demand for additional indicators, to show smaller divisions of time, or just to present the existing indications differently, often connected with scientific and especially observatory practice, or for use in navigation. One of the most important was the so-called 'regulator' dial, derived directly from the regulator clock, a high-precision timekeeper used by astronomers. In order to reduce the amount of gearing behind the dial, and thus the friction inherent therein, concentric hour and minute hands were abandoned in favour of an arrangement by which a small dial above centre showed hours and a matching dial below centre showed seconds; minutes were shown on a ring around the outside edge of the dial, by a hand stretching from its centre. Regulator dials first came into use in the 1780s on marine and pocket chronometers and on some of the early lever watches, made by Josiah Emery and his con-

PLATE 44: Two early eighteenth-century movements, respectively by Edward Bodenham and George Etherington. Similarity in the depiction of the masks, which are not of the conventional 'Father Time' countenance, and the deployment of the same decorative motifs on the table, although in a different arrangement, could indicate the work of the same artist in both examples.

COLOUR PLATE 6: Some examples of the use of decorative enamelling on watches. At the top, a watch by Samuel Betts, c1660, has its case enamelled on the inside with countryside scenes, while the outside, albeit somewhat damaged, is quite differently decorated with translucent green enamel with a central white daisy and a border in relief of white flowers with pink markings. The movement, alongside, has a dial with white enamel chapter ring within an engraved gold border, while the centre is enamelled translucent green with a sunflower and border of flowers. The gold 'beetle' hand is a later replacement, but the original outer shagreen case of this watch survives. Below and to the left, a watch by John Ramsay, c1625, illustrates the technique of *cloisonné* enamelling, while the watch at right, by Richard Carrington, which dates from 1777, uses the Lion of Scotland as a decorative motif.

temporaries. Other information could be shown using a similar layout, of course; and a small subsidiary dial below centre, if it was divided into no more than five second, could magnify the movement of a 'sweep' seconds hands since it could be subdivided into quarters or fifths of a second, depending upon the escapement. Some multi-dialled watches from this period are marvels of complexity, as well as being fascinating to observe.

MOVEMENTS The eighteenth century saw perhaps less change in the overall structure of the watch movement than any other. Functionally, it had settled happily into the so-called 'full plate' movement; that is to say, the framework consisted of two circular gilt-brass plates, separated by pillars, and between which the wheelwork of the movement, and the mainspring and fusee, were deployed. Superimposed upon the back of this main chassis, and operating outside it, were the balance wheel and arbor, the outer end of which pivoted in the centre of the table of the watch cock, which was screwed through its foot into the back plate. Associated with this was the balance spring and a means to regulate it, the latter requiring initially the slide plate, complete with dial and 'square', over which the watch key fitted in order to apply any necessary adjustment.

All this made for rather a deep movement; and, indeed, the English craft tradition had been founded upon a robust and rugged product, which could withstand a fair amount of rough handling and which would certainly continue operating reliably, if not particularly accurately, for long periods. Not for nothing did the English verge watch, especially in its latter years, come to be known as a 'turnip' watch, even though this was somewhat slimmer in build than its early eighteenth-century counterpart.

Around 1700, the decoration of the watch movement is considered to have reached its peak — what is called 'the golden era'. The watch cock was as big as it would ever be — those used by Daniel Quare on his special watches covered at least three-quarters of the surface area of the plate — and, when engraved and pierced by the best artists, are quite splendid. It is only sad that, so far, no means has been discovered of identifying such people, nor yet examples of their work, for a fine specimen, with its 'wings' flaring, and its scrolling maze of foliage, birds, fishes' heads, and so forth, is a fascinating object that will often repay the most minute inspection. Even the 'pendulum cock' (qv), despite its spurious antecedents, has often a great deal of charm.

After about twenty years, the cock foot started to contract in size; from a state in which there was a 180° 'throw' from one side to the other, it became noticeable that one edge of the foot was drawing in; it was not long before both sides were similarly affected. By mid-century, the angle formed by the two sides had shrunk to about 100°.

With the best London makers, this stage seems to have extended to about 1780. Alongside it, however, there appeared, for only a few years, focused about 1760, a style known as 'lace-edged'. In these, the edge of the cock table had a characteristic filigree treatment which might also be continued around the foot, and the outer edge of the slide plate. The foot maintained what might be called its 'semi-splayed' state, even so.

The form of slide plate regulator throughout the first half of this century remained that favoured by Thomas Tompion from the latter end of the previous one; he had introduced it as a result of his own involvement in the application of the balance spring. Its decoration followed closely that of the cock itself. In 1755, however, one

PLATE 45: Two movements with overall decoration, one anonymous while the other has a panel on the slide plate engraved 'Grand London'. The latter dates from c1760, while the other is rather earlier. Even though both watches might appear of conventional English workmanship, simply the total absence of a name on the one must make it suspect while the name on the other, even though listed by Baillie, is by no means well documented. Both could be Swiss imports.

Joseph Bosley invented a form of regulation that effectively dispensed altogether with the need for a slide plate, by transferring the operative mechanism on to the surface of the back plate of the movement and leaving it uncovered, so that its action was plain for all to see. It is perhaps this single development in the evolution of the English watch which, more than any other, sounded the death-knell of movement decoration, by removing one of the principal surfaces susceptible to such treatment.

Yet another example of that time-lag between one usage and its successor to which attention has already been directed is the Tompion-style regulator with slide plate that is still to be found on watches even after the turn of the century, and that was the form preferred by the best London makers, until well into the 1780s. The overall trend, nevertheless, was towards simplification, with the cock foot contracting until its sides projected at an angle of only about 60°, while retaining a round table even though by now the neck had lost all definition and had been absorbed. It may have been the pioneer chronometer makers who, probably unconsciously, were the main instruments of change on this part of the movement. The chronometer escapement utilises a helical balance spring rather than one of spiral form, and this is almost impossible to house beneath a round cock table, since it is here that its outer end has to be fixed. The best shape of table for this purpose is that universally adopted by leading craftsmen on their pocket chronometers, in which the table has almost parallel sides and a rounded end, with a slot near its extremity for a stud to take the spring. This area was, at least in the beginning, the site of some fairly perfunctory decoration, which was soon discarded; but, in the overall shape, it is possible to detect the first glimmerings of a movement towards the ubiquitous 'wedge of cheese' design, which will be the last to be examined.

Movement pillars, at the beginning of the eighteenth century, were basking in the floodlight of attention given them at the end of the previous one, with the 'tulip' design in favour. This was followed quite soon by the type usually designated 'Egyptian', but there were crested versions of both these basic designs, as well as a transitional style, also crested, which had the outward-thrusting lines of the former but the central division of the latter. In complicated watches, with repeating and other functions, there just was not room for such elaboration, and the pillars tended to be simple round posts with a wide collar at each end to provide a firmer attachment to the plates. It was not too long, however, before the square baluster pillar — a pleasing design when well made, with sharp mouldings and angles — became fashionable, while later still a number of exotic designs flitted in and, as quickly, out of favour, some so extraordinary as to defy description. Towards the end of the century — again, almost certainly as a result of the influence of the chronometer makers — the plain round pillar became usual, its simplicity and functional efficiency having an obvious appeal. Even so, throughout the century, there was always room for the individual approach and the reader is referred to the photographs of movement pillars with appropriate commentary towards the end of this book, for further information.

THE NINETEENTH CENTURY

The dominant theme in this, the last period with which this book is concerned, has to be the Industrial Revolution, which had gained a firm foothold by 1800. Fundamental changes were imminent — the arrival of the railways and the rapid harnessing of steam power for industrial purposes, the gradual decline in the overall importance of agriculture as England's principal source of income, changes in standards of living for a class-conscious society. The necessity for accurate time measurement reached a far wider spectrum of the population than ever before, especially as communications improved countrywide. This inevitably brought in its train a greatly increased demand for cheap but reliable timekeepers; yet the English, and especially the London, trade were loath to abandon all the old and well-tried methods of small-batch production and laborious handfinishing in favour of the newfangled mass production methods that had been pioneered in Switzerland and America. The British Horological Institute, which was founded in London in 1858, was originally intended as an instrument to fight this battle; but the outcome was inevitable. The country was eventually to be flooded with cheap imported timekeepers of all kinds, and the fine clocks and watches upon which the famous and international reputation of the native craft was founded, were gone for ever. The London trade itself never compromised, and so was forced out of existence.

WATCHCASES   As the century started, the ordinary watch was much as it had been for the previous two decades — a plain, heavy, pair-case housing a movement of greater or lesser accuracy, depending upon the price paid. The first development to occur — and this happened even before the turn of the century — was the arrival of the hunting-cased watch. A hunter has a solid cover over the dial, while the half-hunter has a small disc-like glazed window in the centre of such a cover, so that the position of the hands can be detected. In its later manifestations, the half-hunter frequently had a chapter ring engraved around this small window, so that the time could be judged with even greater accuracy. There are various apocryphal stories concerning the origin of this style: the half-hunter is said, for instance, to have been created by Napoleon I, who cut a hole in the middle of his hunter-cased watch to avoid having to open it in rough conditions in the Alps; but it seems more likely that its name reflects its antecedents accurately enough. The earliest surviving examples, mostly dating from 1802–4, show quite clearly that they evolved from the pair-cased watch, since the hunter or half-hunter cover is applied to the inner case, while an outer case is also provided.

Fashions for underpainted horn cases continued unabated, the pictorial scenes being even more topical than heretofore. As to new styles, in the 1820s it was still quite common to find an elaborately cast outer case, the band and bezel encrusted deeply with shell or floral patterns and the pendant en suite; yet the back would be machine-turned on a rose-engine (qv) in a very complex geometrical pattern. Most of these cast cases were made in the north, especially in Chester, another typical 'country' feature from that area being the pendant that has an oval cross-section.

The plain pair-cased watch continued to be made in country districts until well beyond the mid-century, although it was gradually dying out elsewhere. Apart from engine-turning, the watch of reasonable quality might have a reeded band to the case to relieve the otherwise rather colourless impression; and, talking of colour, this could be imparted in new and quite subtle ways. The Clockmakers' Company Collection, for instance, contains a splendid watch by Brockbanks, hallmarked 1812, which has a hunter case in four-colour gold, with chiselled floral ornament and complicated engine-turning. The use, together, of gold alloys of different compositions, ranging in colour from white to copper-red, with several intermediate tones, became very popular until the mid-century, or thereabouts.

So, the last decorative treatments applied to watchcases — cast and chiselled ornament, engine-turning, and only very occasionally, a little hand-engraving — were to lead eventually to an essentially plain product. The watch movement itself had become much thinner during the period; a concept introduced by the French, who associated this with elegance and sophistication, at last caught on in England. In the 1880s, the watchcase had to contend with its last major design change arising from technological advances. The method of winding the watch by inserting a separate key into a keyhole at the back, had never been a very convenient one and various alternative means were devised, including several types of so-called 'pump winding'; but eventually the one that

became universally accepted was that familiar to the present day, by which a stem with a winding 'crown' or button on the end, passes down through the pendant into the movement. Rotating the crown not only winds up the watch but, used in association with a 'push-piece' alongside, can set the hands to the right time. The mechanical watch had reached the zenith of its development and it is difficult to conceive of any modification that might have improved it.

DIALS AND HANDS At the beginning of the nineteenth century, there was some carry over from the previous one, certainly in the unabated popularity of the painted dial, which continued beyond the 1850s. Yet there was really no standard form; every maker probably had his own preferences so far as fine detail was concerned. In general, however, the designs were restrained and could be elegant. By the second quarter of the century there was an unexpected change of style with the hour numerals becoming both larger and thicker, so that the area of dense black on the surface became, in some cases, unacceptably large by modern standards. The result could be very ugly.

Some of the trends in watchcases were also rubbing off on dials, too. Before the mid-century, metal dials were seeing an unexpected revival, incorporating motifs in four-colour gold and also with some engine-turned enhancement. Another treatment allowed the hour numerals to appear as polished gold, raised above a usually matted surface; this was particularly effective when well executed. Gold could still be, and very occasionally was, given an engine-turned treatment as a background for enamelling, in the style termed *guilloche;* and the Brockbanks watch in the Clockmakers' Company Collection, referred to in the last section on cases, has this enrichment with the sunken dial centre engine-turned and covered with translucent red enamel, while the chapter ring is enamelled grey-blue.

A few makers used silvered metal dials as a direct substitute for the ordinary enamel versions, translating the layout in its entirety on to them. In a sense, they were reverting to the practice of clockmakers seventy years before; this type of dial reappears spasmodically until the end of the century, almost invariably upon watches with specialised uses, often by good makers.

PLATE 46: At the turn of the eighteenth century, multi-dialled watches became as popular as they had been more than one hundred and fifty years earlier although quite differently designed. Two examples, by Thomas Martin and Andrew Esdaile, reflect the general trend, but the peak of complexity is surely reached in the astronomical watch by George Margetts.

PLATE 47: John Grant made many splendid watches towards the end of the eighteenth century, giving much thought to design. The purpose of the overlapping dials on this example was doubtless to allow greater prominence and scale to the seconds indicator, so that it could be read more easily and accurately.

In the latter half of the century, and as part of the trend towards thinness, the subsidiary seconds dial above VI was recessed below the surface of the main dial, allowing the seconds hand also to drop. This reduced the clearance necessary for the hour hand, since it no longer had to be raised high enough to avoid the seconds hand. The minute hand, in turn, could be dropped, thus reducing the height of the centre post.

As for any departures from other ordinary detail, some half-hunter dials had an additional hour ring, which showed just inside the window in the case cover, and an hour hand that had two indicators, one behind the other on the same shank, so that the innermost one registered on this extra hour ring when the cover was shut. The same design concept was obtained on the much slimmer minute hand simply by a slight 'waist' at the appropriate place.

Hands throughout this period came into their own, with a variety of different patterns fashionable at different periods. Gold hands generally went with gold cases, and blued-steel ones with silver cases. Most hands, probably, were just polished brass. Styles include spade, serpentine, fleur-de-lys, Breguet and many others.

PLATE 48: Three later English watches, all of the class categorised 'pocket chronometers', showing developments in dial design. Reversion to the fashion for metal dials is shown at the top, in this example by Robert Roskell, of Liverpool. Next, is shown one of John Arnold's classic smaller precision watches, and at the bottom another fine maker's work in this specimen by James Hatton, the case hallmarked 1806. Five-minute numerals remain in evidence, although very subdued, on the Arnold watch, but have disappeared altogether from the other two.

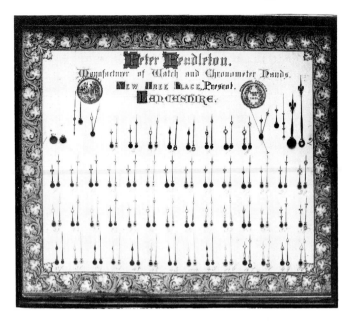

PLATE 49a: Makers of watch hands, a specialised and highly skilled branch of the 'art', often exhibited display frames showing the style and range of their work. Peter Pendleton who supplied the Prescot makers, draws attention to his Prize Medal from the International Exhibition of 1862.

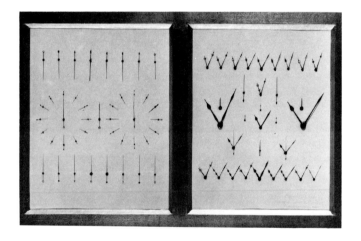

PLATE 49b: A much more restrained display than that shown in Plate 49a is that of R. Haswell & Sons, 48–50 Spencer Street, Clerkenwell, London, EC. It is only just possible to discern, in the bottom righthand corner of this frame, the rubber stamp of identity. Both frames, however, clearly demonstrate the wide variety of patterns of watch hands available during the last century.

MOVEMENTS   As the previous century ended so this one began, with the standard full plate movement still the norm for English watches, no matter what the mechanical make-up, and especially the escapement, might be; yet, in many respects this period was to be the most mechanically innovative of all, reaching its zenith with the perfecting of the lever escapement, which is still in use today as the time-measuring basis of any mechanical watch.

Two other trends, however, affected the development of the movement. Starting early in the nineteenth century, rough and incomplete watch movements — known as *ébauches* — were made in quantity in the Midlands and north of England, from where they could be easily distributed throughout the country to other workshops belonging to the makers whose names finally adorned them; and these makers would 'finish' them, in the terminology of the time. The main centres for these 'movement makers to the trade', as they were called, were in Lancashire, especially in the area of Liverpool and Prescot, and in Coventry, which is less than twenty miles from Birmingham in the industrial Midlands. Joseph Preston & Sons set up business in Prescot in 1829. Coventry was more of a cottage-type industry, with families working in their own homes, which, being mostly terraced houses, constituted small enclosed communities in much the same manner as conventional factories do.

By around 1890, Rotherham & Son, the biggest 'factory' in Coventry, was achieving an output of 100 watches a day. To give some mid-century statistics for added perspective, in 1858 Britain produced about 150,000 watches a year, 33,000 in gold cases and the remainder in silver. Another 99,000 were imported, but some 10,000 of these were re-exported. Of the 10,740 men engaged in manufacture, 4,850 were based in London, 4,020 in Warwickshire which included Coventry, 1,160 in Liverpool, and 710 in Prescot. The centre of watchmaking in London, as it had been for generations, was in Clerkenwell, where several 'makers-up' — firms such as Usher & Cole, and Ashley & Sims — had their premises.

The other trend that materially affected the watch movement in the nineteenth century has already been detected in watchcases during the same period — the technical process of making them thinner. The effect upon the decoration of the movement was immediate, since one obvious means of accomplishing this end was to remove the watch cock and balance, hitherto superimposed upon the movement, and sink them within it. This could be achieved by so designing the mechanism that there would be room to cut away the plate for this purpose; and thus there evolved, during the first half of the century, the so-called three-quarter plate movement, to be followed in the second half by the half plate movement. Meanwhile, the full plate movement continued to be manufactured, but its days were clearly numbered.

In any event, when the century started, movement decoration was already passing into fatal decline. Provincial makers continued the tradition of a cock with round table and somewhat attenuated foot that they had inherited from the end of the previous period. The decoration tended to be very uninspired, mere whorls with a few very stylised motifs, such as six-pointed stars, but generally without form or substance. Rarely, some more experimental operators tried their hands at unusual shapes, especially for the cock table. Liverpool makers developed their own particularly style; and there were also occasional essays into folk-art. London makers tried to preserve their previous restrained and slightly classic styles, meanwhile edging all the time towards the completely plain movement. The precision watchmakers achieved this quite early in the period, but the ordinary everyday watch still retained the most hackneyed remnants of former conventions, now compressed on to the much smaller wedge-shaped cock table that was used in the newfangled movements. So persistent was tradition, however, that an entirely new site for decoration had been opened up by raising a circular 'table' out of the area immediately above the mainspring barrel. This would hardly have been feasible on the old-fashioned full plate movements, but could be executed on the three-quarter plate module: in most cases, the effect is ridiculous.

A further confusion arose, of course, when the balance and cock were lowered into the body of the movement, since the regulator acting upon the balance spring had to descend as well, because it was, by that time, sited upon the cock table itself. As the components became smaller, there just was not room for everything; that is, for the index, as watchmakers call the steel indicating finger, and the scale against which it had to register. Inevitably, decoration suffered. As for the movement pillars, they were simply functional posts, with no pretensions to anything else; for present purposes, they can be ignored.

If nineteenth-century movement decoration needs any sort of epitaph, it can only express wonderment that it survived so long. It must have added to the cost of the finished article; the increasing acceptance of watches as precision instruments meant that the intrusion of dust and dirt into their mechanisms had to be avoided as far as possible, so that no rational excuse remained to open them up for casual inspection. The obstinacy of the craft in respect of its methods and traditions was certainly manifested in other ways, however, and probably this is just another example of that same phenomenon.

PLATE 50: Liverpool, as a watchmaking centre, developed a style of its own. Robert Roskell (left) was a maker of some enterprise, his work characterised by ruggedness and substance, while other wares from that area often possessed rather less intrinsic quality. Both movements date from the second decade of the nineteenth century.

5 The Personal Touch

PLATE 51: A pastor's watch, presented by his parishioners to the Rt Revd Dr Carruthers in 1833, on the occasion of his consecration as Bishop of Ceramis (see p68).

Pride of possession is a universal human frailty. Nowadays, it might be reflected in the 'customised' car with its 'cherished' number-plates or, on a lesser scale, the discreet monogram or even crest, on shirt, briefcase or letter-heading. It is only to be expected, therefore, that the proud owner of a clock or watch, in the days when such things were not only worth a king's ransom but were also frequently conceived as novel items of personal adornment, should wish to identify him- or herself as closely as possible with such an enviable chattel.

The evidence of this pre-dates the survival in Britain of such objects themselves. Reference has been made elsewhere to the remarkable timepieces owned by Queen Elizabeth I, for which our only testimony is to be found in inventory descriptions and the like. The interesting aspect, in this context, seems to be that, while the Queen may well have regarded herself as above such petty foibles — for her clocks and watches do not seem to have been over-adorned with crowns, royal arms and other symbols of her power and person — those who gave such objects to her clearly were not! It is not unusual to find, for example:

> One clock of gold curiously wrought with flowers and beastes, with a queene on the toppe on one side: and on the other side a beare and ragged staffe of sparkes of diamondes, fullie furnished with diamondes and rubies of sundry sortes and bignes; one emerode under it, a faier table diamonde with a ragged staffe in the foyle thereof, and a faier rubie under it squared; and a pearle pendaunt on either side of the clocke.

The 'bear and ragged staff' was the heraldic device of the Earl of Leicester who was the Queen's Master of the Horse.

When the earliest surviving timepieces are considered, it is readily apparent that such practices had become firmly established: they nearly all reflect heraldic connections with their owners; but, over the centuries, there have been a number of different means of 'personalising' the watch, and these will now be reviewed under appropriate headings.

Armorial Devices

It is reasonable to suppose that in the sixteenth century, far more people of that class which could afford to own a watch were armigerous, than would be the case today when, perhaps, the modern equivalent might be the ownership of a Rolls-Royce. Hence, many of the surviving watches from this early period have a coat of arms as evidence of their former owners. Occasionally, these may be combined with a name; and occasionally, too, the arms displayed might appear to be suspect. If, indeed, some of these may have been assumed rather than granted, it was merely setting a precedent for a practice that has been widespread at certain periods.

One of the most flagrant examples to be found among the horological fraternity might seem to have been the 'arms' sported by Sir John Bennett, the controversial Victorian watchmaker whose advocacy of mass production and the use of cheap female labour made him thoroughly unpopular with most of his trade contemporaries, and with the City of London, which three times vetoed his election as Alderman. It was even said of him that he was knighted by mistake! His very ornate personal watch has no less than six coats of arms enamelled upon its cover and one of these, in a prominent position, Sir John appears to have adapted from that of a former namesake, Sir Thomas Bennett, Lord Mayor of London in 1603–4, to whom there is no evidence that he bore any relationship at all.

With coats of arms, as with any other applied symbol of ownership, it has to be remembered that there is ample latitude for fraud. Nevertheless, throughout history forgers and fakers have tended to be careless over detail and entirely concerned with the immediate impression, which may be very convincing. Especially in heraldry, however, the blazon of arms displayed upon any object as evidence of original ownership has to relate to the period of that object; and arms change and develop with each succeeding generation of a family to bear them, so that they can be dated with reasonable accuracy. The heraldic detective, therefore, having established within acceptable limits, even if only stylistically, a bracket of dates for the object itself, must then confirm the currency of the armorials applied to it; and if he cannot do that, he has to suspect the worst.

Dates

At all periods, symbols of ownership of the ordinary watch may be accompanied by a date; and here again the wary must take nothing at face value. There is no obstacle to prevent a date being 'added' to an existing name or

PLATE 52: A coat of arms dated 1620 on a watch by Cornelius Yate. Although the armorial appears to be foreign, the date is consistent with Yate having been one of the original petitioners seeking the formation of the Clockmakers' Company in 1622.

armorial device; but the whole purpose of such a fraud is likely to be to enhance the value of the object so treated by suggesting that it is earlier than in fact it is. In the days before research had built up a substantial bank of data on periods, styles and the working lives of prominent craftsmen, it was relatively easy to perpetrate such deceits. As a result, nineteenth-century catalogues of important — often national — exhibitions contain descriptions of objects for which the stated provenances are chronological impossibilities. The sad thing about this is that such assertions, even when shown to lack credibility, tend to pass into the history of the object concerned, thereby becoming accepted as fact — which, of course, they most certainly are not — and eventually, if it should come on to the open market, being quoted as such.

The last notable occasion upon which all sorts of dubious curiosities were paraded as genuine relics of this and that, was the loan exhibition, *Royal Treasures,* shown in London during April and May, 1937. Very few of the horological exhibits included therein would match up to

the provenances stated were they subjected to present-day scholarship. It is also true that by no means all such paradoxes are deliberately fraudulent. What has sometimes been described as 'the scourge of the professional historian', that curious hotchpotch of fact and fiction, which usually masquerades under the authentic-sounding title of 'family tradition', is just as much to blame. If all the watches that Charles I is said to have bestowed as scaffold gifts upon those about him, were laid end to end, they could have encircled the Greenwich Meridian!

NAMES

On by far the great majority of Englishmade watches of any significant age, there appears upon the movement — and usually upon the dial as well — the name of the maker, with the town or city where his business premises were situated. This can be of enormous help in dating the watch. Of recent years, however, there has been much argument among horological historians as to how much — if any — of the watch itself was actually made by the person whose name appears thereon. Some of the names are known to be those of mere retailers while, conversely, it is also known that, certainly from the latter half of the eighteenth century, some craftsmen manufactured solely for other members of the trade and never actually put their own names to anything.

In the present context, this need not worry us. All that is significant is that there is likely to be, on any English watch that can boast of some antiquity, a name and town connected with its manufacture and/or sale, but unrelated to the owner. If another name is also found upon this same object, it can be reasonably inferred that this must have some connection with its ownership. From time to time it has been suggested that a master craftsman might, on occasion, permit an underling to put his name to a piece if it was his own unaided work and was of special merit, but there is no real evidence of this.

Such secondary names do frequently appear, and there is a choice of several different sites for them. Names will sometimes be found upon the watchcase, inside or out, usually depending upon the period. Pair-cased watches — those in which the movement is enclosed within two separate cases, one inside the other, for strength and protection from shock as well as to exclude dust and dirt — are most likely to have such identification upon the outside of the inner case. Later types of watch, being enclosed within one case (although this may have a double back), may well have the name upon the inner cover over the back of the movement, which is usually called the dome, or cuvette, the outer cover being referred to simply as 'the back'.

Equally, secondary names may appear upon the dial and, if the number of letters involved permits, in place of the 'chapter numerals' or hour figures, as they may more generally be known. In this context, the word 'chapter' is used in a general sense of division, as the chapters of a book. This substitution of letters for figures is of long usage, and will even be found occasionally upon metal dials of the early eighteenth century; but it is much more common on enamel dials, as found throughout the rest of that century and well into the one that followed.

PLATES 53: The substitution of the letters of the owner's name for the hour numerals on a watch dial is by no means uncommon; less common is the inclusion of his town in place of the five-minute numerals.

Direct substitution of letters for numerals upon the dial requires that a full name have no more than twelve such and, for preference, divided equally into six each for forename and surname. However, this type of limitation is very restrictive, and various devices were employed in order to circumvent it. Eleven letters could be accommodated by placing a star or other symbol at XII, the name then reading from I clockwise round the dial. Most arrangements allowed for the name to start from I clockwise, or else there might have been considerable problems of orientation, since no provision for punctuation between first and second names will usually be permitted. A complete name of thirteen letters could also be contained, provided that there was a double letter somewhere within it. The example shown in Plate 53 not only demonstrates this — using what printers call a ligature to represent the double 'l' in William — but also, most untypically, has a comma and a full stop to indicate where the inscription begins and ends.

An interesting variant of this style, which has been noted upon the work of several London makers including Dent, Nicole & Capt, Barraud and Nicole Nielsen, is the reversal of colours, so that the chapters appear in white on a black ground. This is a very effective treatment, with considerable visual impact due to the element of surprise it generates.

Perhaps most rarely, secondary names appear upon the watch movement. Usually these will be found upon the cock; one watchmaker who is known to have had the purchaser's name engraved thereon was Thomas Cummins, the maker of lever escapement watches of quite exceptional quality in the 1820s. However, this practice was known long before Cummins's time, certainly from the middle of the eighteenth century. It should not be confused with a similar-seeming practice, to be found on some early nineteenth-century watches, by which the name of a patentee of some mechanical aspect of the watch is inscribed on the cock.

MONOGRAMS AND CYPHERS

There appears to be little difference in the dictionary definitions of these two terms, which are said to mean 'an interweaving of the initials of a name'. In practice, however, the first is a relatively simple exploitation of the concept, while the second can be so complex as to be quite indecipherable to the uninitiated.

In their simplest manifestation, monograms can be just a combination, in a flowing and artistic manner, of two initials, which are read from left to right. The example shown in Plate 54 is from the outer case of a watch made by the eminent London firm of Mudge & Dutton; and

PLATE 54: A cypher inlaid in gold into a tortoiseshell-covered outer case. The watch, by George Graham and dated 1751, must have been one of the last made in his lifetime. It formerly belonged to Sir William Knighton (1776–1836), who had been variously Physician, Keeper of the Privy Purse and Private Secretary to George IV. The same sort of device, carried out in *piqué* work on a leather-covered outer case, is nowhere near so effective. The simplest monogram, just two letters, is illustrated by the outer case of a repeating watch by Mudge and Dutton made in 1783. Its owner, Thomas Raikes, was Governor of the Bank of England from 1797 to 1799.

PLATE 55: The addorsed-C cypher on the cock table of this watch by Thomas Tompion of date c1675, probably refers to the Cottrell family, who were courtiers for five generations from the early seventeenth century onwards. The idiosyncratic dial of this watch appears in Colour Plate 11.

the initials 'TR' stand for Thomas Raikes, who was Governor of the Bank of England for a time during the last quarter of the eighteenth century. When more than two initials are involved, however, it becomes necessary to 'read' the monogram as if it were three-dimensional, the first letter being that nearest to the 'front' and the last one at the back. This concept is as difficult to explain as it is to put into practice; it is further complicated by the fact that some monogram designers were only indifferent practitioners of the art. If one can imagine that each letter is detachable and an entity in its own right, and that it is actually possible to interweave them physically rather than on the drawing board, then the first letter will be that which is least obscured by those that follow and is, therefore, most visible to the viewer, ie at the front. Correspondingly, the one at the back, which is the last letter of the monogram, will be the one that is most obscured by the other letters. Letters in between — and there is usually only one, since most monograms consist of no more than three letters — fall into the order dictated by their relative obscurity. Thus, the device is read from front to back, as if the letters were layered in what seems an apparently random, but is actually a highly organised, order.

Cyphers, on the other hand, were never intended to be literally read, but simply recognised. Rees's *Cyclopaedia* (1818) notes that:

. . . formerly, when merchants and tradesmen were not allowed to use armorial bearings they had cyphers thus artificially composed in their stead; which mostly consisted of the first letters of their names, curiously inter-twined about a cross, &c. of which many instances remain on ancient tombs: but the custom still obtains among persons of various ranks in life, as an ornamental device, especially on seals, or carriages. This practice has, indeed, been increased of late, to avoid the annual tax of two guineas imposed in Great Britain on those who paint their family arms upon carriages.

Another school of thought regarding the purpose of cyphers maintains that they were intended more as symmetrical patterns, capable of easy recognition by the otherwise-illiterate retainers of those who owned them, and the actual letters from which they were formed were largely an irrelevancy.

There appears to be one convention, in this context, which is that members of a royal house invariably have a cypher rather than a monogram, even when the depiction is simply the letters 'GR'. There is an appropriate exclu-

PLATE 56: Personalised watches, taken to extremes, can be quite unintelligible to the uninitiated. (left) This watch, by Webster, appears to have some kind of 'true love' symbolism; roughly translated, the inscription reads 'If fidelity is lacking, then love will perish', while the clasped hands across an anchor, the Cupid with heart and arrow, all go to reinforce this sentiment. All that is lacking is the identity of the owner! The other watch (right) is by Tompion himself and must be one of the earliest recorded with contemporary symbolism relating to freemasonry. Why this had to be orientated at right-angles to the XII–VI axis of the watch is one more mystery, unless it was to avoid undue interference to the decoration from the winding holes.

siveness about this that can be compared, perhaps, with the correct description of the crest traditionally adopted by each Prince of Wales: the device should consist, not of three feathers, but of that number of 'plumes'.

THE ALLUSIVE WATCH

This is a very rarely encountered category, by comparison with some of the other methods of imparting the owner's individual touch to his or her watch. It might be argued that armorial bearings fall within it, and these have already been considered. Masonic watches, too, might be said to indicate the predilections of their owners, but then only in a general way — rather like a club tie.

This particular class, however, goes somewhat further by incorporating something decorative but at the same time, personally allusive, into the overall appearance of the timepiece.

The feature that immediately strikes the viewer about the watch shown in Plate 51 is the depiction of the Paschal Lamb in the centre of the dial. This watch could belong only to a cleric, and that, of itself, greatly limits its currency. In fact, the watch was a gift — as is shown by the presentation inscription upon the cuvette — to the Rt Rev Dr Andrew Carruthers (1770–1852) from his parishioners at St Peter's, Dalbeattie, upon the occasion of his consecration, on 13 January 1833, in the Catholic Chapel, Edinburgh, as Bishop of Ceramis and Vicar

Apostolic of the Eastern District of Scotland.

The watch is signed Chas Spears, Liverpool, and numbered 1844. The 18-carat gold case is hallmarked for Chester, 1833 and the casemaker was John Helsby. All in all, a splendid and expensive gift, even at the time it was made, and an excellent example of the Liverpool 'school' of watchmaking. A remarkable testimony, too, from a relatively small number of people, since there are seats for only 252 people in St Peter's, and in 1833 these would have been almost exclusively poor Irish workers in the local granite industry.

Presentation and other Inscriptions

This is one of the most fruitful sources of information about the 'pedigree' of a watch, and by no means uncommon. Again, it is necessary to sound a modest warning; but, since the difficulties inherent in substantiating a fraudulent inscription of historic importance are greater than in any other similar deceit, such things are few and far between and, usually, easily detected.

The presentation inscription upon the Bishop's watch even today conjures up the depth of feeling which must have existed towards that particular pastor. As might be expected, royal presentation watches are fairly frequently encountered; it is such a convenient and universally acceptable gift to mark some particular service rendered. Queen Victoria was a prolific bestower of watches upon those around her, and one notable example passed through the London sale rooms in 1973 and again in 1977. Of good average quality, but no more than that, the gold watch and accompanying chain were probably Swiss although retailed by a London firm, whose name appeared thereon. The inscription on this timepiece ran: 'To my faithful & devoted personal attendant John Brown Esqre in grateful remembrance of the presence of mind and courage he displayed at Buckingham Palace Feb.29 1872, from Victoria R.'. On that day the Queen, returning from an afternoon's drive in an open landau, was accosted at the Garden Entrance to the palace by a student brandishing a pistol in one hand and a document in the other. He was restrained by John Brown until he could be arrested by the police.

A rather less common type of inscription is that which is solely intended to establish the eminence of the original owner, presumably in order to pander to the conceit of a subsequent one. The watchcase illustrated in Plate 57 carries a legend stating that it had been worn by Princess Charlotte until the age of twelve and then passed on, although who Henr^y. Kuper may have been is not recorded. As for the unfortunate Princess, born in 1796 and the only child of George IV and Caroline of

PLATE 57: A young Princess's watch by Samuel Houston, London, 1807. The Princess Charlotte was then nine years old.

Brunswick, she died in childbirth in 1817. This type of inscription can, of course, be readily faked but usually gives itself away through lack of attention to detail.

Some Obvious Frauds

Throughout the foregoing sections, there have been frequent references to, and warnings against, too naive an acceptance of the evidence presented by the watch that has been 'personalised'. Much depends upon whether the viewer, being a person of reasonable judgement, who is deliberately preserving an objective approach to the appraisal of such objects, feels that their credibility is complete. If in any doubt, then the apparent attribution has to be treated as suspect. Admittedly, there has to be an element of subjective judgement involved, so that two equally qualified individuals may disagree in specific cases; yet this rarely occurs. The reason, as has been mentioned already, is that the forger is careless about fine detail — probably being more concerned with acquiring quick money and as quickly leaving the scene, than with acquainting himself with the skills required to establish a proper historic background for his deceit, and then executing it in a style appropriate to the period concerned. Very few examples are necessary to illustrate this.

For some — not immediately obvious — reason, more

patently spurious attributions of the ownership of watches have been made to Oliver Cromwell than to almost any other major figure of British history; and several of these are now, by the coincidence of bequests rather than by deliberate policy, in the care of the British Museum. One such is a plain oval watch in a silver case with a circular opening in the cover, through which the dial can be seen; above this opening appear the initials 'O' and 'C' with a crown between, and below the opening, a sword. On the back is the legend 'God and the Commonwealth' while on the dial plate itself, above the chapter ring, is 'T. Hooke 1661'. This heterogeneous matter has been imposed on the watch in such an execrable way, that it is inconceivable that the object ever belonged to the Lord Protector.

The same can be said of another oval watch, which is now only known through the catalogue of the Evan Roberts Collection, of which it once formed part. This large alarm watch in a silver case, which was itself enclosed within an outer protective case of wood covered with shagreen, has engraved upon the dial above XII, the words 'Olliver Cromwell'. Even if the mis-spelling can be dismissed as simply a contemporary aberration, the date '1648' which accompanies it post-dates that of the watch by at least twenty years. Having said all this, however, there is certainly one watch in the British Museum that can believably be assigned to Cromwell.

Shown in Plate 58, this watch by John Midnall, who worked in Fleet Street, London in the second quarter of the seventeenth century, is of good average rather than exceptional quality — a credible feature when related to its purported owner — while the simple accessories, a short fob chain incorporating a medallion engraved on each side, on one with Cromwell's crest and initials and, on the other, a shield with his arms appear wholly in keeping. This watch is so unostentatious yet, at the same time, so lacking in stylistic or other anachronisms, that its provenance is quite acceptable.

PLATE 58: Credibly believed to have belonged to Oliver Cromwell, this typically 'Puritan' watch was made by John Midnall.

COLOUR PLATE 7: The engraved floral dials beloved of Edward
East, among other makers active in the mid-seventeenth century, are often held to be the most beautiful of their kind; yet
how much greater is the visual impact when such designs are
rendered instead in polychrome enamel colours. This possibly
unique example, known as the Ashburnham Watch, has a
movement by Henry Jones.

COLOUR PLATE 8: However unlikely a material porcelain might seem for use as a watchcase, it was doubtless so employed during the mid-eighteenth century, although survivals today are very rare indeed. This example is almost certainly a product of the Chelsea factory, and can be compared with the back of a similar case — all that now remains — in the British Museum. The maker of the watch itself is James Grantham.

6 Materials and Techniques for Enriching the Watch

PLATE 59: Embossed or *repoussé* decoration at its most impressive, in this watch garniture by James Rousseau of London, 1734. The watchcase was chased by I. V. Haidt, and is signed; the scene depicted is of Zephyrus and Flora in a woodland glade, in the company of *putti* holding symbols of love. The gilt-metal hook of the chatelaine is stamped 'Bourne Raynes'. Haidt, born in Danzig in 1700 and died in America in 1780, worked in London from 1724 to 1740, marrying a London-born Huguenot, Catherine Compigne. John Raynes was apprenticed to Samuel Bourne in 1717 and was registered as a smallworker in 1736.

The pages that follow review some of the procedures commonly used from the seventeenth to the nineteenth centuries for enhancing the appearance of the English watch. Deliberately included among these are such fundamental processes as enamelling of watch dials since, although these last constitute an important functional element, their legibility and visual impact contribute enormously to the quality of the finished product. Enamelled dials are much appreciated — or reviled — by collectors today, who will appraise with the greatest care such features as the proportions of the hour numerals and the accuracy of any divided circles, as well as the overall merit of the surface colour and finish, not to mention that of the dial painting itself.

Most of the information is either based upon, or directly extracted from, contemporary printed sources. These tended to be sparse during the seventeenth century and not nearly so explicit as those that came after. It is likely that as the processes used were basically the same throughout the entire period while, during the later years, there were important additions to the range, such as engine-turning, it might have been excusable to have omitted the earliest references altogether. However, it would be invidious to exclude the great flavour of their era to be obtained simply from reading the words used by these early craft writers, and so a compromise has been adopted. Seventeenth-century references have been confined to what is probably the most important single source of such information; they have all been gathered together at the beginning of the review, rather than scattered throughout the various sections, where they might tend to obscure the very much more detailed matter that came later. Students of horology know from experience that it is a field that, to this day, remains full of surprises. To that extent, therefore, it may well be that this review will prove to be far from comprehensive, and that unseen and unsuspected methods of enriching watches still await discovery. They will emerge in their own good time, that is certain, to confound the experts.

THE SEVENTEENTH-CENTURY CRAFTSMAN-DECORATOR

One of the most useful contemporary sources of information concerning a variety of methods of decorating three-dimensional objects at this period has the slightly unpromising title of *A Treatise of Japaning and Varnishing.*

Written, 'Printed for and Sold by' John Stalker and George Parker, it appeared in 1688. Little seems to be known of the authors, apart from the fact — to be discovered from the title page — that Stalker resided in London 'at the Golden Ball in St James's Market', while Parker was 'at Mr Richard Woods House over against the Theater [sic] in Oxford'. It was, however, so much more than its title implies, with information on such varied topics as counterfeiting tortoiseshell and marble, staining ivory and horn, and gilding, burnishing and lacquering all manner of things, that it is a veritable mine of information on the techniques used in its day, of which the following extracts are simply samples:

Of Guilding Metals I acquainted you before with a controversy between the Guilders, concerning the Terms of Art, who denied the name of Guilding to that of Wood, and confined it to Metals only: upon which account we promised you to treat of the latter too, and thereby comprehend both; although tis no question but one laies as just a claim to that title as the other. They are certainly fine inventions, that serve to please us with the shadow, when the substance can't be purchased. We are all of us great admirers of Gold, and by consequence must be enamoured with Guilding, which is so nearly related to it. For Guilding is Gold in miniature, with which as with a golden Ray, we beautify and adorn our viler Metals . . .

To guild Silver, Copper, Brass or Princes-metal
Whatsoever you design for guilding, should be first well scrubbed with a Wier-brush, sold by the Ironmongers. Wet the piece with water or beer, and continue scrubbing and wetting it, until all filth and dirtiness be fetched off, that the two metals may more closely hug and embrace each other . . . [there then follows a rather more archaic version of the usual way of gilding with a mercury-gold amalgam, for which see page 78]. But still, if you would have the work more rich and lasting, you may again quicken it with quicksilver and aqua fortis, and guild it over again after the former method, and repeat it so often, if you please, till your gold lies as thick as your nail upon the metal.

To Silver-over Brass or Copper, as the Clockmakers do their Dial-Plates
Having Leaf or burnt-silver in readiness, put it into as much Aqua fortis as will cover it; after an hours standing pour off the Aqua fortis as clean as may be from the silver; wash the silver three or four times with water, let it dry, and then mix it with one part of fine Argal [= argil, potter's clay] to three of silver with a little fair water. When you make use of it, rub it on the work with a cork, until tis all silvered, and lie as fair as you could wish. Next, dry it well with a linnen cloth, and

having made it warm, wash it over three or four times with the best white varnish, spoken of in this book, and it will not fail to secure it from Tarnishing, and other injuries.

To Stain a Green colour on Wood, Ivory, Horn or Bones
First, prepare either of them in Allom-water, by boiling them well in it, as you were just now instructed. Afterwards grind of Spanish-green, or thick common Verdegreas, a reasonable quantity, with half as much Sal-Armoniack; then put them into the strongest wine-vinegar, together with the wood, keeping it hot over the fire till tis green enough: if the wood is too large, then wash it over scalding hot, as in the other instances.

Thus, Courteous Reader, are we at length arriv'd at our desired Port: Our Performances have been no way inferior to our Promises. What we engaged for in the beginning, we have punctually accomplisht; and nothing certainly remains, but that you convert our Precepts to Practice; for that will be the ready way to examin, and try, whether they are false or insufficient. We have all along been directed by an unerring Guide, Experience; and do therefore advise you, upon the least miscarriage, to make a diligent review, and doubt not but that second thoughts will convince you of too slight an observance. We desire you'd be as exact and regular in your performances as we have been in ours; for by these means, Satisfaction will attend both Parties, all our designs must succeed to our wish, and our Labours shall be crowned with success and reputation.

1 METAL ALLOYS AND SIMULATIONS

As in other types of jewellery, metals used in watch decoration are never pure — in the fine state, as it is called — but always mixed with others to improve the properties of the finished article, usually in the matter of hardness, colour, durability and weight. Of the more valuable metals, those identified as 'precious' — gold and silver — can be found in varying alloys; platinum, sometimes called a 'noble' metal, is not found at all in English watches in the decorative context — at least during the period with which this book is concerned — and only very rarely in the mechanical one, when it is used for the making of rather specialised springs. Some comparatively modern Swiss dress- and wristwatches have been fitted into platinum cases, but this is by no means common.

GOLD has been regarded with awe, and respected as of great value, since time immemorial. Occurring naturally in various parts of the world as flakes, dust or nuggets, or as veins in several different kinds of rock, it can also sometimes be found ready alloyed with silver, when it is known as electrum. It is extraordinarily ductile, so that a single grain can be drawn into a wire 500ft (150m) long, while its malleability is legendary, especially when beaten into gold leaf, which can be as little as four-millionths of an inch (·0001016mm) thick. It cannot be melted below 1,065°C and even at that temperature retains its main properties. Fine gold — the unadulterated metal and too soft and heavy for ordinary use — is defined as being of 24 carat quality, while the most usual amalgams are 9, 18 and 22 carats. Gold of 22 carats purity is conventionally made up with one part of silver and one of copper. In Victorian usage, 12 carats — a half-and-half alloy — and 14 carats can also be found, but these have tended to suffer over the years from cracking due to crystallisation. The colour of gold can be dramatically modified by the make-up of the alloy, copper producing a reddish effect, while silver makes it much more yellow even than the pure metal. Modern so-called 'white' gold is an amalgam of platinum and gold in the proportions of one-quarter to three-quarters, thus producing the 18 carat quality. Golds of different colours are sometimes combined in the same article, and in watches this effect can be observed most readily in some nineteenth-century dials. The groundwork, for both the best alloys and colour changes, seems to have been laid by an extensive series of experiments carried out under the aegis of the Royal Society, and reported in its *Transactions* for the year 1803. In charge of these was a certain Mr Hatchet, starting from the premise that gold is capable of forming alloys with most metals; his findings concluded that gold should only ever be alloyed with copper and silver, other metals tending either radically to diminish its ductility or considerably to alter the colour beyond the limits of acceptability. The main reason for these experiments, it should be noted, was to determine the best alloys for use as coinage.

SILVER has been regarded, historically, as having a value second only to gold. Occurring in the pure state, it is also found as an alloy with gold (electrum), and as a compound in lead ore (galena). It is much too soft, when pure, for normal metal working use, and it is generally alloyed with copper, the proportions of the alloy varying according to country and period. The customary English standard, always known as 'sterling silver', and established by law in the year 1300, requires a 92.5% purity; but from 1697 to 1719 the Britannia standard was compulsory, and optional thereafter, and this consists of 95.8% silver. Less rare than gold, silver is only slightly less malleable, ductile and permanent, and it melts at a temperature of about 1,000°C.

HALLMARK is the symbol, or series of symbols, punched into an article of gold or silver, after assay by a properly constituted assay office, and guaranteeing its standard of purity. Sometimes this mark reveals not simply the particular assay office or guild carrying out the assay, but also the degree of fineness of the metal, the year in which it was assayed, and the name of the maker, this last being intended to guard against malpractice. The particular benefit all this confers upon English watches is contained in the consequent capability to date precious-metal watchcases and, by implication, the watches contained therein, as well as to establish the casemaker, who was usually not one and the same person as the watchmaker. Tables of hallmarks for all the English assay offices are easily obtainable, and very little practice is needed before they can be used with confidence. The British system of hallmarking is admired universally for its total reliability over a very long period of time, but most other countries have instituted some system or another for similar purposes. Of the Western countries, the United States is the only one where hallmarks have never been used.

BRASS AND BRONZE are alloys of copper with, respectively, zinc and tin. The proportions may be varied in order to obtain different shades of colour, especially of brass, which is the more difficult alloy to obtain since zinc is excessively volatile and combustible and is driven off as flames before the copper has melted. To obviate this difficulty a process called 'dry cementation' was devised, by which small pieces of copper were strongly heated in closed vessels, with the zinc being nearly in the vaporised state; this produced an excellent alloy. In the case of bronze, a simple amalgam of copper and tin tended to produce an alloy that was extremely brittle, so that small quantities of other metals, and in particular zinc, antimony, silver and arsenic, were added, depending upon the end-use, which ranged from the casting of statues to bells and cannon. Both brass and bronze accept water-gilding (qv) and certain alloys of this nature are sometimes referred to as gilding-metal. Brass is used extensively in watches for the main elements of the movement, including such decorated components as the watch cock and slide plate, and is nearly always gilded save for those areas that are not readily visible. Bronze is sometimes used in the movement, generally for wheels, but is most often to be found as the basis of gilt-metal watchcases.

STEEL is a somewhat imprecise term for an alloy of iron and carbon, sometimes with the inclusion of other metals such as manganese. In watchmaking, steel is used widely in the mechanism, principally for pinions and arbors, and sparingly for decorative purposes. On early movements, openwork steel decoration was usually 'blued' to reduce rusting, this being a hardening and tempering treatment by heat. Later, during the eighteenth century, decorative watchcases made from cut and polished steel formed part of the large output of novelties, jewellery and trinkets from the manufactory at Woodstock, in Oxfordshire. These are nowadays very rarely encountered, as so much steelwork suffered from the consequences of being cheap and expendable.

SIMULATIONS Historically, the motive for these has been the desire to find a cheap substitute for gold; yet they are all alloys whose ingredients are those already described, the differences being only in the proportions used. References can be found to such products as tombac, Manheim or Dutch gold, tinsel, similor, Prince Rupert's metal, and many others, the precise composition varying according to the intention of the inventor and the end-use. Dutch gold, for example, is said to have been capable of being beaten into extremely fine leaves, which were a very passable imitation of gold leaf so long as they remained fresh; unfortunately, they tarnished very quickly. Tombac was especially noted for its malleability, and is said to have been an alloy of 16 parts of copper with one of zinc and one of tin. Prince Rupert's metal was supposed to have been invented by him in 1680, but was eventually brought to perfection by two Frenchmen, Messieurs La Croix and Le Blanc, although their products were by no means identical, the first being described as the brightest and of the most elegant and lively colour, while Le Blanc's alloy was superior in softness and ductility, so that it was very easily malleable. In addition, Le Blanc had invented a special varnish or lacquer for his metal, which added a somewhat deeper tinge to it, as it was naturally rather too pale; and had this further advantage, that while it remained on the metal it preserved it from rust or decay. This is a very material point in regard to a metal of which copper is the basis, since that is, of all metals, most subject to be injured by the air, or by the contact of liquids of almost any kind.

Easily the best known of all these gold substitutes, however, was pinchbeck, or, in the inventor's words, the 'curious metal which so nearly resembles gold in colour, smell and ductibility [sic]'. There were two Christopher Pinchbecks, father and son, and until very recently it was unclear which had actually invented this alloy that, more by clever contemporary publicity than on account of any inbuilt advantage, became so sufficiently established as to enter the English language as a convenient term for any base metal alloy resembling gold, albeit in a pejorative sense. When Rita Shenton wrote her interesting little book *Christopher Pinchbeck and his Family* in 1976, she was clearly of the opinion that, since no reference to 'the true and genuine metal' as 'pinchbeck' appeared before the death of Christopher Pinchbeck senior in 1732, it must have been invented by the son. In 1981, however, two enterprising members of the staff of the Public Record Office, Susan Lumas and Jane Cox, published an article in *Country Life,* in the issue dated 24 September, describing a newly discovered inventory of the stock-in-trade of Pinchbeck senior, taken at the time of his death, which included the item 'Mr. Pinchbecks Metall fifty pounds'. The Pinchbeck family, incidentally, probably best known today as clock- and watchmakers, had many other irons in the fire, especially 'toys', by which was meant, in those days, all kinds of novelties and trinkets, and the elder Pinchbeck had, in fact, been apprenticed to a fisherman, and then to a pastry-cook, and he was still following this latter trade when in his mid-30s. It even becomes quite difficult to see how the clock and watch business was ever fitted in.

There were other, less salubrious, methods of making substitute-gold, one of them requiring the treatment of silver with putrefied urine; the result was a product that so resembled the real thing that, in France, several edicts were issued forbidding such frauds, especially in respect of wire and lace. Other recipes originated from a Mr Homberg and from 'the celebrated Mr Pott'; and even the genius of Dr Robert Hooke had not been averse to postulating a mixture of verdigris, Alexandrian tutty (crude zinc oxide), nitre and borax, mixed with oil and melted in a crucible, to produce his *aurum sophisticum.*

2 HEAT AND CHEMICAL TREATMENT OF METALS

BLUING For use only on steel, this process is part-decorative and part-protective in that, by altering the chemical construction of the surface treated, some small defence against corrosion from the atmosphere can be achieved. This is by no means total, however.

Bluing of iron as a decorative treatment for buckles, swords and the like, is a technique that has been practised for centuries. The steelwork on the back of watch movements which, in the early periods, was usually designed in the form of openwork tracery, was also susceptible to such treatment, the resultant flowing blue ornamentation contrasting splendidly with the flat gilt surfaces of the backplate and cock.

The method is well set out by F. J. Britten in *Watch & Clock Maker's Handbook, Dictionary and Guide* (12th ed, 1920). The components to be treated were placed in a bluing pan, described as 'a piece of thin copper, shaped something like a frying pan', the latter having first been well warmed to disperse any moisture. Britten goes on: 'Many pieces to be blued are not sufficiently flat on the underside to become equally coloured in a flat pan. If fine brass filings are laid thickly in the pan, and the part to be blued is pressed into them, the colour will then be more even.'

Next, the pan with its contents was held over the flame of a spirit lamp, at the same time being protected from draughts or currents of air. As the temperature rose the steel changed colour, the stages being pale straw (430°F/221°C), straw (460°F/238°C), yellow brown (490°F/254°C), red brown (510°F/265°C), purple (540°F/282°C), blue (560°F/292°C), with a final stage of dark blue available at 570°F/299°C, if desired.

Britten concludes: 'Steel for bluing should be finished with medium red-stuff [a paste made up of sesquioxide of iron with oil] and the last few rubs given not with a metal polisher but with a piece of boxwood or horn, and plenty of red-stuff and oil. Pieces that have been cleaned in dirty benzine, (ie benzine charged with oil) will become specky in bluing'. Rees, however, advocates grinding indigo and salad oil together, and rubbing the mixture on to the work with a woollen rag while it is heating, leaving it to cool of itself.

GILDING AND ITS REVERSAL Before the advent of electro-deposition it was yet possible, albeit more complicated and time-consuming, to gild an enormous variety of different types of material; and it was a treatment that was extensively used on watches. As can be seen from Appendix III the Watch Gilder was a clearly defined and well-established branch of the trade, and the craftsmen so engaged had to become specialists if only on account of the small size of some of the components upon which they exercised their skill.

Cases, dials and movements of watches were all susceptible to being gilded, and, since gold does not tarnish, the reasons were not solely decorative but also protective. There could also be economic considerations. Silver-gilt watchcases, for example, were obviously cheaper than their solid gold counterparts, while the superimposed coating of gold prevents oxidation of the silver and the unattractive discoloration that can result. If desired, both case and dial could be made of a base metal alloy, often simply called 'gilding metal' — it was, in fact, a kind of bronze — to which a coat of gold could then be applied; again, a rich appearance could be simulated at least cost. Watch movements were almost invariably gilded — those that may appear to have lacked this are either unfinished or may have been 'scoured', probably by chemical means — since movements 'in the grey', as discussed elsewhere, are unattractive both in colour and finish. Polishing them alone, while possible, would probably have been even more time-consuming than gilding and, much more serious, would have left the way open not only for tarnish but, much worse, for the development of verdigris, the green coating of cupric carbonate that forms as a result of atmospheric action on copper, brass and bronze.

Gilding of the movement, even so, was always carried out with due attention to economic considerations. So far as the main frame was concerned, the potence plate — the one customarily in full view on the back of the movement — was gilded on both sides. The other main frame plate which, because the dividing pillars are riveted into it, is known as the pillar plate, was gilded only on that side which could be readily seen, that is to say, the side furthest from the dial and facing into the movement. The gilding would be run just over the edge of this plate and then would cease abruptly in an irregular border around the side under the dial. The so-called dial-plate or 'brass-edge' — a kind of cutaway rim which could be fixed to the pillar plate, and into which the dial is fitted — would be gilded around its edge, and just running over on to both sides where it would stop equally abruptly. All the otherwise-decorated components — cock, slide plate, pillars, etc — would be gilded on all the visible areas. All the wheels that could be seen were gilded, too, the exceptions being the centre wheel and often the crown wheel, both of which, being located towards the middle of the between-plates space, were largely out of sight. The crown wheel has sometimes been replaced, however, and, in that case, the substitute seems never to have been gilt.

So, what was the process used? It is generally called water-gilding, and the best contemporary description of this will be found, once again, in Rees's *Cyclopaedia*, which states:

> In order to this operation, they heat some pure quicksilver [metallic mercury] in a clean crucible and, when it is nearly boiling, put about a sixth of its weight of fine gold in thin plates heated red-hot, and stir them gently about, till the gold be found melted and incorporated into a mass with the mercury. It is then allowed to cool; and when cold, it is to be put in a piece of soft leather; and by gradual pressure the fluid part of the amalgam, consisting almost wholly of mercury, may be forced through the pores of the leather, while the gold, combined with about twice its weight of mercury, will remain behind, forming a yellowish silvery mass, of the consistency of soft butter. This, after having been bruised in a mortar, or shaken in a strong phial with repeated portions of salt and water till the water ceases to be fouled by it, is fit for use, and may be kept for any length of time, without injury, in a corked phial. It is of indispensable importance that the materials of this amalgam should be perfectly pure; and, therefore, the mercury employed in the preparation of it should be procured from the distillation of the red precipitate (nitrous red oxyd of mercury) either alone or mixed with a little charcoal powder.

Slightly different procedures were necessary, depending upon the metal to be treated. Silver had first to be soaked in warm, dilute hydrochloric acid to make the surface absolutely clean. Next, it must be freed from any last trace of the acid by washing two or three times in pure water. It is then thoroughly dried, and warmed, as is also a little of the mercury-gold amalgam. This is then spread evenly upon the silver, to which it will immediately adhere. The tool used in this operation can be either a special small knife, or a brush made of brass wire. Giving the work some gentle heat, the operator 'dabs' or spreads the amalgam farther and more evenly upon it.

Taking up the story again, Rees continues:

> Thus far advanced, the metal is set over the fire, upon a grate or in a sort of cage, under which is a pan of charcoal yielding heat just sufficient for evaporating the mercury; by which means the mercury is raised in fumes, and leaves the gold alone adhering to the work; in proportion as the mercury, evaporating and flying off, discovers places where gold is wanting, they take care to supply them, by adding new pieces of amalgam with knife or brush.

This basic process could be continued several times if necessary, in order to build up an increasingly thick coating of gold; and the effect can be quite startling and far more impressive than any similar laminate obtained by electro-plating. It is hard to describe the effect, save to quote one opinion, of a magnificent silver outer case heavily gilded by this means: 'It looks as if the gold was put on with a trowel!'

However, simply applying the coatings was not the end of the matter. The final colour and lustre had to be heightened to relieve the uniformly pale yellow appearance that resulted merely from the evaporation of the mercury, by first rubbing with a fine brass-wire scratch brush until the surface was clean and smooth but still pale yellow all over. Next, it was covered with a substance known as gilding wax and again exposed to the fire, which burnt the wax off; and this application could be repeated until the desired final effect was achieved. Gilding wax appears to have been composed of a mixture of bees' wax, red ochre, verdigris and green vitriol — which is iron sulphate — or alum, and its effect was to produce 'a perfect dissipation of some mercury remaining after the former operation'. If, however, this was insufficient for gaining the required effect, there was yet another stage. The gilt surface was covered with a saline paste made from equal parts of nitre (in this context, probably sodium carbonate), sal ammoniac (ammonium chloride), green vitriol and verdigris, mixed with water or urine. The work was then heated until it smoked, and quenched in water or urine; and the chemistry of this part of the process seems to depend upon the nitric acid released during the exposure to heat acting upon any particles of copper lying on the gilt surface. There is yet a further refinement available for use on carved or embossed work, where the original gilding may not have penetrated fully into all the hollows and recesses. This consists of dipping the work in a liquor obtained by boiling certain yellow materials such as sulphur, orpiment (which is arsenic trisulphide) and turmeric. This is said to impart a rich and solid finish to any article so treated.

So much for the gilding of silver. Copper, and its alloys with zinc — which includes brass, of course — were treated in a somewhat similar manner, but taking account of their much smaller affinity for mercury, by comparison with silver, which made it less easy to obtain a complete and even adhesion of the gold coating. The process required the use of nitric acid, and the object to be treated was first cleaned and washed, and then burnished on a lathe.

> After this, it is dipped in a neutralised solution of nitrate of mercury and, in a few seconds, on account of the strong affinity of nitric acid for copper, the mercurial salt is decomposed. The copper takes the place of the mercury and at the same time the mercury is deposited in the metallic state on the surface of the copper, covering it entirely and strongly adhering to it. The gold amalgam is now applied and the rest of the process is the same with that which has already been described. Thus a given quantity of gold may be made to cover a larger surface than in any other way of gilding on metals, five grains of gold completely gilding both the upper and under surfaces of 144 copper buttons, each of them an inch in diameter.
>
> (*Philosophical Magazine,* vol ix, p20)

Dr J. Lewis, a well-known technical authority in the early part of the last century, highlighted the principal disadvantages of gilding by amalgamation, as this process was sometimes called. He wrote:

> There are two principal inconveniences in this business; one, that the workmen are exposed to the fumes of the mercury and generally, sooner or later, have their health greatly impaired by them; the other, the loss of the mercury, for though part of it is said to be detained in the cavities made in the chimnies for that purpose, yet the greatest part of it is lost. From some trials I have made, it appeared that both these inconveniences, particularly the first and most considerable one, might be in a good measure avoided, by means of a furnace of a due construction.

He then went on to describe the ideal furnace.

> If the communication of a furnace with its chimney, instead of being over the fire, is made under the grate, the ash-pit door or other apertures beneath the grate closed, and the mouth of the furnace left open, the current of air, which otherwise would have entered beneath, enters now at the top, and passing down through the grate to the chimney, carries with it completely both the vapours of the fuel and the fumes of such matters as are placed upon it. The back part of the furnace should be raised a little higher above the fire than the fore-part, and an iron plate laid over it, that the air may enter only at the front, where the workman stands, who will be thus effectually secured from the fumes and from being incommoded by the heat, and at the same time have full liberty of introducing, inspecting and removing the work. If such a furnace is made of strong forged (not milled) iron plate, it will be sufficiently durable. The upper end of the chimney may reach above a foot and a half higher than the level of the fire; over this is to be placed a larger tube, leaving an interval of an inch or more all round between it and the chimney, and reaching to a height of ten or twelve feet; the higher the better. The external air, passing up between the chimney and the outer pipe, prevents the latter from being much heated, so that the mercurial fumes will condense against its sides into running quicksilver which, falling down to the bottom, is there caught in a hollow rim, formed by turning inwards a portion of the lower part, and conveyed by a pipe at one side into a proper receiver.

It is, perhaps, necessary to append an epitaph to this process. So dangerous to health was it, despite the best intentions of Dr Lewis, that untold numbers of operators died a lingering and painful death from the accumulative effects of inhaling mercury vapour, as toxic a substance as can be imagined. It is often said — but without any real foundation, so far as can be discovered — that water-gilders were usually women. What can be said with truth is that many apprentices to this craft seem to have run away (see Appendix III). It was as unwholesome a process as can be envisaged and not practised today even by restorers intent upon utilising only the contemporary procedures, when renovating period pieces. Long may that philosophy prevail.

It may also not be without significance, that it was sometimes felt desirable to reverse the process and ungild, if that is the right term. Rees deals with it in the following way:

> There are various methods of separating gold from gilt works: it may be separated from the surface of silver, either by spreading over the gilt a paste made of powdered *sal ammoniac* [ammonium chloride] moistened with *aquafortis* [nitric acid] and heating it till the matter smokes, and is nearly dry; throw it into water, and the gold will easily come off by rubbing it with a scratch-brush; or, by putting the gilt silver into common *aqua regia* [a mixture of nitric and hydrochloric acids], nearly boiling, and turning the metal frequently, till it becomes all over black; then wash it with water, and rub it with the scratchbrush, which will disengage the gold left by the *aqua regia.*

Gold may be separated from gilt copper by applying a solution of borax to the gilt parts with a pencil, and sprinkling over the place thus moistened a little powdered sulphur; when the piece is made red-hot and quenched in water, the gold may be wiped off with a brush.

SILVERING In the formative years of English watchmaking, solid silver components — dials, cocks and so forth — were commonplace. At later periods, however, it became more usual, as well as much cheaper, to impart a silver coating to a base metal foundation, when making these same parts.

Theoretically, silvering may be carried out using a similar technique to that described for gilding (qv), but, in Rees's words:

> . . . as works of this kind are liable to tarnish and speckle, they are seldom used. But when this is the case, the coating of silver should be much thicker than that of gold, because otherwise the friction which is necessary for removing the tarnish would soon wear off the silver from the most prominent parts, and expose to view the subjacent copper or brass. In order to avoid this inconvenience, some have recommended, when silvering is admitted, a strong varnish, formed of some of the compositions of mastic, sandarac, the gums animi or copal, and white rosin, to be put over it.

Rees then goes on to postulate three methods for silvering in use in his day — the early part of the last century — these being, respectively,

> by amalgamation, by muriated silver, and by silver in substance. The first mode is performed by adding plates of copper to a solution of nitrated silver, which will precipitate the silver in its metallic state and very finely divided; scrape this from the copper and let it be well washed and dried. With half an ounce of this powder, of common salt and sal ammoniac two ounces, and one drachm of corrosive sublimate, well rubbed together, make a paste by the addition of a little water, then clean the article to be silvered with a small quantity of diluted aqua fortis or by scouring it with a mixture of common salt and tartar. Rub it, when perfectly clean, with the paste already mentioned, until it is entirely covered with a white metallic coating; which coating is an amalgam produced by the decomposition of the corrosive sublimate by means of the copper, to the surface of which it applies very closely and expeditiously. The copper thus silvered over is then to be washed, dried and heated nearly red, for the purpose of driving off the mercury; the silver remains behind and adheres firmly to the copper, in a state capable of receiving a high polish.

The second method described by Rees — silvering by *luna cornea* — was the one most used for treating dials. *Luna cornea* is the white, curdy precipitate produced when a soluble salt of silver comes into contact with muriatic acid. If this is exposed to heat, the acid carries off with it a portion of the silver and the remainder melts, to become a hornlike substance. Rees describes this second method of silvering, then, as first to prepare the *luna cornea* by pouring a solution of common salt into nitrate of silver, so long as any precipitation occurs, and boiling the mixture. Next,

> . . . mix the white curdy matter thus obtained with three parts of good pearl-ash, one part of washed whiting, and a little more than one part of common salt. After the surface of the brass, cleared from scratches, has been rubbed with a piece of old hat and rotten stone, in order to remove any grease, and then moistened with salt and water, a little of the composition, being now rubbed on with the finger, will presently cover the surface of the metal with silver. Then wash it well, rub it dry with soft rag, and then, as the coat of silver is very thin, cover it with transparent varnish to preserve it from tarnish. As this kind of silvering is very imperfect, it is only used for the faces of clocks, the scales of barometers, or similar objects.

Finally, there were methods described as 'silver in substance'. One of these consisted of

> . . . mixing together 20 grains of silver precipitated by copper, two drachms of tartar, two drachms of common salt, and half a drachm of alum; and rubbing this composition on a perfectly clean surface of copper or brass will cover it with a thin coating of silver which may be polished with a piece of soft leather. Another and better method, called French plating, consists in burnishing down upon the surface of the copper successive layers of leaf-silver to any required thickness. Although the silver in this operation is more solid than in any of the former modes, the process is tedious nor can the junctures of the leaves of silver be always entirely concealed.

Rees describes one method of cold silvering, which is perhaps closest to that most commonly used by restorers today, when re-silvering dials.

> Silvering in the cold is performed by the following composition: 3 lbs of cream of tartar; 3 lbs of common salt; and 1 oz of muriate of silver, which is the precipitate formed by adding common salt to nitrate of silver till no more is precipitated. This composition is made into a similar pulp. The surface of the copper or brass to be silvered must first be cleaned with dilute acid, and then made dry and kept free from grease. The surface, being now rubbed with the above paste, will assume a white colour by the silver adhering to it. The surface should always be varnished to prevent its tarnishing, as the silver is too thin to bear cleaning.

This method, too, according to Rees, was commonly used on dials and scales.

LACQUERING AND VARNISHING   It is surprisingly difficult, in contemporary texts, to discover any practical difference in definition between a lacquer and a varnish, if indeed there was any. Rees, for example, begins his article on the former with the words: 'LACQUER, or Lacker, is a varnish applied upon tin, brass or other metals to preserve them from tarnishing and to improve their colour.' It might appear, however, from ordinary usage, that the incorporation of any colouring into such protective coatings tended to designate them lacquers, although this is by no means invariable. Nowadays, varnishes have a resinous base while lacquers can consist of any film-forming substance in a suitable solvent, at least, that is the difference according to dictionary definition.

Whatever they were called, these coatings must have been much more widely used, even in the basic stages of manufacture, than is generally supposed. It has already been mentioned in 'Casting' (qv) that when an article of brass had been removed from the sand mould, it was always necessary to handfinish it, first correcting the blemishes caused by the process, and then 'heightening' the work with a specially designed tool, which the workman continuously dips in a lacquer made from turmeric dissolved in spirits of wine.

The same source — Martin, in *The Circle of the Mechanical Arts,* (1813) — continues:

> To keep brass works from tarnishing and getting black by exposure to the air, the brass-workers have recourse to lacquering. Lacquering consists in covering the brass, moderately heated over a stove containing an open charcoal fire, with a liquid, also moderately warm, composed of saffron and Spanish annotta [a red dye made from seeds], each two drams put into a bottle with a pint of highly rectified spirits of wine, which when together should be placed in a moderate heat and often shaken, from this a very strong tincture will be obtained, which must be afterwards strained through a coarse linen cloth, to take out the dregs of the annotta and saffron; it is then to be returned to the bottle, and three ounces of seed-lac, powdered, must be added to it, and the whole again heated until the seed-lac be completely dissolved; after which it is fit for use and will form a good and pale-coloured lacquer, which will prevent the brass from changing colour by exposure to air. It is laid on the brass by a camel's hair pencil as thin as it can be spread, and requires nothing to be done to it after it is so spread but a moderate rubbing. If the brass be required to be of a redder colour, increase the proportion of annotta in the lacquer and it will be accomplished. All the best kinds of brass-works are gilt to prevent their changing colour, and this constitutes the desideratum.

This last sentence comes almost as an aside but gold, of course, was an expensive alternative so that, for most purposes, lacquers and varnishes had an established place in the scheme of things. Even these were not necessarily all that cheap, however. It is clear that one formula, which was much favoured, envisaged the colouring being imparted by the use of amber, a fossil resin with a colour range varying from yellow, in a number of different shades, to red and even white. This substance had to be imported since, although occurring here and there in Britain, the quantities were insignificant. Rees gives the following details of this technique:

> The composition of a gold-coloured varnish, used by the English artists for brass and silver, was communicated to some of the French academicians in 1720, by Mr. Scarlet, and in 1738 by Mr. Graham, and published in the volume of the French Memoirs for 1761. It is as follows: Take two ounces of gum lac, two ounces of yellow amber, forty grains of dragon's blood in tears [a blood-red resin, the best kind being obtained in tear-shaped globules from a certain type of palm tree found in the East Indies] half a drachm of saffron, and forty ounces of good spirit of wine: infuse and digest in the usual manner, and then strain through a linen cloth. The piece to be varnished must be heated before the liquid is applied: it receives from the varnish a gold colour, and may be cleaned, when sullied, with warm water.

Reverting again to Rees's article on lacquers, there can be detected some logical derivation of the term as well as useful instructions on the techniques involved. He continues:

> The basis of lacquers is a solution of the resinous substance called seed-lac, or rather shell-lac, in spirit of wine. This spirit ought to be very much dephlegmated [phlegm, one of the principles of old chemistry, was a watery, distilled liquid] in order to dissolve much of the lac. For this purpose, some authors direct dry pot-ash to be thrown into the spirit. This alkali attracts the water, with which it forms a liquid that subsides distinctly from the spirit at the bottom of the vessel. From this liquid the spirit may be separated by decantation. By this method the spirit is dephlegmated: but at the same time it becomes impregnated with part of the alkali, which depraves its colour, and communicates a property to the lacquer of imbibing moisture from the air. These inconveniences may be prevented by distilling the spirit; or, if the artist has not an opportunity of performing that process, he may cleanse the spirit in a great measure from the alkali, by adding to it some calcined alum, the acid of which uniting with the alkali remaining in the spirit, forms with it a vitriolated tartar, which, not being soluble in spirit of wine, falls to the bottom together with the earth of the decomposed alum. To a pint of the dephlegmated and purified spirit, about three ounces of powered shell-lac are to be added; and the mixture to be digested during some days with moderate heat. The liquor ought then to be poured off, strained and cleared by settling. This clear liquor is now fit to receive the required colour, from certain resinous colouring substances the principal of which are gamboge [a gum-

resin chiefly obtained from Garcinia morella] and anotto, the former of which gives a yellow and the latter an orange colour. In order to give a golden colour, two parts of gamboge are added to one of anotto; but these colouring substances may be separately dissolved in the tincture of lac, and the colour required may be adjusted by mixing the two solutions in different proportions. When silver-leaf or tin are to be lacquered, a larger quantity of the colouring materials is requisite than when the lacquer is intended to be laid on brass. There are sundry other materials, from a due mixture of which a like colour may be produced, as turmeric, saffron, dragon's blood, &c . . . Instead of shell-lac, used in the composition of varnishes for lacquering, resin or turpentine is substituted for the coarser uses. The following composition for brass-work, designed to resemble gilding, has been much recommended: take of turmeric ground, as it may be had at the dry-salters, one ounce, and of saffron and Spanish anotto each two drams: put them into a bottle with a pint of highly rectified spirit of wine, and place the bottle on a moderate heat, occasionally shaking it, for several days; then strain off the yellow tincture thus obtained, through a coarse linen cloth, and putting it back into the bottle, add three ounces of good seed-lac grossly powdered; place the bottle again in a moderate heat and shake it, till the seed-lac be dissolved. The lacquer strained as before will be fit for use, and must be kept in a bottle carefully stopped. By increasing or diminishing the proportion of anotto, the lacquer will be rendered warmer and redder, or cooler and nearer to a true yellow. A cheaper composition little inferior to the former, may be formed of one ounce of turmeric root ground, half a dram of the best dragon's blood, and a pint of spirit of wine, managed as the former.

3 The Decorative Tooling of Metals

BURNISHING AND POLISHING Burnishing is described by Rees as 'the operation of giving an uniform and brilliant surface to a variety of substances by friction, with a polished hard instrument usually called a burnisher.' The same source then continues with a typically splendid contemporary aphorism, as euphonious as it is illuminating:

> The modes of politure in use amongst artisans may, perhaps be all reduced to four:– the asperities of a rough surface may be removed by cutting off the protuberances, as in *planing;* by abrading them, as in *filing* and *polishing;* by obtunding them with the hammer as in *planishing;* and by accomplishing the same purpose in the manner now under our consideration.

Burnishing is only feasible on substances that possess some degree of malleability, and those that are brittle — glass, hardened steel and so forth — cannot be treated in this way. Having said that, it would have been difficult to find any artisan working with metal, in the last three hundred years or so, who did not use this process. The instruments used, too, varied in accordance with the surfaces to which they were to be applied. For present purposes, therefore, the process as applied to plane surfaces only will be described. Rees puts it as follows:

> It [the burnisher] is a piece of very hard steel three or four inches long, and about one eighth of an inch thick, with a somewhat convex edge, not much unlike that of the steel which is commonly used for striking fire, all the angles of it being smoothly rounded off, so that the longitudinal section of the part to be applied to the subject is a semi-ellipse of great eccentricity, the edge of which is nearly semi-cylindrical. It is applied in different ways according to the nature and extent of its use in the workshop.

These included inserting the instrument into the lower end of a wooden pole suspended over the workbench from one end of a strong wooden spring fixed horizontally in a frame attached to the ceiling, and pressing downwards. The workman passed it backwards and forwards horizontally at right angles to its own plane, over the surface of the objects being treated — in this case, ornamental plates for stoves — its application being assisted by the action of the spring. Other artisans fix the burnisher to the underside of a lever with a handle at one end, and hooked at the other into a fixed staple; others again fix it obliquely into one end of a staff, of which the other end is curved like a scythe. This passes over the right shoulder of the workman, enabling him to exert a very considerable pressure. Yet others merely insert it into a handle, or a short bar with a handle at each end, using it just like a rasp or file, or on occasion, as if shading a drawing with a black lead pencil. 'In whichever of these modes the burnisher is applied, the direction of its motion should be always rectilinear, parallel to itself, and at right angles with the edge of the instrument.'

There was also a practice by which the burnisher remained stationary, while the surface being treated was turned in a lathe. The one essential in all these processes was to keep the semi-cylindrical edge of the instrument as highly polished as possible — a leather buff charged with *crocus martis* was advocated for this purpose, to be frequently used — while the surface being burnished had to be constantly lubricated during treatment, the recommended lubricants including milk, oil, and soap-solution, the last-named being the one considered most efficacious. Failure in this regard caused the surface to ripple up before the burnisher, the ridges thus formed being laminated by any continuance and forming flakes or scales; this, in turn, being followed by the emergence of dark-coloured iridescent spots and streaks, and consequent failure of the process.

Although the basic principles remain the same, the

foregoing procedures would have been used to treat base metals and common alloys. The burnishing agents for gold and silver included a wolf's or dog's tooth, or a bloodstone; tripoli powder, fine emery and white wood were also favoured.

In practice, there seems little differentiation in the definitions of burnishing and polishing; it is partly a matter of degree, in the brilliance of the effect produced, and partly one of discrimination between materials being treated. Only some metals can be burnished, but many materials of varied kinds can be polished. Gilders, according to Rees, use an iron polisher to prepare the metal they are to gild; and after gilding they burnish with bloodstone to produce a brilliant finish.

ENGRAVING, PIERCING, CHASING AND CHISEL-LING Many techniques are used to decorate a plain metal surface without the need to introduce or apply any other material. In watches, and especially watchcases, most of them are mutually compatible and are to be found in various combinations on one and the same object. Because of their relative importance and the frequency with which they will be encountered in the context of the English watch, several are being described under their own headings, among these being, for example, casting, *repoussé* or embossed work, and engine-turning. This last is, of course, simply a particular type of engraving by machinery. In this present section, conventional engraving will be considered and the techniques allied to it, using only the relevant hand-tools now.

The art of producing designs on metals, as well as other materials such as wood, and certain gemstones, by means of lines inscribed upon the surface, has origins going back into antiquity. The Bible contains numerous references to seals, signets and other products of the engraver. In more recent times, engraved woodblocks, or plates of copper or steel, have been the bedrock of the printing industry. The basic techniques remain the same, however; and many engravers worked as both decorators

PLATE 60: The beauty of the early pierced, engraved and chiselled watchcase becomes more apparent the more examples are seen. These four range over the period from c1650 to perhaps 1680. The early versions, on watches by Jeremie Gregory and Henry Mott, as well as the quite superb example by John Bayes, all show the preoccupation with floral designs of great detail and complexity which were high fashion at that time. Even the small central vignette of buildings on the Mott watch hardly disturbs the general theme. Later, however, much more of the case back was left solid, as on the fine clock-watch by Solomon Bouguet, c1680, even though floral ornament continued to dominate the work.

of gold and silver, and as printmakers. In the watch trade, there seem to have been specialists available for this type of decorative work, certainly from the early eighteenth century onwards, and these are reflected in the categories listed in the Appendix, which include 'watch engraver', 'watch chaser' and 'watch piercer'. How much overlap there may have been in these related fields is by no means clear.

Described by one writer as 'a mode or species of sculpture performed by incision', the root of the term 'engrave' is variously said to derive either from the Greek or Hebrew tongues. In the latter case, its meaning is 'to plough', and since this is such a very apt description of the process, this perhaps seems the more likely. The basic tools consist of a range of cutting implements called gravers, of different sizes in relation to the thickness of the lines to be incised, but a set of the same was usually as many as nine, together with a scraper to remove the burr which the graver turns up. A burnisher was also necessary on occasions to rectify small errors. The work to be decorated was placed upon a 'cushion' — a leather bag about 9in (23cm) in diameter and filled with sand — having previously had the outline of the design to be engraved traced upon it. The first cuts were designed to transfer this outline on to the article, albeit in the finest degree — little more than mere scratches. Once this state was achieved, the operator could give full rein to his talent and technique, building up the design with lines of varying thickness, hatching and shading as deemed necessary by the artistic content of the depiction. The technique itself was slightly contrary to expectation, since the curving cuts were made by holding the graver stationary and turning the cushion as needed, while straight cuts necessitated exactly the opposite procedure. Although this gave much greater control and decreased the likelihood of accidental slipping of the graver, it also seemingly produced great physical stress. An Italian inventor and artist, one Joseph Longhi, reflecting upon this, states: 'It too often happens that those artists who apply themselves the most assiduously to their art, fall early victims to their diligence, so that their first essays become their last works.' He found that this situation

> . . . proceeded from the very hurtful attitude in which the engraver is placed at his work; for, in engraving a plate, even of middling size, if the plate be placed horizontally upon a cushion, it is not only impossible to perform the work without a very injurious curvature of the body; but it lays the foundation of those complaints which so often prove fatal to artists.

Abbé Longhi — for such he apparently was — could not bring himself to be more specific about the latter. To correct this hazard, he invented an engraver's table, which was articulated in such a manner as to enable the operator to work either standing or sitting, without any injurious bending of the body; but there is no evidence that it ever found great favour with engravers.

Abraham Rees's *Cyclopaedia* gives some thoughtful advice to novice engravers, in the following terms:

> As the principles of engraving are the same with those of painting, a person cannot expect to attain any considerable degree of perfection in this art who is not a good master of design, and therefore he ought to be well acquainted both with perspective and architecture, for the former, by the proper degradations of strong and faint tints, will enable him to throw backward or bring forward, the figures and other objects of the picture or design which he proposes to imitate, and the latter will teach him to preserve the due proportion of its several orders, which the painter often entrusts to the discretion of the engraver.

This is then followed by detailed instructions as to how to engrave certain commonplace features — hair and beard, flesh, architecture and sculpture, textiles, and metals, especially armour, and finally, water and sky, in various manifestations ranging from still to rough, and clear to cloudy. The landscape, too, comes in for particularly detailed treatment; and, since all these elements or any combination of them can be found in the decoration of watches, the methods represented are full of interest to anyone bent on emulating them.

Chasing should, more properly, be termed 'enchasing', and it has a close affinity with embossed, or *repoussé,* work (qv), the main difference being in the depth of the relief obtained — chasing is essentially a low-relief technique — and in the methods used, although both employ hammer-and-punch procedures. In chasing, which according to Rees, is only practised on thin hollow-ware like watchcases, the design is raised by surface hammering, the term 'flat chasing' being used of surface decoration in low relief produced by hammering with small blunt tools.

> It is performed by punching or driving out the metal to form the figures from within side, so as to stand out prominent from the plane or surface of the metal. In order to this, they have a great number of fine steel blocks, or puncheons, of divers sizes; and the design being drawn on the surface of the metal, they apply the inside upon the heads or tips of these blocks, directly under the lines or parts of the figures. Then, with a fine hammer, striking on the metal sustained by the block, the metal yields, and the block makes an indenture or cavity on the inside, correspondent to which there is a prominence on the outside, which is to stand for part of the figure. Thus the workman proceeds to chase and finish all the parts, by successive applications of the block

and hammer to the several parts of the design. And it is surprising, with what beauty and justness, by this simple piece of mechanism, the artists in this kind will represent foliages, grotesques, animals, histories, &c.

In modern usage, chasing is also the term used for finishing cast (qv) metalwork, by filing or cutting away any blemishes or roughnesses.

Chiselling is a technique rarely used on its own, its purpose being to remove, as expeditiously as possible, relatively large amounts of metal in order to obtain special effects, usually in relief work. A gouging chisel, sometimes called a scorper, is generally employed for this purpose.

Similarly, piercing is simply an enrichment, to be combined with the more common methods of decorating metal surfaces. In certain cases — especially with some types of watch cocks — it can be very fine work indeed, and it has been said that, for that very reason, it was often carried out by women, on an outworker basis. It is difficult to find any real evidence to support this, however likely it might appear circumstantially. The tools were relatively simple ones — fine drills and needle files, together with special saws, called piercing saws, in which the blade could be likened to serrated wire only, of course, very sharp and hard. When working with thin-gauge metal, it was essential to provide some kind of support against the distorting effects of drilling, sawing and filing; this usually took the form of a wooden template, fixed firmly to the work, into which the drills and files also penetrated, thus absorbing any injurious effects.

ENGINE-TURNING   To speak of 'mechanical decoration' in the context of the arts might almost seem to be a contradiction in terms; yet, certainly in the latter half of the last century, engine-turned decoration, that is to say, engraved decoration applied by machinery, was virtually the principal means of relieving the plain metal surface of the average watchcase. As practised by the finest experts, this type of work can be of the greatest imaginable complexity and calls not only for consummate skill in its execution, but also for the most intense concentration on the part of the operative, since there is no latitude whatsoever for mistakes and it is easy to ruin many hours of work with an ill-considered stroke. Of recent years, it has been possible for the layman to glean for himself something of the mysteries of engine-turning — as well as its hazards — since a rather advanced toy, the parts made in plastics but based on the principles of the rose-engine, has enabled quite a good approximation to this technique to be contrived, though using a pencil on paper rather than any kind of cutting tool on metal.

PLATE 61: Overall piercing of watchcases was not abandoned easily, as this later example (top left) by Ben Wolverstone illustrates. The swivelling keyhole covers are themselves engraved to fit into the general decor. The adjoining watch, by Charles Gretton, actually makes a feature of the winding holes by positioning them in the centres of flowers. No tiniest detail of such watchcases must ever be overlooked, and the band of the case will frequently be found to incorporate choice minutiae such as this fearsome warrior, from the inner case of a watch by Brounker Watts. An entirely different style is reflected in this pair of early eighteenth-century cases of a watch by Thomas Windmills, the pendant and bow being later replacements. The rustic scenes are after Teniers.

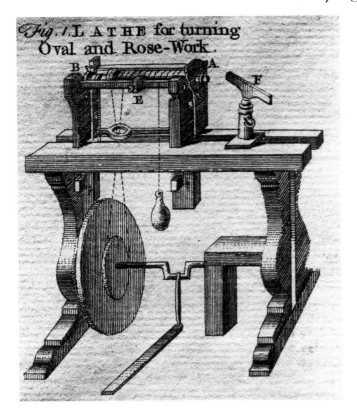

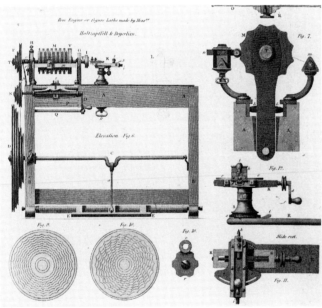

PLATE 62: Engine-turning demanded a special kind of machinery and it is clear that this developed quickly from the rather primitive version, taken from Owen's *Dictionary* in the mid-eighteenth century, to the sophisticated design with any number of accessories, supplied by Holtzapffell & Deyerlien seventy years later.

The process known as engine-turning — in French, *guilloche* — despite its reliance on precision machine tools, nevertheless has quite a long history. The earliest work to touch upon it is *L'Art du Tourneur* by Charles Plumier (Lyons, 1701) but, in its most primitive state, it probably starts to appear from around 1670. So far as watchcases are concerned, however, it is rare indeed before the last decade of the eighteenth century, and did not really come into its own until the succeeding one.

The machine employed is usually called a rose-engine, presumably because the most elaborated rosette designs were particularly popular and appropriate to the technology concerned. The rose-engine is a specialised lathe, and its properties are well summarised by Rees in his *Cyclopaedia*, in the article under that heading. This states:

> This machine contains all the parts of the lathe and, in the same manner as in turning, the work is caused to revolve whilst the cutting tool is kept stationary; but the difference between the rose lathe and the common lathe is that, in the former, the centre of the circle in which the work revolves is not a stationary point, but a slight motion is given to the centre whilst the work is revolving upon it, the tool being all the while stationary; the surface of the figure which it forms will be, of course, out of round, i.e. it will deviate from the circular figure as much and as often as the motion is given to the centre.

Rees goes on to say that:

> The art of turning curiosities . . . is one of those which is best adapted, of any of the mechanic arts, as an amusement for persons who either have leisure to apply to such subjects, or who require relaxation from mental studies: it has long been a favourite pursuit of many gentlemen, and the machines they employ are very ingeniously constructed. The curious in this art reckon two points of perfection in their works, one where the extreme delicacy, or elegance, of the object renders it admirable; and the other is considered from the difficulties of the execution; the former may be judged by all persons possessed of good taste but to judge of the latter requires some knowledge of the art or at least, so far as to know that the lathe will form only such articles as are perfectly circular, all parts having a common axis; therefore the specimens of [ornamental] turning are to be more or less esteemed in proportion as they are more opposed to the circular figure.

The gentleman-turner was a species peculiar to the nineteenth century and is rarely to be found today although a Society of Ornamental Turners survives. The origin, in England, of most of the finest equipment for engine-turning, both for the gentleman practitioner and for the trade, was Messrs Holtzapffel & Deyerlien, of Cockspur Street in London, and their equipment is today much prized and sought after. The Holtzapffel family were prominent in this business from 1780 until as recently as 1914, but the principal and most important member of it was Charles Holtzapffel, who was born in 1806 and died in 1847. His son John Jacob carried on with the family business of engineering and manufacturing after the relatively early demise of his father.

Apart from some of the surviving machines and tools, Charles Holtzapffel's most valuable contribution to the understanding of lathes, common and ornamental, as well as to other methods of shaping and working everyday raw materials, was his inception of the standard printed work of reference, eventually to run to a monumental five volumes, entitled *Holtzapffel's Turning and Mechanical Manipulation*. The chronology of this *magnum opus* is a little sketchy in places, as the volumes appeared either in their original versions or in revised and enlarged ones, over a period of half a century. It seems most likely that Charles Holtzapffel only published Volume I himself, in 1843, although he had almost completed Volume II, which was published by his widow in his name. Volume III is generally credited to John Jacob Holtzapffel if, as appears probable, this volume first appeared in 1864. However, it has been said that it first came out early in 1851, in which case the son would have been too young to have been involved, but no copies of such an edition have seemingly been recorded. When Volume III was republished in 1894, as a second edition, it had almost double the number of pages of its predecessor, and is stated to have been 'revised and enlarged' by the son, under whose name both Volumes IV and V appeared. The enlarged second edition of Volume III is comparatively rare, while Volume V is almost never to be found in its original version, although an unabridged facsimile has been published in recent years.

It is Volume V with which we are concerned here. Entitled *The Principles and Practice of Ornamental or Complex Turning,* it is considered to be the last word in the English language on this most esoteric subject. It will already have become apparent that the main principle underlying engine-turning is the eccentric rotation of the object, or of the cutting tool, or both, while they are in continuous or intermittent contact with one another. The variants of this technique are explained by Holtzapffel in the following terms:

> The cutting action may be divided into three principal methods. The work may be held at rest while the tool revolves and is advanced into simple contact with it, or during such contact is traversed along it; secondly, the work may traverse or may make a complete or partial rotation while the point of a fixed tool is advanced to it; and thirdly, the work may make its complete or partial revolution while a revolving tool is in simple contact with it or is traversed along it.

The index to this volume bespeaks the complexities of the machinery and tools involved, with references to 'double eccentric differential counting', 'elliptical and epicycloidal cutting frames', and the like, but it is beyond the scope of this present work to investigate them.

REPOUSSÉ OR EMBOSSED WORK 'EMBOSSING or Imbossing, the act of forming or fashioning works *in relievo,* whether they be cast, or moulded, or cut with the chisel, etc.' (Rees's *Cyclopaedia*)

The decoration of metal surfaces by embossing, that is, hammering up from the underside, was one of the first techniques to be learnt by metalworkers, and exceptionally fine early examples include the Vaphio Cup made in Crete c1600BC, which is now in the National Museum in Athens, and the Scythian animal reliefs dated to the fifth or sixth centuries BC, which are in the Hermitage in Leningrad.

In this type of work, the design is first drawn on the visible surface of the metal object, after which it is transferred through to the back by exerting pressure with a tracing tool. The object is then turned over from front to back and set face downwards on a support, which can be either asphalt, pitch or wood, usually in block form. Those parts of the design that have to be raised are then hammered down into this resilient support, using specially-shaped punches and a light hammer with a fairly elastic haft. When all the raised parts of the design have been embossed in this manner, the object is removed from its support and turned over, so that the front surface is now visible again. This time the back is filled with asphalt, so that the relief of the pattern can be further enhanced by hammering down portions of the background from the front.

When treating hollow-ware, which includes watch-cases, recourse may be had to a snarling iron. Made of steel, this has one end shaped to produce the required pattern and bent upwards at right angles to the bar from which it has been fashioned, and the opposite end is bent downwards and either held in a vice or driven into a block of wood. The shaped end being placed inside the hollow-ware article, the iron is given a sharp blow near to the end where it is secured, and this causes the other, patterned end, to strike the inside of the object being treated. The pattern that is rough-worked in this manner is finished by filling the object with asphalt and reworking the outside surface with chasing (qv) tools. This final process is accompanied by the employment of special punches that have a particular raised form on their faces. Much skill is needed in this work, which can produce scrolls and leaves with the most unlikely seeming tools.

4 OTHER TECHNIQUES IN ORNAMENTAL METALWORK

CASTING In the early nineteenth century, a mould was defined as 'a cavity artfully cut, with design to give its form, or impression, to some softer matter applied in it.' The terms 'cast' and 'moulded' were synonymous, and closely related to the operation of the foundry. So far as watches are concerned, cast elements were often used to add depth to the 'band' of the watchcase, which is that part that separates front and back covers; and even an entire case could be cast, in several parts, of course. The watch movement was not so susceptible to this technique, save for the pillars, which were always cast and could hardly be made any other way, unless simply of the turned baluster pattern. Where precious metals were concerned, casting techniques seem to have fallen within the prerogative of the goldsmith, whereas clock- and watchmakers often did their own casting in the base metals, and especially brass.

The best contemporary description of casting small brass objects seems likely to be that given by Thomas Martin, in *The Circle of the Mechanical Arts* (1813). In his essay entitled 'Founding', he first draws attention to the number of different processes even then available:

> Founding is as multiplied as there are metals susceptible of fusion by elevation of temperature; and as all those that are present known are in some way or other so, it follows that all may be foundered.

He describes briefly what is now known as the 'lost wax process', in which larger brass models are cast, and which was sometimes of use to the clockmaker. For smaller work, however, the common practice seems to have been relatively simple.

> Founders in brass require an exact model, in wood or otherwise, of the article to be founded; and this is most frequently required to be in two parts, exactly joined together, and fitted by small pins, and the casting, in such a case, is performed by two operations, that is, one half at one time and one half at another and in manner following, viz. The founder provides himself with a yellowish sharp sand, which is required to be well washed, to free it of all earthy and other particles. This sand is prepared for use by a process called tewing.

None of the authorities consulted gave any direction as to the origin of this particular sand — which Rees describes as 'yellowish and pretty soft' — but it seems clear that the exact quality was important.

'Tewing' means preparing or working up, and is the equivalent of 'tawing', the term applied to preparing skins and pelts. In the present context, the dampened sand is worked over a board, said to be about 1ft (30cm) square, placed over a box that receives the debris. The sand is rolled about using a roller 2ft (60cm) long and 2in (5cm) in diameter; and a long-bladed knife is also required, the sand then being alternately rolled and cut until it is considered free from any impurities and fit for use. It is clear that much work went into this preparatory stage, as a faultless impression was a prerequisite of the moulding procedure. Martin continues:

> When the sand is so far prepared, the moulder provides himself with a table or board which in size must be regulated by the castings about to be performed on it. The edges of the table or board are surrounded by a ledge, in order to support the tewed stuff; the table so previously prepared is filled up with the sand as high as the top of the ledge, which is in a moderately moistened state and which must be pressed closely down upon the table in every part.

The slightly archaic language nevertheless suggests a kind of shallow tray, filled to the brim with wet sand and smoothed over firmly.

> When the operation has so far advanced, the models must be all examined to see that they are in a state to come nicely out of the mould, and if not found so, they must be cleaned or altered until the founder is satisfied with them. All models require the greatest accuracy in their making, or it will be vain to suppose any good thing can be performed by the founder. When the models are found to be in a state to be founded, one half, generally longitudinally, is taken first, and this is applied on the mould, and pressed down into the tewed stuff or sand, so as to leave its form completely indented in it, and which must be very carefully looked to and examined minutely, to see that there are no small holes, as every part in the indented sand must be a perfect cameo of the models submitted and pressed into it. If it should not be found perfect, new sand must be added, and the model re-indented and pressed into it, till it leaves its impression proper to receive the metal. In the same manner, other models intended to be founded on the same table, must be prepared and indented into the sand.

COLOUR PLATE 9: One of the greatest expressions of art on the English watch has to be the exceptional instance where a well-known conventional artist has used this artifact as his medium. In this magnificent watch garniture, the neoclassical decoration, including the heads of George III and his consort, is carried throughout the chatelaine and on to the back of the watchcase. The artist is William Hopkins Craft, the enamel painter, who lived c1730–1811, exhibited regularly at the Royal Academy, dwelt for a time in Paris and later worked for Wedgwood. Several clock cases decorated by him are recorded, including one in the Royal Collection. The associated watch was made by John Leroux, of Charing Cross, and has a quarter-repeating movement. The complete garniture dates from 1777, and was made for Sir James Napier, FRS, FSA.

The next stage is the inclusion of the so-called master jet through which the molten metal will be carried throughout the mould. This is inserted by the 'melter' after he has thoroughly examined the condition of the mould and the impressions contained in it and satisfied himself that all is as it should be. This master jet is 'the half of a small wire of brass, pressed into the sand so as to form a small channel for the melted brass to flow in'. Rees, in his account, recommends a half-pipe — presumably a pipe split lengthways — of brass for this same purpose. The master jet 'is so disposed as to meet the ledge on one side, and far enough to reach the last pattern on the other; from this is made several lesser jets or branches, extending themselves to each pattern on the table, and by which means the fluid metal is conveyed to all the different indented impressions required to be cast on the table . . . the whole is sprinkled over with mill-dust and . . . is placed in an oven of moderate temperature till it gets dry'.

So far, so good. Now it is necessary to make a second mould, which is to incorporate the counterparts of all the patterns included in the first. The principle employed is identical to that already followed, the indented impressions being obtained by the simple expedient of turning the first mould upside-down on to the surface of the second, or by extracting the models from the first mould, having slightly freed them from the cloying sand with a knife, and using them to make the impressions afresh in the second.

COLOUR PLATE 10: Four watch garnitures illustrate the wide variety of treatments that could be applied to this type of artifact. (Top left) A splendid example of the work of G. M. Moser (qv), enamelled in the neoclassical manner with an *en grisaille* depiction of 'Love taming a lion', based upon an illustration in a volume published in Amsterdam in 1724 which is known to have been owned by Moser; the same work provided the inspiration for 'Medusa', the subject of the uppermost medallion. The watch movement was made by George Philip Strigel. (Top right) This treatment for a watch and chatelaine is quite frequently encountered, although this is a particularly fresh example. The translucent dark blue enamelled decoration is laid over a chiselled ground. The quarter-repeating watch is by Thomas Mudge, No 389. (Bottom left) This, too, is a more conventional style of decoration, based upon the use of dark blue enamel on a guilloche ground, together with diamonds and half-pearls. The maker of the watch was Thomas Gray, of Sackville Street. (Bottom right) The quality of the enamelling as well as the attractive accoutrements on this watch garniture make it especially outstanding. The quarter-repeating movement is signed Willm Allam, a maker who was working in London during the period 1743–85, while the pair-cases are stamped with the incuse mark of Peter Mournier, of Frith Street, Soho, first registered in 1761.

This economy in founding, of making one half of each pattern to be cast answer the purpose of the whole pattern, is a very common practice in brass founding and enables the manufacturer to sell his goods at a much cheaper rate than he would otherwise be enabled to do if he was obliged to have a full pattern of all goods to be founded.

The frame in which the counterparts of the objects will be moulded is identical to the previous one 'excepting only that it is prepared with small pins, to enter holes which are made in the first half of the model, and into which the pins enter and secure the two halves together. It is obvious that the accuracy in the joining will depend wholly upon the neatness and truth of fixing and boring for the pins.' This second frame is also taken to the 'melter', who enlarges the principal jet and ensures the cross-jets are properly made, after which it also is sprinkled with milldust and set to dry in the oven. When everything is sufficiently dry and ready, the two frames are joined together by the pins and holes; and, further to prevent any possible movement when the molten metal is introduced, they are 'locked down' in a kind of screw press or, if too large, fitted with wedges to ensure their rigidity. They are then taken to the vicinity of the furnace.

The raw metal — brass is a compound of copper and zinc, but the proportions vary enormously due, apparently, 'to the excessive volatility of the latter' — is prepared by being heated to the molten state in an earthenware crucible, usually about 10in (25cm) high and 4in (10cm) in diameter. The furnace is equipped with large bellows worked by a lever, and a chimney for the smoke to escape, and in these respects resembles a smith's forge.

The hearth of the furnace is of masonry or brickwork, secured by an outer rim of iron, in the centre of which is the fire-place and which consists of making a void or cavity from twelve to eighteen inches square and reaching quite down to the bottom or floor of the foundry. The void or cavity is divided into two parts by an iron grating, on the upper side of which is placed the fuel, and in the midst of it the crucible containing the metal; the lower part of the cavity is appropriated to admit the air to the fire, and also to receive the waste or cinders falling from the fire. The fuel consists of dry beechen wood cut into small billets, and previously baked to make them more readily combustible, and which are, when a fire is required, put into the cavity in the hearth, and well lighted. The crucible, when full of brass, should be placed down in the centre of the fire so that it may play all around it, and it should be covered with an earthen cover or tile, to promote the heat of the fire upon the metal.

Throughout this part of the process the attendant continually 'blows up' the fire with the bellows and also prevents any heat escaping up the chimney by placing a tile over the furnace aperture. As the first charge of metal in the crucible melts, it tends to shrink, leaving a considerable space above it, which has to be topped up. This is done by introducing pieces of brass that have been previously hammered in a mortar to break them down, and by means of an iron ladle that has a long hollow cylindrical shank of small diameter, yet sufficiently large as to admit of the brass fragments rolling through into the crucible. Once the metal has completely fused, the crucible is lifted by means of special iron tongs which have inward-bending 'feet', and carried to the moulds.

The molten brass is then poured into the master jet of each mould, until they are filled or the crucible emptied; but it was customary to melt rather more brass than would actually be needed in order to avoid the latter eventuality, since this entailed inevitable delay.

> As soon as the moulds are run, water is sprinkled over the tables to cool and fix the metal; after which the presses or wedges are removed from the frames, and the works just founded are removed out of the sand, to be cleaned and finished for sale. The tewing-stuff or sand is afterwards taken out of the frames to be worked up again for another casting. The sand, by a repetition of use, becomes quickly black, by reason of the charcoal that it collects from the foundry; but its blackness does not render it unfit to be employed in other tables for moulding or casting.

This condensed version of Thomas Martin's early nineteenth-century account of brass casting necessarily omits much incidental detail, which is not relevant in the present context; but it is interesting to note that, even at this relatively early date, many larger-scale brass founders were employing steam engines to punch articles out of sheet metal, using specially prepared dies. This technique could certainly have been applied to small watch components. Martin comments, however, that 'the punched goods are very cheap, but of very little strength or durability, as may be noticed in many of the brass articles employed in our domestic economy'.

An article, once cast, was not then immediately ready for use; some handfinishing was invariably needed. Martin goes on:

> All brass, as well as other foundings, require, when taken out of the sand, to be cleaned up and made complete, as they seldom come out exactly perfect. This is done, in brass founding, by filing off the cores [nowadays called 'flash'] and filling up the small holes with melted metal or solder. These imperfections frequently occur by air-bubbles, which are generated by the heat of the metal. Some brass works are cast to a rough pattern, for instance, all those which are cylindrical in shape; and such kinds of goods are put into a lathe and turned, and smoothed up afterwards. Articles in brass which are sculptured, are generally left in a mat-state

on their grounds, and the raised parts burnished up by hand; the mat-state refers to such parts only which are left without polish, or in a state in which the brass is found when it first comes out of the sand, with the addition of cleaning and perfecting only. The burnishing consists in making the raised parts quite complete, and afterwards laying them down tight upon a bench, or in a vice, whichever is most convenient; and working up the face of the brass with a bent tool composed of a shaft of steel, about half an inch wide and eight or nine inches in length, fixed firmly in an handle of wood. The end of the tool is turned up about a quarter of an inch, and ground away on its inner edge. With this tool the workmen rub the part that is to be *heightened,* as it is termed. They have these heightening tools of various widths, some one-eighth of an inch wide only, others as much as three-quarters of an inch. With such tools they operate upon all the various sized parts to be heightened; and as the part is thus rubbed, the workman dips his tool in a lacquer, which is standing near him in an earthenware dish. This lacquer is commonly prepared from turmeric dissolved in spirits of wine . . . Chasing, or enchasing [qv] as it is called, is also employed in brass works. It is a similar operation to heightening except that it is employed in the more delicate works to give them greater sharpness and effect.

PLATE 63: The watchcase with complex cast decoration and employing gold alloys of three or more colours, even — as in this example — further heightened with turquoises and garnets, found much favour in the early decades of the nineteenth century. This specimen, which houses a watch by Rundell, Bridge & Rundell, of Ludgate Hill, London, dates from 1817.

So much for the treatment given to complex castings, before they were ready to pass on to the next stage towards an end-product. The plain work, however, also had to be finished off before it could be sold. This involved filing or turning to produce a smooth surface, and then polishing, by rubbing first with emery — this would remove any remaining very small surface blemishes — and then with tripoli, to bring out the sheen.

In watch-work, much of the casting is done in precious metals, as has already been mentioned. Martin was concerned that people undertaking this work were properly qualified, expressing himself in the following terms:

> The business of founding or casting these [precious] metals is consigned to the artists known as the gold- and silversmith. In the City of London they are formed into a company, and enjoy many particular privileges. Their business consists in manufacturing gold and silver into numerous vessels and utensils both for utility and ornament, which they do either in the mould, or beat it out with a hammer or other engine. All works requiring to have raised or embossed figures are cast in moulds, the subjects for which are previously designed by an artist, and modelled afterwards in wax. Messrs. Rundell and Bridge, who are the most extensively employed of any house in London as goldsmiths, keep constantly in their employ, for this purpose, several very ingenious artists, whose whole time is taken up designing and modelling different articles to be cast in gold and silver . . . W. Theed, Esq., A.R.A., is their principal designer . . . Every goldsmith ought to be capable of designing and drawing, with a knowledge of modelling sufficient to understand its effect when it comes to be founded in metal. He should also be somewhat expert in the chemistry and metallurgy, to enable him to assay the mixed metals, and to alloy the pure ones with address. He will also require a knowledge in mathematics to defend himself from fraud in his purchases of the virgin-metal.

Despite all these requirements, Martin points out that the technique for casting in precious metals was the same as that used for brass. Rees, in his account, appears to dispute this, at least where small and delicate articles are concerned:

> The goldsmiths use the bones of the cuttle-fish to make moulds for their small works; which they do by pressing the pattern between two bones, and leaving a jet or hole to convey the silver through, after the pattern has been taken out.

In another part of the same work, however, there is given a variation on this, which suggests that cuttlefish, 'when dried, being reducible to a kind of fine pumice, very susceptible of all impressions', could be used in place of sand as the casting medium.

FILIGREE   Many collectors may spend a lifetime with their hobby and never see a true filigree watchcase, so rare are they — yet they are known and should not, therefore, be excluded from this survey.

Derived from two Latin words meaning, respectively, 'thread' and 'grain', the ornamental work called filigree consists of fine wire, which is twisted and plaited and soldered into a design. Usually employing gold or silver wire, in late Roman times bronze was also used; this alone illustrates the great antiquity of this process. Yet, by the post-medieval period, the technique had declined to the extent of becoming a product of the lowest end of the goldsmith's trade and, eventually, became little more than a peasant craft for cheap jewellery and novelties. Such trivia were made all over Europe, and the craft, even to this day, lingers on as a tourist attraction in Tuscany and Norway.

PLATE 64: A rarity among watchcases, this filigree example in gold contains a watch by Charles Gretton.

Even in the first quarter of the last century, Rees comments that filigree work 'was formerly much more employed than at present in the manufacture of small articles, which served more for show than for use; such as vases, needle-cases, caskets to hold jewels, small boxes' and he then goes on to describe the contemporary practice in countries such as Turkey, India and Malaya, where it was still a flourishing craft despite the primitive crudity of the tools used by its practitioners. However:

> . . . they are very inexpert at finishing and polishing the plain parts, hinges, screws and the like, being in this as much excelled by the European artists, as these fall short of

them in the fineness and minuteness of the foliage. The price of the workmanship depends on the difficulty or uncommonness of the pattern. This art is now neglected and little esteemed in Europe.

Despite the pejorative attitude towards filigree adopted by Rees and other contemporaries of his, it was clearly a skilled process that could be either executed upon some kind of forme or carcase, which was not necessarily of the same material, or left on its own, like a spider's web, yet shaped for some visible purpose. It may be that so few filigree watchcases have survived simply because this type of work was, even in its own day, held in such low regard.

5 OTHER DECORATIVE MATERIALS EMPLOYED

ENAMELLED WORK There is a delightful, if rarely encountered, little book by one Charlotte Matilda Hunt, which was published in 1826 and specifically dedicated to HRH The Princess Augusta. Seemingly intended originally for the sole use of her own children, Mrs Hunt's book was published almost by public, not to mention royal, command; and, if its substance could be epitomised in a few words, these could only be 'enquire within on everything'. *The Little World of Knowledge,* in its 350 or so small octavo pages, is a remarkable digest of contemporary information 'designed . . . as an Introduction to the Arts and Sciences, History, Natural Philosophy, Belles Lettres, &c. &c. &c'. This is what the author had to say about enamelling:

> By the custom of trade, rather than from any principle of utility, enamelling is divided into two branches, viz. DIAL-PLATE enamelling, and TRANSPARENT enamelling. The former includes the manufacture of watch and clock plates, with fluxed plates for enamel painting; the latter comprehends the enamelling of watch-cases, brooches, pins, and other bijoux: latterly, the making of these lesser articles has grown into disuse in this country.

Mrs Hunt then goes on to discuss the great antiquity of this art, but without specifically drawing attention to its use as a decorative medium in watches from the very earliest times. For example, one of the few surviving watches signed by Michael Nouwen has its chapter ring enamelled in dark blue with the numerals picked out in gold; this object can barely post-date 1600 and is certainly a product of the very beginnings of English watchmaking. Later in the development of the English watch, the enamel dial came to have a far more functional than purely decorative significance: it would be difficult to envisage a more legible combination than black numerals on a white ground. It is perhaps this distinction between the functional and the decorative that provides the right introduction to a process that is not only highly complex, using a variety of techniques, but must always have been very expensive in its more extravagant manifestations, otherwise it would not have been necessary to encourage cheaper substitutes, like underpainted horn (qv).

Functional use

> For clock and watch dials there is probably no substance that can equal enamel in permanence and beauty; in several respects, it possesses advantages even over the rich metals of silver and gold. Within the last thirty or forty years, an imitative enamel has been used and through the scarcity of real enamel is now in much demand . . . but it is by no means comparable with its prototype: for, being chiefly composed of flake white, ground up with spirits of turpentine and afterwards mixed with copal varnish, it will neither assume an equal brilliancy in colour, nor continue unchanged in different climates; on the contrary, the action of the air occasions it to become dingy and yellow. In fact, imitative enamelling is nothing more than a branch of the art of japanning.

So begins the article on this subject in Rees's *Cyclopaedia.* The author then proceeds to castigate the secrecy that surrounds those arts that lack any formal scientific basis, and the jealousy with which the professional practitioner conceals information, profit being the only motive, so that 'the amateur seldom acquires an insight sufficiently minute to enable him to unfold the modes of operation.' He goes on to promise that, however inadequate his own explanation of the processes may be, it is much better than anything that has hitherto been available!

There are, so it appears, two kinds of dial-plate enamelling; the first, usually called hard-enamelling, uses only Venetian enamels and requires a much greater input of time, labour and skill than the second and hence is much more highly esteemed. The second, called soft- or glass-enamelling, uses English or glass enamels.

The first part of the process is concerned with preparing the material to which the enamel is to be applied and the principle is the same, whether this be gold, silver or copper. The metal is initially evenly 'flatted' in long strips of the required thickness at the flatting mill, where it is effectively mangled between steel rollers. According to the size of the finished articles, pieces of these strips are cut off and annealed in the fire to soften them and make them pliable.

They are then accurately shaped with the use of brass dies, small evenly turned circular plates varying in thickness from $1/16$ to $1/8$in (1.5 to 3mm), or even more according to their diameter. Some of these are flat, some are convex so as to impart a slight curve to the dial. The edges of the dies are turned off obliquely, and have at the centre a hole rather larger than that required in the finished dial-plate. A complete set of such dies is said to range from about ³/₄ to 2¹/₂in (19 to 63.5mm) in diameter, the difference between each die and that immediately following it, whether larger or smaller, being very slight indeed, possibly as little as ¹/₃₂in (·8mm).

The method of using the dies consists, first, of placing a piece of prepared and softened metal strip of the appropriate size on a suitable die and making the 'eye', or centre hole. This is done by forcing the metal up into the hole in the die with a round-headed punch, the resulting bulge being then opened up with a smooth-grained file. Placed once again on the die, the hole is gradually opened up and pressed tighter into the aperture with an oval burnisher; and the process is repeated once again, this time using a round broach, care being taken each time to remove the burr with the file, and to prevent the eye from cracking. The punch, burnisher and broach are each made of steel, and the two last-named are tapered towards the handles.

Once the eye is completed, the edge is trimmed so as to leave only a tiny rim projecting beyond the die — as little as ¹/₃₀in (·85mm). This is then turned up and burnished against the edge of the die, and filed evenly round and reduced as may be necessary to make a good fit with the brass-edge to which it will be fixed when in the watch. The inside burr is then removed with a graver and finished with a scratch-brush. 'The purpose for which the eye of the copper is formed and the edge turned up, is to retain the enamel in its proper place so that the plate may be finished both square and neat.'

The degree of curvature of the finished product is governed by such factors as the design of the gearing immediately beneath the dial; when a subsidiary seconds indication has to be provided for, it is desirable to keep the dial as flat as possible. Any curvature must, of course, be regularly and accurately formed and a small so-called setting-die is used for this purpose. Made of box or other hardwood, and turned out to the required concavity, it also has a hole in the middle to receive the eye of the plate when placed within it. When this is in place, the required curvature is obtained by rubbing it gently but firmly with a spatula formed of a thin slip of steel, about 5in (127mm) long.

The next stage is to solder on to the plate the 'feet' by which it will eventually be fixed to the brass-edge or frame of the watch, their positions having first been marked on the plate through the holes provided for them in the brass-edge. The feet are always made from wire of the same metal as that to be enamelled, which is drawn into different thicknesses according to the size of the dial being made. The range of such wires is from ¹/₁₀ to ¹/₁₆in (2·5 to 1·5mm) in diameter. One method of cutting corners at the cheaper end of the product range was to use copper wire plated with silver, which formed the solder when exposed to the lamp and blowpipe — for that was the method of soldering used then and is still in use today. In the best work, however, plain copper wire was used, with silver solder or spelter, an impure form of zinc. It is said that feet soldered with spelter take the firmest hold, those with silvered wire the slightest. The ends of the feet are filed to correspond with the surface to which they are being attached, and they are held in position sufficiently to permit of soldering, by first dipping in a mixture of borax and water. Great care has to be exercised concerning the degree of heat being applied to fuse the solder as, if it is too powerful, the dial-plate is likely itself to melt. Similarly, it is essential to see that the feet retain their correct positions from the outset, as replacing them can be a very troublesome operation.

The heat from this part of the process having inevitably produced a scale upon the metal surfaces, a pickling solution is used to remove it. This can be either oil of vitriol (concentrated sulphuric acid) or 'double aquafortis' (concentrated nitric acid), which will reduce the scale sufficiently to allow it to be removed with a soft brush, water and white sand. When all these impurities have been washed away and the plate dried with a soft cloth, almost invariably it will be found to have lost some of its shape. Irregularities are corrected by further recourse to the brass die and setting block; the consequent rubbing with the spatula at this stage can be beneficial, in that it tends to harden the metal being treated.

Such are the basic means of preparing the dial-plates of watches for enamelling; if done in quantity at one time, it is quicker to turn up the edges on a lathe rather than to file them by hand, as previously described. Indeed, there were two other kinds of dial-plates, known as 'solid French edges' and 'laid-down French edges', in which the lathe was used to facilitate turning out the unwanted metal from the original blank and thus provide the edges to contain the enamel; but these were usually restricted to watches of the kind where space for the dial was limited so that they had to be fixed directly to the main frame of the movement rather than to an intermediate brass-edge. As for the dial indicators, where a seconds hand was required or some other complication made an additional hole, apart from that at the centre, necessary, this could be quite simply accomplished. Having marked its position with the greatest accuracy on the underside of the plate, the hole would then be 'bulged' upwards by striking it with a small hammer and punch, into a piece of lead about three times the thickness of the die; the lead provides sufficient resistance to prevent the eye from cracking yet is soft enough to permit the plate being bulged up evenly. Any such small eyes are afterwards evened up with a file and further opened up, if necessary, with a small needle or round pin.

The plates are now ready to be enamelled. As it came from the makers, enamel was usually supplied in round cakes from 4 to 6in (10 to 15cm) in diameter, and it was necessary to reduce this to a form in which it could most conveniently be used. To do this, a small hammer with one end flat and the other of that shape commonly used for riveting, was used to strike the edge of the cake sharply, while it rested upon the forefinger of the left hand. This caused thin flakes of the material to break off, which were then put into an agate mortar and pulverised with a pestle of the same material, the enamel meantime being covered with water to prevent splinters from flying about. The exact fineness of the ground enamel thus produced is said to have been judged only by experience of the process although, in general, the backing should be much finer than the first coat, and the second coat of an intermediate fineness. Hard enamels had to be considerably finer than glass enamels, and the flux finer still, since the effect of the fire on this was much less than on either of the other substances. In all these procedures it was vital to exclude any dust or dirt, and the slight fluff which grinding generates had to be washed away as many times as might be required during the operation, and until the washing water came out clean. A small teapot was customarily used to pour out the water and, after sufficient grinding, the product was stored in a small cup, the surface being kept just covered with water.

Rees provides a graphic description of exactly how the grinding operation was performed, from which it is clear that both strength and skill were involved. The mortar was placed on the bench upon a piece of coarse flannel or linen, twice or thrice doubled and made wet to prevent its slipping. The handle of the pestle being grasped firmly about its middle with one hand, the palm of the other was then placed upon the top while the operator inclined his body over the mortar and crushed the enamel by pressing forcibly with his chest upon that hand that covered the end of the pestle. This action had to be repeated in quick succession until all the larger pieces were reduced to coarse and uneven grains. When this stage was reached, the mortar was held firmly down with one hand while the other, working the pestle in a circular motion, and using as much strength as could conveniently be exerted, reduced the material to the requisite degree of fineness and evenness.

The manufacture of watch dials was clearly what would nowadays be termed a small-batch process: a number of plates would be treated at the same time, saving time, labour and materials. The first stage, after the plates had been scrupulously cleaned with the 'pickle' and then water, was to place them, face downwards, on a soft cloth or smooth napkin. Next, the 'backing', as it is called, of ground enamel paste was spread over the underside of the plate — that is, the side facing upwards — with a bone spoon or specially cut quill. It was essential that this paste should be smoothly and evenly spread over the metal surface, most usually copper. This was done by alternately applying another soft cloth or napkin to the ground enamel to absorb some of the water with which it had been mixed into paste, and then smoothing with the rounded side of a steel spatula. After this had been done several times, the proper degree of smoothness and evenness would be achieved; but considerable judgement had to be exercised to ensure that not all the moisture was absorbed from the ground enamel, otherwise it would revert to the powder form and drop off the plate before the next stage in the process was reached. The final operation in 'laying the bottoms' was to clear away the loose particles of enamel from the edge and eye of each plate with a spatula and the pointed end of a quill.

The next stage was to lay the first coats, by spreading a bed of glass enamel over the upper sides of the plates. After first brushing the surface with a camelhair brush or hare's foot, to remove any extraneous matter that might have accumulated thereon — especially any particles of hard enamel which, if mixed with the glass, would completely spoil the work — the latter is evenly spread to a thickness equal to the height of the brass-edge and the eye. The water content must be reduced slightly after this, and the same method is used as before, with absorption by a cloth or napkin and smoothing with a spatula until all unevenness has been removed and the surface runs regularly from edge to centre. Finally, the edge of the plate being gently tapped two or three times at different places with the spatula, any residual water can be brought to the top and absorbed with the cloth, followed by further smoothing, the intention now being to take up as much of the water as possible without disturbing the enamel. The plates are now ready to be placed upon rings for firing.

These rings are generally made of a mixture of pipemaker's clay and Stourbridge clay that has been rolled into a cylinder and turned in a lathe by means of a cylindrical piece of wood forced through the centre of the mass when wet. Each ring is about a ¼in (6mm) thick, and the same wide. The underside is nearly flat, but the upper side has to be specially prepared to make it slightly concave, and this is done by rubbing it carefully upon a half-sphere of lead sprinkled over with fine silver sand. The purpose of this concavity is to ensure that only the edge of each copper plate touches the ring, thus leaving its enamel backing undisturbed. The edges are prevented from sticking to the rings by rubbing the surfaces of the latter with soft chalk or whiting.

The rings, with the plates which they support, are next placed in a shallow tin vessel, about ³⁄₄in (19mm) deep, and called a 'tin cover'. All the remaining moisture is then slowly driven off by placing near a fire; this process has to be gradual and properly controlled since, if dried too quickly, the work will suffer from blistering. This is occasioned by air bubbles rising to the surface, caused partly by lack of care in laying on the enamel but also, seemingly, by the air that has been trapped in the water used in the process.

Next comes the firing, beneath a muffle placed in a small furnace, which is fuelled with coal and charcoal. When this has reached a sufficient heat, the plates are placed carefully upon thin slabs of clay or iron, chalked over, and then gradually introduced below the muffle, which is simply a fireproof arched cover designed to protect anything placed beneath it from falling ashes or coal. In a short time the enamel melts — the technical term is 'runs' — and once it is properly consolidated, the first coat is complete. It is very important that the enamel is not over-fired, as this produces loss of opacity and other defects. In practice, the slabs are placed at the back of the muffle by using a pair of tongs, and, as soon as fusion is seen to be occurring, carefully turned round so that every part can be equally affected. These slabs, or planches, are usually circular and concave, so that the work can be moved without any danger of shaking off the enamel before it has become fixed.

The enamel in its ground state occupies a greater space than when solid. As a result, the action of fusion produces a depression in the enamel of the first coat, so that the edge and eye of each plate once more project above the surface. The second coat is designed to remedy this deficiency. After cooling, therefore, the work is next descaled at edge and eye by means of a fine-grained Lancashire file or a smooth 'greystone' (pumice). After washing and drying, each plate is then put upon a small round wax-block, of sufficient bulk to be held in the hand and about 4 or 5in (10 or 12·5cm) high, the feet being firmly pressed into the wax covering one end of the block, and care being taken not to strain the enamel by pressing too hard. A second layer of ground enamel is then spread with a quill and prepared for firing by napkin and spatula, exactly as before, followed by placing the plates on the rings, evaporating the moisture in the tin-cover, and then firing in the furnace. This time, however,

a procedure known as 'coddling' is added, giving a rotary motion to the work by holding the planche lightly with the tongs and gently drawing the edge of it towards the mouth of the muffle, and then returning it to its former position. The work is now ready for polishing, and then painting.

In this context, the polishing process has a twofold purpose. It is not solely concerned with procuring a glossy surface, but also with ensuring an absolutely even and regular one. The glossiness is easily obtained and maintained, since it derives wholly from the act of fusion by heat. If it should be lost, it can simply be reintroduced by applying sufficient heat to cause fusion to recur. To achieve an even and regular surface, however, requires the use of a variety of different grades of abrasive. Rees specifies the materials needed for this purpose, as 'grey-stones, rag-stones, sometimes called burrs, fine ground silver sand, and water', the second ingredient in this list apparently being a kind of vitrified brick.

First, the edges and eyes were rubbed down, the former to a state of universal smoothness and the latter until the centre of each plate is even and 'square' — a strange term (but in general use in the trade) to apply to a round hole! This initial operation is done with various grades of greystone after the surface irregularities are removed either with the greystones or ragstones, the latter being only used for the more common types of dials. The method is to hold the plate upon the fore and middle fingers of one hand, giving it a circular motion with the thumb, meantime using the other hand to rub the polishing medium backwards and forwards over all parts of the surface. Another method is to hold the polishing stone on the work bench with one hand and with the other to rub the enamel surface upon it; yet a third method is to fix the plate upon a cork by its feet or with a piece of wet flannel, and giving it a rotary motion with the fingers while applying the polishing medium to it as previously described. The ground silver sand wears away the enamel with greater rapidity than any other medium, and it is also used to sharpen up the other polishing stones. Whatever method is used, inevitably the polishing destroys the glossiness of the enamel surface, and great care has to be exercised to ensure that the pressure upon it is never too powerful, as the plates will then crack in the fire and can only very rarely be properly restored thereafter.

Once the enamel is sufficiently polished — and this is judged to be when all the gloss has disappeared — the plates are thoroughly washed and any specks of dust or dirt picked out with a sharp graver. They have then to be well rubbed over with some fine ground glass in order to remove the discoloration left by the polishing stones, this medium being applied with a cloth or a smooth piece of fir wood. The plates are then once again washed and thoroughly dried, and placed upon the rings for further firing. Since the re-fusion is much facilitated by the enamel being free from blemishes, the degree of heat needed depends upon the particular method by which they were prepared; when the enamel is properly 'run', that is, when it becomes perfectly smooth, even and bright, the plates are allowed to cool. They are now ready for painting.

So much for the preparation of dial-plates for, as Rees calls it, 'the best kind of work'. Two other methods of enamelling, used for the less expensive products, were known as 'run-down plates' and 'run-down second coats'. In these, sufficient enamel was used in the initial operation to obviate any need for a second coat; but the finish left much to be desired, and completely flat plates could not be treated by this method at all. Run-down plates were not polished so that, in the firing, more 'coddling' was required and a longer continuation of intense heat to encourage the enamel to run to the requisite evenness of surface. A slight improvement was obtained with 'run-down one coats', which were polished with ragstone and then underwent a second firing; while 'run-down second coats' had their final surface imparted by the second firing, were not subsequently polished, but were then sent straight for painting.

The above deals with English enamelling using soft, or glass, enamels; but by far the most expensive process employed Venetian enamels, also called hard enamels and, if genuine, originating from Venice. Thomas Martin, commenting in *The Circle of the Mechanical Arts* (1813), on the difficulty of obtaining such quality products because of the Peninsular War, states that 'what used to fetch only two or three shillings per lb., are not to be had for twice as many pounds'.

In enamelling hard plates, as they were called, all the preparatory stages up to the first coat were the same as for soft enamels, save that the first layer is slightly thinner than previously described. The nature of the enamel, however, requires small differences in its preparation if anything other than a very small quantity is needed. For larger quantities, after breaking off sufficient flakes from the cake with a hammer, they are pounded in a steel mortar to obtain coarse granulation, but must then be exposed to a strong magnet to remove the particles of steel that the act of pounding will have broken from the mortar wall, otherwise these would rise as black specks to the surface upon firing, and ruin the appearance of the product. Even this was not considered wholly adequate, and it was usual also to steep the enamel in strong acid solution for some hours to dissolve any remnants of steel, before washing it thoroughly to remove the acid. Finally,

PLATE 65: The enormous versatility of which enamel is capable, is demonstrated by this and the following two illustrations. Here, a gold watchcase, London-made in 1791, has its back decorated with a chain spiral in translucent blue enamel against a white ground. It has a matching chain and key.

the particle size of the enamel was reduced to the required fineness by grinding in an agate mortar.

The coating and firing proceeded much as before, but polishing required different agents, including bluestone and sand. With the former, a kind of half-polish could be obtained, and the glossier this was, the better, since the amount of heat required in the third firing could then be modified. Throughout this process, much care had to be taken to prevent scratches, since firing could often not fuse these over without subjecting the enamel to a greater heat than it could stand. Any small specks or other blemishes had to be picked out with a small diamond point and the resulting hollows very carefully filled with enamel from a sharp quill to such an extent that they would remain level with the surrounding area after firing. Should this not be achieved, it was necessary to use the bluestone to smooth out any irregularities, followed by a fourth firing to obtain uniformity in surface texture and glossiness. The other problem area, which affected the polishing of both glass and hard plates, was the separation between the enamel and the metal base, which could be caused either by too much pressure or by too coarse an abrasive destroying the adhesion. With glass enamels these defects can sometimes be remedied, but with hard ones, practically never.

Ornamental use In his *Chemical Dictionary* (1807), Arthur Aiken says:

> The reader may conceive how much the difficulties of this nice art [enamel painting] are increased, when the object is not merely to lay an uniform coloured glazing on a metallic surface, but also to paint that surface with figures and other designs that require extreme delicacy of outline, accuracy of shading and selection of colouring. The enamel painter has to work not with actual colours, but with mixtures which he knows from experience will produce certain colours after the operation of the fire; and to the common skill of the painter in the arrangement of his pallet and the choice of his colours the enameller has to add an infinite quantity of practical knowledge of the chemical operation of one metallic oxyde on another, the fusibility of his materials, and the utmost degree of heat at which they will retain not only the accuracy of the figures which he has given but the precise shade of colour which he intends to lay on.

The spelling may be archaic in places, but the problems come through loud and clear. Painting in enamel involves a succession of firings, the first two of which will be solely concerned with the ground that is to receive the design. After that, the different parts of the design will each require its own firing. There can well be additional complications, too. Thomas Martin, for his part, writes:

> The operations of 'transparent enamelling' are nearly similar to those that have been already described in the manufacture of watch dials. But, as the work is generally of a more minute kind, greater delicacy of handling is required. Watch cases are usually enamelled on gold, as well as the superior articles of the fancy kind; and the surface of the gold is frequently engraved into different figures and compartments, before the enamel is laid on; hence the work has a beautiful variegated appearance, through the enamelled coating.
>
> In ornamental transparent work, a good effect is produced by applying small and very thin pieces of gold or silver, cut or stamped into different figures, as acorns, oak-leaves, vine-leaves, bunches of grapes, fruits, &c., upon the surface of the first coating of enamel, where they are fixed by fire, and are afterwards covered over by the second, through which they make a beautiful appearance.

Most early nineteenth-century treatises on this subject then go on to discuss the nature and composition of the various colours, virtually all metallic oxides, and it is surprising how many were available. The basic nature of opaque white was considered so important that it was explored in great detail:

It should be of a very clear fine white, so nearly opaque as only to be translucent at the edges, and at a moderate red heat should run into a kind of paste or imperfect fusion, which allows it to extend itself freely and uniformly, and to acquire a glossy even surface, without fully running into a thin glass.

A number of different formulations of the essential ingredients, the oxides of tin and lead, were described and evaluated and Martin even commissioned 'our chemist' — one can sense the pride with which he wrote this — to try to find a substitute for marine salt, which is also a part of the mixture. Interestingly, in the end it was concluded that the French had solved the problems of white enamel best, and the reader was especially referred to the account by Monsieur Clouet in the thirty-fourth volume of *Annales de Chemie*.

PLATE 66: This repeating watch by Conyers Dunlop, c1780, not only has pierced decoration — to allow the sound of the bell to be heard — but the back has been enriched with translucent blue enamel leaves in the *basse taille* manner, after which further enamelled flowers have been added in relief.

Attention then focused upon other common colours; it was considered that virtually every colour could be simulated provided the oxides being used did not lose their oxygen too quickly, and that those that did were unsuited to enamelled work. Specifically, it was possible to render purple, red, yellow, green, blue, violet and, of course, black without difficulty. The techniques for employing them, however, were quite complex. It seems that there were two methods of painting on enamel, one on a raw enamel surface and one on already baked enamel, and both could, in fact, be used for the same object. Martin writes:

Solid colours, capable of sustaining the fire necessary for baking the enamel ground, may be applied in the form of fused enamel on that which is raw, and the artist may afterwards finish with the tender colours. The colours applied on the raw material do not require any flux.

The meaning of 'tender' is connected with the melting point of different enamel colours, the tender ones being those that resisted heat the least. The principle, therefore, was to apply the colours strictly according to the degree of heat that fused them, starting with the highest temperatures and working through them in precise order to the lowest, with a firing in between each heat level. Arthur Aiken, from whose *Chemical Dictionary* of 1807 the opening of this section was extracted, puts it in these words:

Painting in enamel requires a succession of firings; first, of the ground which is to receive the design, and which itself requires two firings, and then of the different parts of the design itself. The ground is laid on in the same general way as the common watch face enamelling already described. The colours are the different metallic oxides melted with some or other vitrescent [tending to become glass] mixture and ground to extreme fineness. These are worked up with an essential oil, that of spike [a type of lavender] is preferred, to the proper consistence of oil colours, and are laid on with a very fine hair brush. The essential oil should be very pure, and the use of this rather than any fixed oil, is probably that the whole may evaporate completely in a moderate heat, and leave no carbonaceous matter in contact with the colour when red-hot, which might affect its degree of oxydation, and thence the shade of colour which it is intended to produce. As the colour of some of the vitrified metallic oxides, such as that of gold will stand only at a moderate heat, while others will bear and even require a higher temperature, to be properly fixed, it forms a great part of the technical skill of the artist to apply different colours in their proper order; fixing first those shades which are produced by the colours that will endure the highest degree of heat, and finishing with those that demand the least heat. The outline of the design is first traced on the enamel, ground and burnt in; after which the parts are filled up gradually with repeated burnings to the last and finest touches of the tenderest enamel.

Mechanical aids to ornamental enamelling Enamel painting, as has been seen, relies mainly on using enamels on plain metal surfaces, with all the special technology required by considerations of the temperatures of fusion, but using painters' methods. Over very many centuries, however, other techniques have been involved that treat the basic metal suface being enamelled either by decorating it in a manner that can be seen through a translucent enamel topcoating, or by compartmentalising the surface so that different enamels are physically prevented from coming into contact with one another, thus simplifying the firing procedures. Another technique, which has already been mentioned, involves 'floating' small decorative motifs by firing them on to one enamel surface and

PLATE 67: Perhaps at the other end of the social scale, three painted enamel dials, all found on provincially-made watches. In the centre, a typical farmer's watch, on which the sails of the windmill rotate with the seconds. Flanking this are two watches with obvious fraternity associations, probably of masonic significance. The dates of the hallmarked cases, from left to right, are 1845, 1798 and 1839, sufficient of a span to show the long-lived popularity of the painted dial.

then covering them with a further, translucent, coating which was fired in its turn to provide a glossy veneer to an interesting optical effect.

Engraved or chiselled decoration of the metal surface before enamelling is the technique always known as *basse-taille*. It is not without significance that all the major enamelling techniques are described by French names, for which there are simply no English equivalents. In *basse-taille* work, sculptural effects were applied to the thickness of the metal, and the coating of translucent enamel, which was subsequently used to coat them, seemed to reflect different shades of its particular colour according to the depth of the sculptured area underneath. Probably the commonest form of *basse-taille* to be encountered on watches is symmetrical engine-turned decoration (again, usually called by the French term *guilloche*) which, at its best, can produce considerable visual appeal.

There are two main methods of compartmentalising the metal surface to provide 'cells' for the enamel. The first, known as *cloisonné,* involves creating cells, or cloisons, by fixing metal wires or fine strips of metal laid edgewise, to the metal carcase. These cavities are filled with finely powdered glass enamel, in paste form, which is then fused to the metal in a furnace. As with other methods, the enamel tends to shrink on fusion, so that the filling and firing may have to be repeated several times. After this, the surface has to be levelled and polished. With the *champlevé* method, however, the cells were gouged out of the metal sheet itself, instead of being attached to it; otherwise, the principle was the same. The simplest form of *champlevé* work to be found on English watches must certainly be the treatment of metal dials, especially during the twenty or so years either side of 1700, in which the numerals have been cut out and filled with black material, although this can just as easily be engraver's wax as true enamel. Nevertheless, these are always referred to as *champlevé* dials.

So versatile was enamel as a medium that its possibilities were limited only by the ingenuity of the executant. With or without cells, variants or combinations of the foregoing techniques certainly exist; sometimes enamel is simply run into engraved, or pierced — or pierced *and* engraved — metal, the designs ranging from the purely geometrical to the fully representational, and the quality from the brilliant to the indifferent. Watch decoration would, even so, have been much the poorer without it.

NIELLO   A technique akin to, but technically different from, enamelling, niello is a black substance made up of powdered silver, lead, copper, sulphur and often borax.

This is used as a filler for *champlevé*-style engraved silver, the effect being of a brilliant black decoration on a bright silver ground — provided that this last is not allowed to tarnish, when all contrast is quickly lost. Heat is used only to the extent that the niello is run in a molten state into the engraved metal. While by no means common, niello is to be found as a decorative treatment on watch cases.

HARD STONE AND LAPIDARY TECHNIQUES   Two materials not infrequently found in fine antique watches, and employed primarily for their appearance, are worked by methods deriving from the lapidary: these are rock crystal and agate. Rarely, a variety of the former nowadays called smoky crystal, and sometimes known as topaz, can also be found. The latter is generally categorised as 'hard stone', and can include varieties of minerals similar, but not necessarily identical, to agate.

Rock, or mountain, crystal is the purest known form of quartz, and differs from commoner varieties by virtue of its exceptional transparency and, in chemical terms, the more regular form of its crystalline structure.

Agate, on the other hand, does not denote a single type of mineral but rather a combination of those types whose main constituent is silica. Such combinations may be formed of two or more ingredients from a list that might include flint, chalcedony, amethyst, jasper, carnelian, and others. The main characteristic of agate is its stratified construction; in banded agate, the colours are deployed in straight lines, while in fortification agate, they are arranged in wavy and angular concentric zones. Other versions include landscape and moss agates, descriptions that speak for themselves.

Agate is neither wholly transparent, like rock crystal, nor opaque, like jasper; as it differs in the colour of its constituent parts, so it does in its transparency. Both agate and rock crystal can take a very high polish, and both can be successfully simulated in glass which, on occasion, can provide problems for the unwary.

When cutting and shaping stones, the lapidary's principle is always to use a harder substance for the cutting or grinding edge, than that being worked. For rock crystal a copper wheel, charged with olive oil and diamond dust, was preferred; a polish could then be obtained by using a second copper wheel charged with tripoli powder — an abrasive, naturally occurring product chiefly consisting of fine particles of silica — and water. In the case of agate, it was customary to employ a lead wheel, using as the abrasive a substance called smalt, which was a kind of glass, together with water. Polishing was accomplished with a wooden wheel and again using tripoli and water.

In case it should be thought that this kind of highly specialised skill was mainly to be found abroad, it is interesting to hear Rees stating the situation as it prevailed around 1820:

> The art of cutting precious stones is very ancient; but, like others, its origin was very imperfect. The French have succeeded in it the best; and the lapidaries of Paris, who have been a corporation since the year 1290, have carried it, especially in cutting of diamonds called brilliants, to a very great perfection, but not superior to that of the English.

The use of encrusted brilliants — defined as octohedral crystals — to enrich watchcases is well recognised but rarely found on Englishmade timepieces. A rose diamond — which has one flat side — is to be found, on occasion, to give emphasis to the push-piece by which the case of the watch may be opened. It is small but important details of this kind which add immeasurably to the inherent quality of an object.

PLATE 68: The range of decoration to be found on underpainted horn outer cases is enormous — see also Colour Plate 4. In these examples, heraldics — in this case, the arms of the Clockmakers' Company — are rare; the theme of jungle ferns and insects is quite commonplace. Specimens from the second half of the eighteenth century often use the device of an oval panel within which to contain the principal motif.

HORN AND TORTOISESHELL The basis of all horn-like materials is a substance called keratin; and the method of working them, despite differences in superficial appearance, is the same. The technique is well summed up in David Brewster's *The Edinburgh Encyclopaedia* (1816) in the article entitled 'Horn-Pressing'. This states, of both horn and tortoiseshell, that:

> . . . these animal substances are capable of being so softened by the application of a moderate heat that they can be moulded by pressure into any required shape, and the surface may be imprinted with any design in the sharpest and most delicate relief. Another valuable property is that pieces may be made to adhere firmly together without any cement . . . for making hollow articles, such as snuff-boxes, tooth-pick cases, powder-flasks, tubes of opera-glasses, inkhorns &c [and, although Brewster does not specifically mention them, watchcases] a screw-press is used. The process is extremely simple: the horn or tortoiseshell is boiled in water until it becomes softened, and is then put into moulds of iron or brass, made in two or more pieces, and with cavities between them to correspond with the article which is to be fabricated, and with all its intended ornaments engraved in the interior surface of the mould. This mould being made hot, the horn or shell is put between the two halves, and the mould being put in a small screw-press,

the halves are forced together to imprint the horn and press it into the cavity of the mould. If the article has any considerable relief, this cannot be done at one heat, and therefore the press, with the moulds in it, is put into a copper, and boiled still longer; it is then taken out, and, by a lever applied to the screw, it is screwed tighter, so as at length to obtain the impression desired. When a single piece of horn or tortoiseshell is not sufficiently large to fill the mould, two or more pieces are put together: they are cut to fit to each other with a proper degree of overlap, and when sufficiently softened by boiling in water, the surfaces are forcibly pressed together, and they will thus be united as firmly as if they were originally in one piece. The screw-press employed for this business is very simple, being only an iron frame with a screw through the top of it; and, for the convenience of putting it in or out of the boiler or copper, a small tackle of pulleys is fixed just over the copper, and by the side of it is a block of stone, with a hole or cavity in it large enough to receive the press, and hold it firmly upright, whilst a lever or wrench is applied to the screw to turn it round and produce the pressure, which being done, it is again returned to the boiler.

The horn used for the purposes under discussion comes from the upper part of the skull of the bovidae group of animals — that is to say, cattle — and from stags, although staghorn is, in fact, a true bone. Paula Hardwick, in her *Discovering Horn* (1981) says:

In the early days horns were often soaked for a period of months to encourage separation from the [bone] core. The horns were afterwards sorted according to size and quality. The next stage was for the presser to cut off the solid horn tips before dividing the horns by sawing into varying lengths. Each section would then be cut along its natural curve and afterwards soaked in hot water or oil for a time which considerably softened it before it was subjected to a fire where the constant movement over a flame prevented any scorching taking place, but made the horn very malleable, after which it could more easily be pulled open by the use of pincers. It was then spread nearly flat and placed between hot iron plates, previously coated with tallow and pressed with great force. The amount of pressure varied dependent upon the thinness required.

Further refinement could be done by hand using a draw-knife with a wire edge. The quality of the finished article and the degree of translucency which might be required in it, together governed the gauge of the 'leaves' being manufactured by these means.

Tortoiseshell, on the other hand, traditionally comes, not from the tortoise, but from the Far Eastern hawksbill turtle, *chelonia imbricata*. *Spons' Workshop Receipts* (1909 edition) notes that:

The hawk's-bill turtle has a shell which consists of a number of plates, overlapping at the edges like the tiles on a roof,

thirteen full plates on the middle of the back with 25 smaller ones around the edge. In the trade these are known as blades, and are mottled in colour. The under or belly plates are plain yellow. None can be considered true shell, as in substance the material more nearly approaches horn. To detach the blades from the bony base fire-heat is employed, which causes the shell to come away, a thin knife completing the operation.

The working of tortoiseshell is virtually the same as horn, but 'some care is needed, as too long a treatment spoils the colour. A little salt in the water does much to prevent injury from this cause, though some care is again needed, as a strong solution of salt makes the shell brittle'.

Abraham Rees's *Cyclopaedia* (1805–18) gives a little more detail about the nature of hawksbill turtle shell, stating that its

. . . plates [blades] are much stronger, thicker, and clearer than those of any other kind, and constitute the sole value of the animal. They are semi-transparent, and elegantly variegated with whitish, yellowish, reddish, and dark brown clouds and undulations, so as to constitute, when properly prepared and polished, one of the most elegant articles for ornamental purposes. These laminae form the external coating . . . [and] vary in thickness, according to the age and size of the animal, measuring from an eighth to a quarter of an inch. A large turtle is said to afford about eight pounds of tortoiseshell [another estimate suggests from five to fifteen, or even twenty pounds] and unless the animal itself be about the weight of 150 pounds, the shell is not worth much.

The business of working with this kind of material was an unsavoury one. Collyer (see Bibliography) describes the horner's craft as 'an ingenious though stinking business which requires more ingenuity than strength', while Campbell, in 1747, says: 'It is none of the most polite trades though a very useful one, for the stench of horn which they sometimes manufacture with the heat of the fire keeps them from the Hyp, Vapours and Lowness of Spirits, the Common Malady of England'.

Used decoratively, horn has acquired the reputation of being 'the poor man's substitute' for other, more expensive, materials; and this is not without some justification, so far as watchcases are concerned. Suitably stained, it can be made into a very acceptable simulation of tortoiseshell, while, when the transparent form is underpainted with appropriate motifs, it might just — provided it is not seen under brilliant lighting conditions — pass for enamelled work.

The vast majority of horn outer cases — or consular cases as these also occur — are allied to watches of indifferent to 'good ordinary' quality, but practically never to the best. The only watchmaker who, very occasionally indeed, combined a really splendid horn case with one of his invariably fascinating timepieces, was Daniel de St Leu, who was appointed Watchmaker to the Queen in 1765, and who is best known for the idiosyncratically elaborate enrichment he bestowed upon all his watches. Otherwise, it is quite common to find horn cases that have been deliberately stained to resemble tortoiseshell, such was the perceived attraction of the latter. To do this, Rees says that, after first pressing the horn into proper plates or scales, it is necessary to:

> temper two parts of quicklime and one of litharge to the consistence of a soft paste with soap-ley. Let this paste be laid over all the parts of the horn, except such as are proper to be left transparent, and thus let it remain until it be thoroughly dry; when, the paste being brushed off, the horn will be found partly opaque and partly transparent, like tortoiseshell. Semi-transparent parts may be added, by mixing whiting with some of the paste to weaken its effect in particular places, by which means spots of a reddish-brown will be produced, which will increase the beauty of the work as well as its resemblance of real tortoiseshell.

Spon gives several other recipes for this purpose, and in all cases emphasises that it may prove necessary to repeat them until the desired effect is achieved. It is interesting to note that, following its discovery in the last century, the preferred cheap substitute for tortoiseshell became celluloid.

Horn and tortoiseshell — further decorative techniques
a) *Inlaying* Tortoiseshell, in particular, can be enormously enriched when extra ornament, usually in silver, is inlaid into the surface. There must have been some systematic designing of such work, since a number of themes and motifs are commonly encountered, sometimes in almost identical arrangements, at others employing the same basic devices but in differing combinations.

PLATE 69: Very rarely indeed, a tortoiseshell outer case is enriched with outstanding ornament. This one, from a watch by Charles Gretton and displaying the arms of the Lee family, incorporates the techniques of *piqué,* inlay and the application of pierced and chiselled circular reserves that reflect the style to be found on watch cocks of the period, that is to say, the last quarter of the seventeenth century.

PLATE 70: Some designs in inlaid tortoiseshell outer cases recur constantly, with some slight rearrangement of the principal elements, normally birds and flowers. Even so, there is no evidence that this bespeaks the existence of pattern books.

The effect can be reminiscent of the style known as chinoiserie; in other examples, however, it is much less organised, even random, in its impact. If pattern books, or similar means, were utilised to this end in English practice, they do not seem to have survived.

The technique for inlaying into the surface, as given in contemporary sources, requires the making of a bed of tortoiseshell filings within the mould or press, over which is placed a thin sheet of paper. On to this goes the 'plate' or shell to be decorated, with all the pieces of the inlay — which have been separately manufactured — located in their correct positions upon it. The top die-plate is then lowered until it presses upon the shell, and the whole is then plunged into boiling water. After an hour, careful examination is made to see that none of the ornaments has been displaced, after which the press is again closed and returned to the boiling water. After a short time, the pressure is substantially increased and while under this pressure the press is plunged into cold water. If all has gone well, the ornaments will be perfectly inlaid into the surface, which can then be smoothed and finished.

It is often assumed that inlay is unique to tortoiseshell watchcases and that horn cases were never so treated. In fact, inlay is often to be found on *simulated* tortoiseshell work, that is to say, on horn that has been stained to resemble the more expensive material. The inlaying process was almost the same, except that, the shrinkage of horn being nothing like as marked as that of tortoiseshell during the moulding procedure, the inlay could not be as firmly and permanently embedded; indeed, it was usually considered necessary to glue it into place. Despite this, where excessive damage in the form of missing pieces of the decoration are found in this type of work, it will often be the result of using horn as the basic material.

b) *Pinwork (piqué)* The term '*piqué* work' embraces both the inlaying and the super-surface embellishment of tortoiseshell with gold or silver. With watchcases, though, it has been customary to divide the techniques into inlay (qv) and pinwork. In inlay, pictorial themes are represented by the use of small motifs shaped from strips of precious metal, if necessary engraved with extra detail, which are then embedded into the shell surface under heat and pressure. In pinwork, the design is built up from a large number of pins inserted through both the shell and the metal carcase it encloses. The heads of these pins, either plain or quite often ornamental in their own right — and more appropriately called studs — lie proud of the surface of the tortoiseshell, and problems of shrinkage encountered with inlay do not arise, since the ends of the stems are simply bent over inside the case. This same technique is equally applicable to horn, of course,

PLATES 71a,b: Both tortoiseshell and leather outer cases decorated with *piqué* work also suffer from repetitive designs, although occasionally the purely symmetrical gives way to swirling foliage, and even fruit.

although it is never met with save when the cheaper material is being employed to simulate the more expensive. The one exception is the simple border, a single row of pins at most, which is more functional than artistic since it is the usual method of attaching any horn covering to the metal foundation of its case.

The tortoiseshell *piqué* technique was first developed by a Neopolitan jeweller named Laurentini in the mid-seventeenth century, and it was soon adopted in both London and Paris. Essentially a handicraft, nevertheless Matthew Boulton started to produce it by factory methods from the mid-1760s. While inlay provides splendid opportunities for quite complex pictorial representations, pinwork is far more stylised in its use. Simple motifs like the crown lend themselves to it quite happily but anything more ambitious presents problems.

c) *Polishing*   Although they can be turned on the lathe, the main processes for shaping both horn and tortoiseshell have been shown to be cutting, heating and moulding; there is, for instance, no means of melting them. Both, however, will take a high polish. Spon recommends that as perfect a surface as possible is obtained first by scraping:

> The scraper may be made of a razor-blade, the edge of which should be rubbed upon an oil-stone, holding the blade nearly upright so as to form an edge like that of a currier's knife, which may be sharpened by burnishing. Work when properly scraped is prepared for polishing. To effect this it is first rubbed with a buff made of woollen cloth perfectly free from grease. The cloth may be fixed upon a stick to be used by hand; but a 'bob', which is a wheel running in the lathe and covered with the cloth, is much to be preferred on account of its rapidity of motion. The buff may be covered either with powdered charcoal and water, or fine brickdust and water. After the work has been made as smooth as possible with this, it is followed by another bob on which washed chalk or dry whiting is rubbed. The article . . . is slightly moistened with vinegar, and the buff and whiting will produce a fine gloss, which may be completed by rubbing with the palm of the hand and a small portion of dry whiting or rotten-stone.

Alternative processes designed to achieve the same effect involve combinations of the same polishing media, together with powdered pumice, linseed oil, 'Trent sand', applied with a variety of buffs ranging from 'old cloth' to 'felt hat'.

d) *Underpainting*   By far the most popular method of embellishing horn watchcases was by underpainting. Since the material could, if required, be virtually transparent and clear, it could be used exactly as is glass to

protect the artist's work; and the results are often visually intriguing and delightful. There has never been any pretence, in such applications, at great art nor, indeed, are there any well-known names associated with it; yet it must have given the humble workman charged with its execution a great opportunity to exercise his artistic talent, albeit on such a small scale, and doubtless it brought with it its own kind of satisfaction.

While it is attractive to dismiss underpainted horn depictions as artless, there are always surprises. Most of the pictures in this context tend to be stylised, as might be expected — the sailor home from the sea, the uniformed soldier on sentry duty, the sweetheart left alone to bemoan her solitude, and other such naive themes. There are also some splendid, almost tropical, representations incorporating jungles of ferns, insects and multicoloured butterflies. The occasional armorial version will be encountered; and, perhaps least expected, the most powerful expression of this genre can be the naval battle, delineated in all its detail. Such artistry as this simply cannot be relegated to the insignificant.

It is generally considered — and indeed the name of the technique suggests it — that 'underpainting' means applying the picture to the underside of the horn, using appropriate paint media. While not exactly like mirror-image painting, this technique must, nevertheless, have

---

COLOUR PLATE 11: Unlikely as it might seem, watch dials are capable of very unorthodox treatment, as these four examples show. (Top left) This remarkable dial comes from a watch by no less than Thomas Tompion himself and dates c1677. It is a version of the 'regulator' pattern with, on a silver-gilt matted ground, a peripheral minute ring enclosing a subsidiary six-hour ring above and sixty-second ring below, each ring with only two of its conventional numerals aligned against the alternating polished silver and black waxed divisions. (Top right) The conventional 'regulator' dial seen on a much later watch, this time by Thomas Cummins and dating from 1825. On this, minutes are indicated by the centre hand against the outermost ring, which in turn encloses a chapter for the seconds above and the hours below centre. The engine-turning on this gold dial is of the highest quality. (Bottom left) This type of eggshaped watch is associated only with the makers Benjamin Gray and Justin Vulliamy, and is a considerable rarity anyway. Justin Vulliamy married Gray's daughter in 1741 and the two makers then went into partnership until Gray died in 1764. (Bottom right) Dating from c1810, this gold, enamel and pearl-set watch by London maker William Anthony, its articulated gold hands expanding and contracting within the long and short axes of the chapter oval, will almost certainly have been originally intended for one of the Far Eastern markets where such novelties were greatly in demand. The subsidiary dials are for seconds above centre, and quarter seconds below.

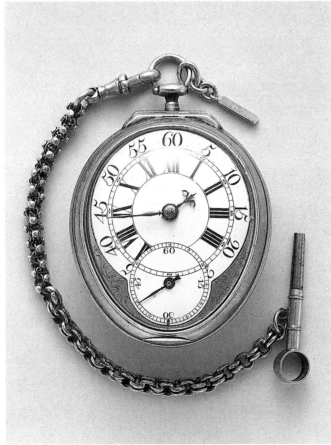

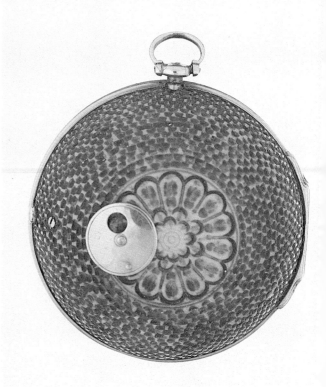

been quite challenging. However, there is also reason for thinking that much of this painting was done directly on to the metal carcase of the case — usually a base alloy of the type generically known as gilt-metal — and, in this instance, the purpose of the horn is precisely analagous to the use of glass to protect a conventional picture. It is impossible to demonstrate the truth of this supposition without unacceptable risk of damage to specimens selected for trial, since only total dismantling, which would involve destruction of the border of pins attaching the horn to the metal, would suffice. Examination of any representative number of such cases will, however, reveal some in which the paint surface has an almost enamel-like quality and it is these which, it is thought, may have been decorated on the metal rather than the horn surface.

Shagreen, fishskin and leather The term 'shagreen' has been much misused and misapplied, over many years, especially in auctioneers' catalogues. Said to be derived from the Turkish word *saghri,* which means the crupper or hindpart of an ass, it has been used indiscriminately both for the product derived from that specific area of leather, and for certain types of fish-skin, notably that of sharks and ray fish. In this latter context, in fact, it has been used since the seventeenth century for covering small boxes, tea caddies and so forth. So far as watch-cases are concerned, anything with a textured green surface is generally described as shagreen, while the original carrying cases of pocket sundials, usually a brownish black, are called fish-skin. This same material on watch-cases is simply called 'leather'. Yet any scrutiny of the advertisements for lost watches in eighteenth-century journals will turn up plenty of examples where the watch in question is described as having a 'black shagreen case'. In horological circles today, such would be considered a contradictory misnomer! However, the historical importance of the material cannot be over-emphasised, as indi-

cated by the fact that the 'shagreen watchcase maker' was a specialised trade-within-a-trade, and the practitioners jealousy guarded their expertise.

It is, therefore, desirable to revert to earlier sources for any true understanding of this paradox; but even at the beginning of the last century, the definition of this term was far from precise. The only common ground seems to be the geographical area from whence this product derives. Rees says that it is prepared in Astrakhan, chiefly by Tartars and Armenians, and mostly used to cover books, cases, etc. It is brought to England from Constantinople, Tunis, Tripoli, Algiers, and some parts of Poland. He continues: 'There has been a dispute among authors, what the animal is from which the shagreen is prepared' — the options ranging from the onager, which is apparently a wild ass, to the sea-calf, to another kind of fish called by the Turks *shagrain,* and finally to the *squatina,* this last being equally well applied, in England, to the monkfish, the angel-fish and the greater dogfish.

Assuming, however, that the more usual raw material derives from horses' or asses' hides — both are said to be equally useful — the procedure is to excise a nearly semicircular piece from the area immediately above the tail, the dimensions of the same being expressed, even in an English work, as 'about an arshine and a half upon the crupper, and rather less than an arshine along the back', an arshine being an old measure of length equivalent to about twenty-eight inches in Russia or about thirty inches in Turkey. This small area is the only part of the poor beast's pelt that can be used 'and the rest is thrown away.'

The skin thus obtained is immersed in a vat of pure water for several days, after which any hair comes away easily. This is done by scraping with a blunt instrument called a *urak,* the skin having first been attached, by the folded-over upper edge, to a sloping board. With the hair also comes away the upper pellicle, a kind of superficial skin layer. The hide is then once again immersed in fresh water. Yet a second time it is spread out as already described, only this time the flesh side is well scraped. After this, the hair side is once again scraped, 'so that nothing now remains of the softened skin but the clean sinewy web which serves for parchment'. All such skins are then stretched upon shaped frames, called *paeltzi,* using equidistant strings to promote uniform tension; meanwhile it is necessary to sprinkle the skin with water from time to time to prevent localised drying out, with a consequent uneven shrinkage.

The skins are then thoroughly wetted once again, and next taken to the work room, where they are laid flat on the floor, with the hair side uppermost. This side is then thickly covered with the very smooth and hard black seed of *chenopodium album,* known locally as alabuta, which

---

COLOUR PLATE 12: The materials used for the cases of these two watches are of interest because the first is highly uncommon and the second, not infrequently encountered, is yet not generally handled in quite this manner. At the top, left and right, is a green-stained engine-turned ivory consular case enclosing a movement by Thomas Windmills, London, No 5152. The continuation of this treatment around the bezel of the dial is particularly attractive. Possibly not the original case of the watch, it was made especially for it. At the bottom, the splendid rock crystal outer case in jointed gold bezels, and with panels of crystal set into the band, is intended to provide maximum visibility for the superb enamel-work on the inner case of the watch, which is by Josiah Roberts, a London maker active at the end of the eighteenth century.

grows in great abundance 'and almost to a man's height' in the farmyards and gardens of the southern Volga. In order to impress these well into the hide being treated, they are then covered with felt, and trodden in with the feet 'by which means they are impressed deeply into the very yielding skins'. Then, without disturbing the seeds, the frames are taken once more into the open air and placed leaning against a wall with the seeds next to it so that they do not receive direct sunlight. The skins are thus left to dry for several days in succession. After no more moisture can be detected, they can be taken out of the frames. When the embedded seeds are then knocked away from the hide, it appears full of little pits and irregularities, all the impressions unique to shagreen and lacking only in the staining and polishing.

Polishing is done on a board on trestles, equipped with a small iron hook, and covered with felt. The hide to be treated is attached to the hook and lies on the felt, with its further edge weighted to permit of some movement but not of any permanent displacement. The polishing, or rasping, is started with an instrument called a *tokar,* which is a sharpened crook-like piece of iron. With this, the most prominent wrinkles — the contemporary word is 'rugosities' — can be removed; but great care is needed in order not to shave away too deeply the impressions of the alabuta seeds which, should the *tokar* be too sharp, is all too easily done. Since the blade of this tool is narrow, it leaves an uneven surface on the shagreen, which must then be smoothed all over with further scraping from the *urak,* the object being to leave only a slight, but nonetheless clear, impression of the seeds equally distributed all over the skin. After this, the shagreen is yet again immersed in water, for forty-eight hours, partly to make it supple and partly to regenerate the 'grain', 'for the seeds, having caused pits in the surface of the skin, the interstices of these pits have lost their prominent substance by the polishing or shaving, and now the points that were pressed down, having lost nothing of their substance, spring up above the shaved places, and thus form the grain of the shagreen'.

After this immersion, the shagreen is floated several times more in a hot and strong solution obtained by boiling a substance called schora, an alkaline and saline earth found near Astrakhan. After this, the skins are bundled up together while still hot, when they swell and soften, only to be plunged into a moderately strong common salt brine for another twenty-four hours. This makes them fine and white, and ready to receive any colour from the available range of sea-green, black, red, blue; or they can remain white.

Rees goes into great detail about the methods of dyeing shagreen in the above-mentioned colours; but since, in watchcases, green and black are virtually the only hues encountered, just these will be dealt with here. The shagreen skins are brushed over, on the ungrained flesh side, with a concentrated solution of sal ammoniac (ammonium chloride) in hot water and, when thoroughly wetted, a thick layer of copper filings is strewed over them and the skins doubled together, so that the treated sides are inwards. Separated by felt but placed uniformly on top of one another, the whole pile is subjected to a considerable and evenly distributed weight, under which the skins must lie for twenty-four hours. If one treatment by this means does not impart a sufficiently deep sea-green colour, a second similar treatment will certainly do so.

As for black shagreen, the process requires that the skins, while still moist from the brine, are covered with finely powdered nut-galls, folded together and laid one upon another for twenty-four hours. Meanwhile, a fresh solution of bitter-earth salts or schora is boiled and poured hot into little troughs. Each skin is then agitated to and fro several times in the solution, and is again covered with pulverised nut-galls and once again laid in a pile for some time. The skins are then allowed to dry, after which the nut-galls are beaten out of them; next, they are smeared, on the shagreen side, with mutton suet, and laid in the sun to allow the fat to be absorbed. Each skin is then separately rolled up and pressed against a solid surface to promote the complete absorption of the 'unctuous particles'. After any surplus has been scraped off with a blunt wooden scraper, the shagreen is rubbed on both sides with a solution of iron vitriol in water, which brings out the full depth of the black colour.

The import of shagreen skins into England was not an entirely painless process, certainly not in the 1750s. Owen's *New and Complete Dictionary of the Arts and Sciences* (1755) concludes its article on this material by observing casually that 'each shagreen skin pays, on importation, a duty of $4\frac{78\frac{3}{4}}{100}$ d. and draws back on exportation, $4\frac{51\frac{1}{4}}{100}$ d.'. What a justification for a computer!

Idiosyncratic materials: Amber, Bloodstone, Glass, Ivory, Porcelain and Puddingstone

There are perhaps a small number of materials, some of them superficially quite unsuited to the purpose, which have been used, at one time or another, as a decorative element in watches, usually in the casework. Watches are fragile enough objects, in any event, and highly susceptible to any shock to the mechanism. How much greater is the risk — probably of terminal damage — if the case also is made of a breakable substance, like porcelain? Possibly, considerations such as these provide the clue to the scarcity of such objects: they have simply been broken and discarded; yet they must certainly have been costly to manufacture and, therefore, not the prerogative of the average citizen.

Amber

> The colour of amber is generally some shade of yellow, as wine yellow, wax yellow, honey yellow, hyacinth red, yellowish white; it is also found occasionally green or brown. It occurs amorphous and in detached pieces. Is shining, or little shining, with a waxen lustre. Its fracture is conchoidal, and when broken it flies into indeterminate, not particularly sharp, fragments. It is commonly transparent, more rarely semi-transparent or translucid. Is brittle, and its specific gravity varies from 1.065 to 1.1. By rubbing, it readily becomes electric. When applied to a lighted candle, it takes fire, swells considerably, but does not run into drops, and exhales a white smoke of a pungent penetrating odour. The only proper mines of this substance that are as yet known, are in ducal Prussia, near the sea coast. They are worked in the usual way by shafts and galleries to the depth of about one hundred feet. The amber is embedded in a stratum of fossil or carbonated wood, and occurs in nodules from a few grains in weight, to three or even five pounds . . . The projecting eastern shore of England, too, and the coast at the entrance of the channel from the north, affords many specimens. Rounded nodules have been occasionally met with in the beds of gravel near London.

Rees then goes on to describe methods tested to convert the more common varieties of amber into the less common ones — some of these almost smack of alchemy; and Rees concludes, 'most of these secrets have perished with the inventors'. In short, amber has all those properties that should militate against its incorporation into watches in any capacity whatever and it is surprising that the occasional specimen does occur.

Bloodstone   This is probably the rarest material of all for watchcases and is almost unknown in English watches although it is not quite so uncommon on the Continent, where usually it appears in the form of panels or reserves together with other stones. The finest English example recorded enclosed a watch by Josias Cuper, a member of a well-known family of watchmakers in Blois, but who came to England about 1620, becoming first a member of the Blacksmiths' Company but, subsequently, transferring to the Clockmakers' Company, to whose Freedom he was admitted in 1632, the year after that company's formation. The main carcase of the case is of oblong octagonal form, measuring 1⅞in (47·6mm) long by 1in (25·4mm) wide, cut with facets and hollowed to receive the movement, the dial of which is protected by a faceted rock crystal cover. This watch formed part of the famous Webster Collection, which was dispersed in 1954. There

is no comparable example of a bloodstone watchcase in either the British Museum or Victoria & Albert Museum collections.

Bloodstone, sometimes called heliotrope, is a green chalcedony more or less liberally sprinkled with blood-red spots of jasper, providing another example of the lack of demarcation between the numerous varieties of quartz. It is said to have been given its alternative title, which is derived from two Greek words meaning 'sun' and 'I turn', because of a popular belief that the image of the sun turned to the colour of blood when seen as a reflection in the stone. In fairly recent history, however, it might appear that the term was reserved for another material altogether, an extremely rich and fine iron ore, also called haematite, which would nowadays be called ferric oxide. Owen (1754) and Rees (1819) both include long dissertations on this substance, which came in various shades of red and had its principal uses in medicine.

Glass   Most watches use glass to protect the dial without affecting the legibility — so much goes without saying. This is hardly a decorative use, however, and there are two other areas where glass can sometimes be found in an ornamental context. The first is on the table of the watch cock, and a note about this will be found elsewhere in this book. Otherwise glass can occur in watchcases, as a substitute for rock crystal: superficially, the two substances can be difficult to differentiate, and the most usual method of detection employs polarising filters. Glass can be cut with faceted surfaces, to resemble crystal, so that it may well be that some such cases are original; but the possibility that they are modern replacements cannot be discounted.

Ivory   The latest edition — the ninth — of Britten's *Old Clocks and Watches and their Makers* revised by Cecil Clutton (Methuen & Spon, 1982) makes the point, on p65, that 'any material other than metal or stone is very rare in a watchcase, but examples in ivory and amber are known'.

In the middle of the eighteenth century, too, ivory was an expensive commodity. At that time, it seems that only elephant-tusk ivory was used, that from Ceylon and from Achem, on the slave-coast of Africa, being preferred to that from Guinea because it retained its white colour with age, rather than turning yellow. Owen's *Dictionary of Arts & Sciences* (1754) specifies that all ivory imported into the United Kingdom had to pay a duty of 1s 11$\frac{10}{100}$ d per lb, which was susceptible to a drawback of 1s 8$\frac{25}{100}$ d per lb on subsequent exportation.

Nearly seventy years later, Rees tells us that, by that time, by far the greatest part of the ivory imported into the country came from Africa, so that the part of Guinea which furnished most of it came to be called the Ivory Coast. The best tusks, according to Rees, are:

> . . . those that are least curved, without spots, and most solid towards the base. Some writers on this subject pretend that such elephants as inhabit swampy places, generally produce blue, knotty and spongy tusks, in every respect inferior to those of elephants living in hilly country or on dry plains. The Ethiopian elephants' tusks . . . are furnished with larger cavities and are therefore less esteemed.

By Rees's time, too, elephants' teeth had also become a useful source of ivory, the quantities imported into Britain rising, between 1776 and 1792, from 690cwt to 2,050cwt (35,052kg to 104,140kg). As to the methods of working ivory then in ordinary use, the same source states:

> The component parts of ivory being the same as those of bones (viz. phosphate of lime combined with a gelatinous substance), and differing only with regard to texture, hardness and whiteness, the preparations it undergoes in the arts are equally applicable to the bones of animals. The whiteness which ivory acquires depends chiefly on the degree of dryness it has acquired. When yellow, its gelatinous matter is altered by the air, and appears to be combined with the oxygen of the atmosphere. Oxygenated muriatic acid will restore it to its original whiteness. Those employed in working ivory, distinguish the *white* and the *green.* The former is known by the whitish or lemon-coloured rind of the tusks, the other by the brown and blackish. The green ivory (so-called from a greenish or faint olive colour pervading its substance) is preferred, it being of a closer texture and known soon to exchange its green hue for the most beautiful white, which is less liable to turn yellow. The green ivory is, however, more brittle than the other.

While heat can be used to soften ivory, it does not make it pliant. It can be divided by sawing, sometimes under water to prevent the build-up of heat or the risk of tearing the material, both significant factors in delicate work. It will also be noted, from the example illustrated, that ivory can be turned in a lathe. Polishing ivory is carried out using pumice and tripoli powder, and softening it is more usually done by steeping in a dilute mineral acid or, alternatively, in an alkaline lye made of soda and quicklime, the latter treatment being also suitable for bone.

Ivory can be stained and marbled, although in horological use this is generally not applicable — sundials, for example, often made of ivory in the early periods, were usually left white, although any engraved matter thereon was frequently filled with black or coloured substances.

The watchcase illustrated in Colour Plate 12, however, has been stained green, and the most common method of achieving this effect was to steep the ivory in two parts of verdigris and one of sal ammoniac, ground well together and with strong white-wine vinegar poured upon them. There were also recipes for staining ivory red, black, purple and blue.

The major defect to which ivory seems particularly susceptible, apart from its tendency to turn yellow from age and long exposure to light, is an aptitude to warp and split easily if exposed to extremes of temperature. There is no suitable remedial action for this latter condition, which is irreversible; but it is worth mentioning that ivory should be kept at a cold but constant temperature to preserve its condition. Extremes of moisture and dryness are equally unsuitable, and commercial storerooms for this commodity are usually below ground and unheated.

Porcelain On present knowledge it must appear that the decade immediately following the year 1750 witnessed the introduction of porcelain as a material for watchcases; it is difficult to be more specific than that. Much of the evidence comes from contemporary newspaper advertisements which, if only on account of terminological ambiguities, are not so reliable as might be expected. However, reading several of these notices together, some glimmering of the course of events can be deduced, at least in respect of one important English factory.

The earliest such announcement comes from *The Public Advertiser,* 16–21 December 1754, and reads:

> To be Sold by Auction by Mr Ford . . . All the entire stock of Chelsea Porcelain Toys, brought from the Proprietors Ware House in Pall-Mall, consisting of snuff boxes . . . Trinkets for Watches (mounted in Gold or unmounted).

Although the wording of this advertisement is somewhat imprecise and the term 'watchcases' does not actually appear as such, it is not unreasonable to suppose that this type of artifact formed part of the stock, if only because, eighteen months later, the same newspaper was announcing (17/18 and 20/21 May 1756):

> Mr Turner will expose to Sale, at his Shop, on the Terras, in St. James's Street, several hundred sorts of Figures, Birds, and Animals, for Desarts or Ornament, with new Patterns of Candlesticks, ornamented with all sorts of flowers; likewise Clock Cases, Watch Cases, Gerandoles, Brackets and Epargnes . . . of the curious Chelsea China, which exceed Dresden.

Finally, there is the announcement in *The Daily Advertiser* for 28 March 1760, which reads:

To be sold by Auction by Mr Ford
This and the following day at his Great Room, the upper end of St. James's, Haymarket, by Order of the Administratrix of the late Sir Everard Fawkener, decd. All his remaining stock of the Chelsea Porcelain Toys, consisting of a large Quantity of Smelling Bottles . . . Watch Cases, Tooth-Pick Cases.

In this particular advertisement, the contents of the sale are likely to have been accurately described, if only because Sir Everard Fawkener had been closely associated with the Chelsea Manufactory, principally, it is thought, as a financial backer.

There are two points to be made in interpreting these extracts. The word 'toys', which appears in two of them, did not have its present-day meaning, but denoted the small novelty or trinket, even something fairly insubstantial and expendable, and certainly not confined to the use of children alone. Christopher Pinchbeck is associated with 'Toys' made from his 'New Metal', to give another example. This alone might well explain the great rarity of porcelain watchcases today; they were never intended to last, being simply a passing craze which, combined with the intrinsic fragility of the material, would have contributed to an enormous rate of loss.

The other point concerns the precise meaning of the term 'clockcases', even though it is perhaps not of vital importance in this present context. Although porcelain clockcases of much the same date do exist — that other great London factory, Bow, made some remarkable ones that can be accurately dated to 1759 — there does not seem to be a single recorded example of Chelsea manufacture from the 1750s. It is unlikely that they can all have been lost to us, and Hugh Tait, of the British Museum, thinks that the term then indicated what we would now call 'watch stands': that is to say, decorative receptacles in which the watch could be placed when retiring to bed at night and which, effectively, converted it into a temporary clock! In this context, it is perhaps not wholly irrelevant to note that the two magnificent and apparently unique Chelsea Gold Anchor period clockcases — a non-identical pair — that are to be found in the Royal Collection, and which are said to date c1760, in many ways resemble watch stands and, indeed, their permanent movements by Strigel are of watch caliper. That they are not is only because they are far too big for such use — the watch stand normally stood on the bedside table — and they have no rear access through which a watch could be inserted.

Even less certain is when the fashion for porcelain watchcases died out, but it seems to have been short-lived. They continued to be mentioned in advertisements throughout 1760 and 1761, a typical example being the

PLATE 72: A surprise inside the porcelain watchcase shown in Colour Plate 8. The housefly, beautifully delineated, was in fact a device used to disguise some minor blemish that might otherwise detract from the final effect.

PLATE 73: Puddingstone is fairly uncommon in watchcases but, as this example shows, the effect can be quite compelling. Of 'consular' pattern and with an unusual feature in the central engine-turned boss with cast border, it houses a watch by John Leroux of Charing Cross, an eminent maker of precision watches during the final two decades of the eighteenth century.

following, heralding the opening of a new emporium in central London. It appeared on 24 June and 1 July 1760, in *The Daily Advertiser*:

> This Day is open'd, The Old Chelsea China Warehouse, opposite the Black Bear in Piccadilly; with Dishes, Plates . . . Variety of Table and Desert Knives and Forks, Clock and Watch-Cases, Epesques.

To summarise, in Hugh Tait's own words:

> There is little doubt that at least one of the London porcelain factories had begun, by the mid-1750s, to produce porcelain watch-cases, and it is probable that it was in Chelsea that the first were made in England . . . I have no doubt that the Clockmakers' Company's porcelain watch-case with delicate flower painting [see Colour Plate 8] is another example of Chelsea's typical '*circa* 1760 work' and it should be compared with the British Museum's un-mounted 'cover of a circular box' . . . never recognised as the back of a watchcase until a few years ago. It is also painted with flowers.

Puddingstone An unattractive material in the raw state, it is slightly surprising to find puddingstone used, on occasion, for watchcases; and its acceptability in that context probably depends upon its finished appearance. Abraham Rees describes it as:

> . . . the term applied by English lapidaries to an aggregate of oblong and rounded pebbles of flint, about the size of almonds and usually black, imbedded in a hard siliceous cement, of a light yellowish-brown. This mineral substance is capable of receiving a very high degree of polish, and was formerly much used in inlaying, and other ornamental works. It is chiefly procured from the county of Essex.

Today's lapidaries term this material 'conglomerate', and the pebbles that constitute it are no longer restricted to flint, but can be compounded of fragments of rock of many different kinds. It almost seems as if it might be one of Nature's waste products, since it is thought to be the surviving parts of ancient beaches.

7 Postscript – the Best of Both Worlds

PLATE 74: Watches encrusted with gemstones are almost unknown in the English practice but, when they do occur, they are most effective. The Imperial State Crown on this watch of 1894, by Hamilton & Co, suggests that it might have been a gift from Queen Victoria.

The world's great decorators of *objets d'art* (in metal) have to be the French. They may not have invented all the principal techniques, but their terms for them are understood in most of the languages of civilisation. Thus *repoussé, piqué, champlevé, cloisonné,* and a host of other, cross all barriers in the field of the applied arts. The world's great mechanics, on the other hand — at least during most of the period covered by this book — were equally unquestionably the English; the technical terms they derived from their innovations have very often been translated literally into other languages. It must follow, therefore, that a watch made by an English craftsman but decorated by a French one should inherently possess all the attributes of perfection. Historically, however, where could such a watch be found?

One example — there may well be others — stems from a gift made by the French Court to our own Queen Charlotte in 1778. A notice of this appeared in several periodicals of the day, and the one illustrated in Plate 75 is typical of their general content. It comes from the January 1778 issue of *The Westminster Magazine,* where it features in the 'Monthly Chronicle' section, at page 55.

Enquiries through the Lord Chamberlain's Office to establish whether this watch was still in the Royal Collection revealed that it was not, and no trace of it could be found in the records of that institution. The next problem was to discover the name of the English craftsman working for the French king, Louis XVI, at that time. More by luck than by serious research, this information came quickly to light, since one of those whose help has been elsewhere acknowledged immediately supplied the answer; but the big question remained — where was the watch itself?

Providentially, at this point, a member of the Lord Chamberlain's staff, who had been on leave when this matter was first broached, recollected that such an object had been offered, some years before, to the Royal Collection by a leading London dealer, but had not been acquired. That was in May 1982. Perhaps that same dealer might be able to help, even at this distance in time.

Indeed, the firm did help most generously, so that the watch, with all its glorious accoutrements and accessories, is to be seen in Colour Plate 16. The watchmaker's name was Gregson; but immediately, yet another mystery is encountered. G. H. Baillie, in his definitive *Watchmakers and Clockmakers of the World,* states that this maker's forename was Pierre. By contrast, Tardy's *Dic-*

tionnaire des Horlogers Français gives the name as Jean, but then goes on to say that one of his watches is signed 'Pierre Gregson, Horloger de la Cour de France'. The royal gift watch is said to be by Jean Gregson, but there are seemingly no pictures of the movement extant, so that whether or not the full name appears thereon is open to question.

Perhaps, for present purposes, we can compromise and assume that the craftsman's name was Jean-Pierre Gregson. He was certainly born in England, and he was appointed to the French Court in 1776. Tardy states that he was associated with a horological manufacturing concern pioneered by the famous French *mécanicien,* François-Jean Bralle in 1773–83, which, within two years, became 'Manufacture Royale' and had its own specially authorised maker's mark. However, it failed in 1788 and Bralle and his partner Vincent, a former pupil of Ferdinand Berthoud, were ruined. Gregson, though, seems to have survived, with his shop in the Rue Dauphine, at least until the 1790s.

The Gregson royal watch has a movement with cylinder escapement, and it is serially numbered '813'. The official description continues:

The case is of matted yellow gold with hidden cover hinges and entirely decorated with diamond foliage in silver settings, the back centred with an oval blue guilloche enamel panel applied with the English Royal Crown and the cypher 'CR' in diamonds. The chatelaine and clip are made entirely of gold with matted decoration in two colours similarly set with diamond foliage, the clip with an enamel panel with applied diamond-set Royal Crown, the intermediate panel with a similar reserve set with the Sceptre and Mace. Four suspended clips with matching key, egg-shaped pill box, seal with agate intaglio of the crown and cypher CR and an urn-shaped pill-box with agate intaglio of a fly or possibly a bee.

The watchcase and chatelaine both bear the Paris marks for 1777, and the casemaker's mark is LL and star, No 474. The chatelaine was made by Charles Quizille in 1776, and it is likely that the watchcase was made by Louis de Levemeur. This remarkable materialisation of an English horologist's daydream speaks volumes for itself, and nobody is going to settle down with a magnifying glass to check the number of rose-diamonds! If there is anything at all to be felt about this astonishing object, apart from the sheer wonder of it, then it must be some slight sense of loss, that it is not in the Royal Collection where it must surely belong. The circumstances of its

tion, the one for five years, and the other for three years.

Monday, *Jan.* 26.

A moſt ſuperb watch, valued at 1700 loiuſ-d'ors, has lately been preſented to our moſt gracious Queen Charlotte, as a preſent from the court of France; it was made by the French king's watchmaker, who is a native of Great Britain; and the outſide caſe is ſaid to be the moſt curious ever ſeen, for its various methods of opening, all of which are inviſible to the eye, and is reckoned a great improvement in the ſcience of mechanics; the watch-chain and trinkets contain 652 brilliants, and 3191 roſe-diamonds.

Thurſday, Jan. 29.

During the courſe of this month, the ex-

PLATE 75: The notice in the *Westminster Magazine* for January 1778, describing the wonders of Queen Charlotte's watch.

PLATE 76: The dial view of the 'hybrid' royal watch.

coming on the market not having been revealed, it would be invidious to make any judgements; but it is understood that it is still in private hands so that one day, perhaps, another chance may present itself to acquire it for the nation's posterity.

If, indeed, the Gregson watch represents a high peak of French achievement in watch decoration, then how does the English practice — which is, after all, what this book has been all about — bear comparison? The simple answer is that it does not; the two cultures, if that is the best term to express them, are as different as chalk from cheese. It may be an example of that reserve commonly supposed to be a characteristic of the English, that their watches are never encrusted with diamonds; it would be considered far too ostentatious and grandiose. By contrast, the English enjoyment of what might be termed a kind of folk-art — as reflected, for instance, in nineteenth-century provincial painted dials and in the imaginative decoration of watch cocks — was nothing like so popular or commonplace in France. The English tended to judge quality by sheer mass; their watch mechanisms remained heavy and substantially made long after their French counterparts had discovered the elegance and sophistication of the thin, lighter-weight watch. Such differences can be extended ad infinitum; but if it is possible to summarise the English achievement in this context, perhaps it was the capacity to house an efficient and reliable timekeeping machine in an attractive, even if sometimes rather workmanlike, setting that offended nobody's sensibilities yet gave great satisfaction to its owner, possibly for a lifetime. That cannot be bad.

Appendices

PLATE 77: Movements in an early stage of manufacture — 'in the grey', as it was called — ranging in date from the mid-seventeenth to the late-eighteenth centuries.

I: Organisation And Working Methods

Relatively little is known about the way the craft functioned during its earliest years in England; but, on the basis of surviving artifacts, it seems reasonable to make certain assumptions. It seems likely that, throughout most of the seventeenth century, 'one-off' production was the general rule. By Thomas Tompion's time, however, it would appear that small-batch production methods had come into use, and experts in the work of this great master claim that groups of his watches can be identified in which at least some parts are interchangeable. The first substantial evidence of the *modus operandi* does not appear until 1747, with R. Campbell's *The London Tradesman.* Sub-titled *A Compendious View of all the Trades, Professions and Arts, both Liberal and Mechanic, now practised in the Cities of London and Westminster,* this informative little volume divides the production of watches among ten specialists, all employed by the so-called watchmaker, whose principal function might seem to have been to judge, on sight, the quality of their work 'and put his Name to nothing but what will stand the severest Trial; for the Price of a Watch depends upon the Reputation of the Maker only'. Thus is the master responsible for the actions of his servants.

There is very little information to be gleaned from this book, even so, about the embellishers of watches. Among the skills listed are those of the 'Silversmith who only makes Cases, and Workmen who cut the Dial-plates, or enamel them, which is of late become much the Fashion'. There is also mention of the Gilder, but only in respect of the brass movement wheels; and after the Finisher, who puts the whole machine together and adjusts it to proper time, the final stage is reached, when 'the Watch-maker puts his Name upon the Plate, and is esteemed the Maker, though he has not made in his Shop the smallest Wheel belonging to it. It is supposed, however, that he can make all the Movements.'

By the early years of the nineteenth century, the practice of the craft had become even more diffuse. As has been mentioned elsewhere, watch movements were produced in quantity in factories, mainly in the north of England, and sent to London for 'finishing' by the fashionable makers having their business there. Abraham Rees, in his remarkable forty-five-volume *The Cyclopaedia; or Universal Dictionary of the Arts, Sciences and Literature,* which appeared in parts during 1805–18, specifies thirteen 'principal workmen' employed by the best movement makers in Prescot, a town at the centre of the provincial branch of the craft. The product of their

industry, the watch movement, was then sent on to its final destination, the so-called 'watchmaker', where it was handled by a further twenty-one specialists before it was fit for the showroom. This applied only to 'plain' watches, though, and any complicated pieces — repeaters and suchlike — required the attention of even more skilled people. Women, it seems, were hardly ever employed in the British watchmaking industry, except to polish watchcases, and were then often the wives of the casemakers. The Swiss, however, used a lot of female labour in their factories, and the subdivision of such labour was carried much further than in Britain. Consequently, in Rees's words, 'the Swiss watches have . . . supplanted the English in many countries of Europe' despite which 'in general, the workmanship of the Swiss watches is exceedingly slight'. A slight display of bias, perhaps?

Even with Rees's help, it is still by no means easy to identify all the skills that enhanced the look of the English watch movement. Of the components that were usually decorated, the watch cock, slide plate and stop work were made in the factory. There is a dial-plate maker, a dial-painter and a hand-maker. Two skilled workers make the case, one of whom specialises only in the 'joint' or hinge. The engraver cuts the name of the watchmaker on the movement plate and also engraves the cock and slide plate or index. Finally, the gilder employs his skills throughout and as required.

The workers who decorated watch movements have, sadly, contrived to remain almost anonymous despite the most rigorous search. Watchcase makers, if they worked in London, were required to register their imprints at Goldsmiths' Hall, and these have been identified and listed by Arthur Grimwade in his invaluable work *London Goldsmiths, 1697–1837: Their Marks and Lives,* in which a substantial section is devoted to their incuse marks. Apart from these, a few isolated individuals have emerged from the shadows and are included in Appendix III.

II: Areas of Art on the Movement

How much would have been lost to us, had watch movements been left completely plain? Some understanding of this can be obtained from a group of movements in the Clockmakers' Company Collection which are, in professional parlance, still 'in the grey'; that is to say, they have been roughed out and assembled so far as is possible at that particular stage of manufacture. They have next to be handfinished and decorated, before being timed and adjusted as necessary.

PLATE 78: Earlier English watches — these three range over the second quarter of the seventeenth century — are notable for their beautiful, albeit restrained, decoration which, nevertheless, pays great attention to tiny features such as the regulating and other dials, and striking count-wheels.

Stylistically, quite a number of these movements purport to originate from the mid-seventeenth century and, indeed, seem always to have been regarded as such, in which case they are a truly remarkable survival. Yet, if only because they incorporate modern screws in places where their use would anyway have been unlikely over three hundred years ago, it must seem more plausible that they are mere evocations, made perhaps as an exercise by some school of horology or for exhibition purposes, in which case the identifying letters inscribed on some of them might serve some purpose. Movements from the later periods, however, do appear much more likely to be authentic; and even with the earlier ones, it cannot be disputed that they would have looked exactly like that, at that particular stage of production.

The first impression that they make upon the lay observer is one of ugliness. It would have been perfectly possible, technically, to finish these watches to the fully functional stage, without any further surface treatment of the areas that are exposed to view; yet any inducement to show them off to friends would then have been reduced almost to the point of being unsustainable. This has to be the only logical reason for incurring the added expense,

which might well have been considerable, of superimposing art on to the English watch movement. Precisely the same thing happened in other advanced countries, and it is sometimes the art, rather than the technology, which helps to distinguish the products of one from that of another, as well as to provide dating indications.

Over the years, quite a number of different zones on the movement have been utilised for greater or less decoration. Those of least importance — because their decoration is, at best, mere 'doodling' and has no real meaning — include the potence, the spring barrel, and certain specialised parts of complicated watches. Those decorated parts that are significant, either because they help to date the movement or simply because of their artistic appeal, are only two in number, viz the watch cock and slide plate, which can be viewed as one assembly, and the pillars which separate the plates of the movement. The first-mentioned, which should always appear en suite, have the functional purpose of protecting the balance, providing the pivoting point for one end of its arbor, and accommodating the mechanism that regulates the watch by acting on its balance spring. Eventually, the slide plate was superseded and its function laid bare

PLATE 79: The turn of the seventeenth century saw the 'golden age' of movement decoration. These two movements by Daniel Quare, from his series of watches with advanced technical features, suggest that he employed two different decorators to enrich them, one preferring his cock foot and slide plate to be solid, while the other pierced them; also, in one, the principal decoration springs from a female head while, in the other, it issues from a cockleshell.

> An ingenious watchmaker, near St. Martin le Grand, has invented and made a dye for executing watch-clocks, by which the expence of drilling, engraving, &c. is faved.
>
> Mon-

PLATE 80: A curious newspaper announcement from 1764. No examples of watch cocks that can be credibly attributed to this process have yet been identified, and the use of 'watch-clocks', a nonsense term, seems to indicate little understanding of the underlying purpose.

upon the movement plate for all to see.

Apart from the simplest forms, round baluster designs, which could be produced on a lathe, pillars were generally cast, and clear signs of this are to be found on the inwards-facing surfaces. Outwardly, once they have been handfinished and gilded, they always appear highly polished and attractive. Although the range of designs of pillars is relatively limited, probably on account of spatial considerations, there are a number of well-recognised types as well as some exotic oddities, and more of these will inevitably turn up in the future.

Watch cocks are of sufficient size as to provide much more scope for enhancement so that, for purposes of description, they are customarily divided into three zones. The two largest of these are, respectively, the 'table', which is that part immediately above and protecting the balance, and the 'foot', often splayed out and always abutting directly on to the movement plate to which it is screwed or, in its earliest manifestations, pinned. Connecting yet dividing these two larger areas is the 'neck', narrow in its early stages, gradually broadening until, come the nineteenth century, it is absorbed and disappears.

At different periods, watch cock decorators arrogated sufficient artistic authority to annex several wholly decorative and functionally superfluous features to the basic pattern. Protruding 'ears' from the edge of the table, and 'wings' or 'streamers' from the neck, add a certain touch of flamboyance to the whole effect; the slide plate, too, was capable of carrying similar extensions. A purely functional addition, however, was the one or more cranked lugs, used to anchor the table more firmly to the plate, and especially favoured, in the earlier periods, by Daniel Quare.

Pillars, watch cocks and slide plates are generally made from gilt-brass but, on occasion, both silver and steel, polished or blued, may be encountered. Steel is very much rarer than silver and is most likely to form only part of a component — the centre of a cock table or the capital of a pillar — whereas silver, where it occurs, usually constitutes the complete article. Visually pleasing colour contrasts result from careful combinations of the metals: for instance, when, conventionally, the slide plate is fashioned from gilt-brass, the regulator dial is always made from silver. However, when the slide plate itself is silver, this tiny dial is given added impact by being made in blued-steel. Either watch cock or slide plate, on its own, can be found in silver, the rest of the assembly being in gilt-brass.

The evolution of the watch cock, in decorative terms, has been dealt with elsewhere in this book; and little is known about those who created them. The work must

PLATE 81: The later eighteenth-century fashion for 'skeletonising' watch movements could have eradicated all the areas hitherto susceptible to decoration; but, as these three examples show, old habits die hard, and only the left-hand movement is totally bereft of ornament.

PLATE 82: By contrast with the previous illustration, some late eighteenth-century makers still chose the most ornate enrichment of their work; this movement by George Margetts even has his initials 'woven' into the intricacies of the cock table.

have been highly skilled and delicate, and it is sometimes said to have been mainly carried out by women. In 1764, a notice in a London newspaper suggested that an unnamed watchmaker had devised a method of stamping out these components, presumably as blanks for subsequent finishing; but little seems to have come of this.

There is one other fascinating factor that must not be overlooked. The survival of the decorative watch cock, as an entity in its own right, and long after it has become divorced from its parent artifact, is a phenomenon that is regularly evidenced by the quantities of these charming objects that appear in the large specialist auctions, both in London and abroad. It is clear that they have attracted the attention of collectors, since the rarer forms command surprising prices; and in the United States they are much in demand as wall decoration, framed upon a suitable textile backcloth. It always used to be held that they survived in such quantities as a direct result of the Depression years of the 1930s, when people in need of ready money pawned their watches and were subsequently unable to redeem them; but this cannot have been the only influence brought to bear since workmanlike articles by watch cock collectors were appearing in arts journals as long ago as before World War I.

It now seems more likely that when watches were replaced, from time to time, for other perfectly plausible reasons such as the dictates of fashion, or simply because they wore out, the jeweller usually removed the watch cock, before sending the rest for melting and recovery of the precious metal content. Subsequently, it would re-emerge as an item of jewellery, mounted up as a brooch or perhaps strung together with others to make a

necklace or earrings. Eventually, this procedure itself became unnecessary, and the watch cock became a collector's piece in its own right, and without any need to dress it up. If there has to be one sad reflection upon this practice, then it is to regret the disappearance of countless thousands of fine watches; but at least their cocks give a tiny glimpse of the quality they themselves once possessed.

The death of a fine watch from 'natural causes', leaving behind only its watch cock by way of an obituary, is at least understandable, however much we may regret it. What is not understandable is the reverse of this process. In 1961, the prestigious Dennison Collection, which had been formed by the son of the founder of the Waltham Watch Company in the USA, was auctioned by Christie's in London. When the 253 lots went on view, it was an unbelievable sight, since almost all of them had been denuded of their cocks. Seemingly this had been done quite indiscriminately, the early, rare and most valuable pieces suffering just as severely as the later and less important ones. No explanation of this dastardly act of vandalism was ever vouchsafed, nor was it mentioned in so many words in the catalogue although the horological press quickly picked it up. At the time, it was regarded by serious horologists as the greatest act of desecration of its kind ever perpetrated.

PLATE 83: The precision watch makers must take their share of the blame — or credit — for the disappearance of watch movement decoration. These two movements, with a gap of half a century between them, both yet demonstrate restrained elegance in their last vestiges of enrichment, but the same cannot be said of many of their contemporaries.

COLOUR PLATE 13: A number of different kinds of stone, given sufficient hardness and capability to take a high polish, can be adapted for use as watchcases. The gold-mounted 'teardrop' at the top is of amber, and houses a watch by Isaac Pluvier, thought originally to have been a Dutchman, who was admitted as journeyman to David Bouguet in 1637, and admitted a Freeman of the Clockmakers' Company in 1652. In the centre, a magnificent gold-mounted carnelian case is associated with a watch signed, simply, 'Strigner, London', a so-far unrecorded craftsman. The remaining three cases, two of them resplendent in scrolling gold mounts, are made in different varieties of agate. The watchmakers concerned are Henry Long, Robert Setter, and John and George Hanet; and all date from the latter half of the eighteenth century.

COLOUR PLATE 14: Indigenous English enamels, epitomised by Battersea and Bilston, are to be found very occasionally on watchcases, as seen in the two examples at the top of this picture. In the centre another example of the very rare filigree watchcase, the movement by B. Chance, c1720. The handsome and unusually heavily gold-inlaid tortoiseshell outer case at bottom left houses a movement by Joseph Martineau Senior, its inner case hallmarked 1754. Beside it is an obvious relative of the English 'tulip' form watch, this type being designated a 'fritillary'. The movement is by Thomas Hande.

III: WATCH DECORATORS — SOME NAMES RECOVERED

The list of names and trades that follows is drawn from two main manuscript sources. In the Clockmakers' Company Library, MS 3338 (Bromley 1071) consists of two substantial volumes containing an alphabetical list of references to eighteenth-century newspaper advertisements concerning not only watch- and clockmakers, but also members of allied trades, in London. This was compiled in the 1930s by a contemporary of G. H. Baillie, by name Francis Buckley, FSA. He published a number of still-useful pamphlets, frequently helped, as in this case, by his father Dr George Buckley, MC. A few names have been culled from MS 3963 (Bromley 960), a manuscript rather grandly entitled *A List of Watch Case, Pendant and Glass Makers, Joint Finishers, Springers and Liners, Gilders and Coverers,* anonymous and undated, but seemingly from the early nineteenth century, which is not nearly so productive as might reasonably be expected. To this, finally, have been added some names extracted from recent and still-continuing research into eighteenth-century insurance policies, being conducted by Mr S. B. Turner, who has kindly permitted their inclusion.

Each entry is accompanied by a reference indicating the trade involved, and care has been taken to preserve the exact wording employed, in accordance with the following legend:

WCM = Watch Case Maker
SWCM = Shagreen Watch Case Maker
WG = Watch Gilder
WP = Watch Piercer
WPM = Watch Pillar Maker
WGM = Watch Glass Maker or Grinder
WC = Watch Chaser
CM = Watch Cap Maker
WE = Watch Engraver
WDM = Watch Dial Maker
TWCM = Tortoiseshell Watch Case Maker
S & GWCM = Silver and Gold Watch Case Maker
WCJF = Watch Case Joint Finisher
SWCMSL = Shagreen Watch Case Maker and Springer and Liner
C & P = Coverer and Pinner
PM = Pendant Maker
WCC = Watch Case Coverer
WCF = Watch Case Finisher
EDPP = Enamel Dial Plate Painter

ACKEMAN—(WGM) 'Gold Ball', New Rents. 1753

ALBERT, Isaac—(WCM) Bishopsgate Without. 1739

ANDERTON, Samuel—(EDPP) 4 Salmon & Ball Court, Bunhill Row, 1802

ARIS, John—(SWCM) Drapers' Court, Lothbury. 1744

ATKINS—(PM) Red Lion Street. Early 19th century

AUSTIN, John—Apprenticed to Mr. SMITH (WG) 'ran away'. 1752

AVELINE, Daniel—(WCM) Seven Dials. 1745–7

BASELL, Richard—(PM) 12 Berkley Court in Berkley Street in Clerkenwell. 1786

BASKERVILLE, John—(WCM) Southwark, 'died'. 1761

BAYLEY, John—(WCM) Warwick Court, Warwick Lane. 1706

BEADELCOMBE, John—(WCM) 3 New Court in St John's Street in Clerkenwell. 1794

BEAN, Edward—(WG) Little Cross Street, Clerkenwell. 1787

BEARE—(WC) Red Lion Street, 'married'. 1763

BELL, Joseph—(WCM) Clerkenwell Close, 'bankrupt'. 1780

BENTLEY, James—(WG) Great New Street, Fetter Lane. 1744

BEYENDORFF, David—(WCM) Late Hatfield Street, London and formerly Dublin, 'insolvent'. 1770

BILLINGSHURST, Henry—(WCM) 67 Aldersgate Street. 1767–8

BINLEY, William—(C&P) 'Shepherd & Shepherdess'. Early 19th century

BLACKMORE—(WC) Salisbury Court. 1746

BLAKE, William—(WCM) 28 Whitecross Street, Cripplegate. 1781

BONNER, William—(WP) Duck Lane, West Smithfield. 1762

BOWERS—(WC) St James's Street, removed to 'Golden Head', Red Lion Street, Holborn. 1755

BRADSHAW—(WCM) Johnson's Court, Fleet Street. 1762

BRADSHAW, Edward—(WCM) Puddle Dock Hill. 1745

BRIGHTRIDGE, Henry—(WG) Butchers' Hall Lane. 1757

BROTHERTON, John—(WCM) 'of Sun Row, Islington'. 1755–65

BROWN—(WE) 'next Lord Cobham's Head in Cold Bath Fields'. 1777

BROWN, Richard—(PM) 'and Key Maker: St John's Street'. Early 19th century

BROWN, Robert—(WG) Fleet Lane. 1755

BROWN, William—(WG) '42 in the Minories'. 1771

BUCKLE, David—(WG) Bridgewater Square. 1802

BUCKLEE, Henry—(WG) 81 Princes Street Barbican. 1771

BURR—(PM) Old Street Square, Bridges Court. Early 19th century

WCM = Watch Case Maker
SWCM = Shagreen Watch Case Maker
WG = Watch Gilder
WP = Watch Piercer
WPM = Watch Pillar Maker
WGM = Watch Glass Maker or Grinder
WC = Watch Chaser
CM = Watch Cap Maker
WE = Watch Engraver
WDM = Watch Dial Maker
TWCM = Tortoiseshell Watch Case Maker
S & GWCM = Silver and Gold Watch Case Maker
WCJF = Watch Case Joint Finisher
SWCMSL = Shagreen Watch Case Maker and Springer and
    Liner
C & P = Coverer and Pinner
PM = Pendant Maker
WCC = Watch Case Coverer
WCF = Watch Case Finisher
EDPP = Enamel Dial Plate Painter

BURTON, John—Apprentice to Joseph SIMS (WG), 'ran away'. 1752

BURWASH, Thomas—(PM) 214 St Johns Street. Early 19th century

BURWASH, William—(PM) 45 Red Lion Street in Clerkenwell, 1782, and at 3 Red Lion Street. 1792

CALVERT, Richard—(WCM) 'of The Sun, Little Old Bailey'. 1771

CARLOS, Henry—(WG) Old Street. Early 19th century

CARLOS, John—(WG) Near Silver Street. Early 19th century

CARPENTER, Thomas—(WCM) 'No. 5 St John Street Turnpike in Islington'. 1785

CATON, Gilbert—(WCM) Cherry Tree Court, Aldersgate Street. 1751

CATTING, William—(WPM) Purple Lane, Holborn, 'insolvent'. 1772

CLARK, John—(WCM) 'Ordered for execution for High Treason'. 1766

CLARK, Martha—(WCM) 70 Bunhill Road. 1807

CLARK, Richard—(WCM) Spitalfields, 'bankrupt'. 1795

CLARK, Robert—(WG) Old Fish Street. 1747

CLARKE, Abraham—(SWCM) From London, at 'The Rose, Thomas Street, Bristol' (?on a visit only). 1784

COLLAMBELL, Anthony—(WCM & C&P) 11 Goswell Street. 1793 to early 19th century

CRAMMILLION, Peter—(WCM) Clerkenwell Green, loses his apprentice, Thos. DREWAPP (age 19). 1744

CREBER, Jeremiah—(WGM) Loses his apprentice James WINTER. 1744

CROKATT, B.—(WG) 32 King Street, Smithfield. Early 19th century

CURRIER—(WGM) Whitecross Street. Early 19th century

DAGLEY, Samuel—(WC) 'of Shug Lane'. 1777

DANIEL—(WCM) At the Golden Ball over against Ivy Bridge in the Strand. 1771

DAVENPORT (or DEVENPORT), William—(WCM) Age 28, accused of counterfeiting. 1799

DAVIS, Samuel—(WE) 'of Shrewsbury Ct., in White Cross Street'. 1771

DELANDER, John—(WCM) 'Over against St Clement's Church in the Strand.' 1675

DESLOGE, Samuel—(WP) 'of Denmark Street in the parish of St. Giles in the Fields'. 1746

DOOREY, Thomas—(WCM) Charles Street, Soho. 1766

DRING—(WCM) Under Norman's Buildings, Old Street. 1784

DUKE—(CM) Brick Lane, Old Street. 1774

EDWIN, John—(WE) Salisbury Court, Fleet Street. 1752

ELY—(WE) Red Lion Street, Clerkenwell, 'died'. 1764

EMMETT—(PM) Albemarle Street. Early 19th century

FERRON, Abraham—(WCM) 'in Church Street, St. Ann's in Westminster'. 1756

FIELD—(PM) 'Son in Law and Successor of W. GOODALL Red Lion Street'. Early 19th century

FOSTER, John—(WCM) 'near the Barrs, in Goswell Street'. 1765

FRENCH, William—Apprentice to Richard PAYNE (WCM), runs away. 1747

FRESHFIELD, James—(C&P) 'Retired'. Early 19th century

FURNEAUX, Lewis—(WCM) 223 St John's Street in Clerkenwell. 1794

GARLAND, Matthew—(WG) Bunhill Row. Early 19th century

GIBBARD, Thomas—(WCM) 'at No. 10 in Quakers Buildings Cow Cross'. 1777

GIBBONS—(WCM) Facing Holloway Mount. 1762

GIBBS, Solomon—(WCM) 'insolvent'. 1731

*GIFFIN, Edward Burr—(SWCMSL) 12 Berkley St, Red Lion Street, Clerkenwell. 1771

GILBERT, William—(WCM) 'at Mr. Hardevilliers, Hog Lane'. 1766

GLOVER, Richard—Apprentice to Mr. SMITH (WG), ran away. 1752

GOOCH, Thomas—(WCM) 23 Coppice Row, in Cold Bath Fields. 1795

GOODALL, W.—(PM) see 'FIELD'.

GOSLING, Thomas—(WCM) 2 Lilly Pot Lane. 1778

GOUJON, Peter—(WCM) Retiring from business. 1774

*GRIFFIN, Edward Burr—(WCM) Loses his apprentice, Henry CAREY. 1770

Note: *probably one and the same man.

GRIGNION, Charles—(WE) Bow Street. 1763

GROVE, Richard—(WCM) 1 Vine Yard Gardens at the corner of Fletchers Row in Cold Bath Fields. 1794

HAMMERTON, Richard—(WE) 'of Shrewsbury Ct, in White Cross Street'. 1771

HAMMOND, Laurence—(WC) 'of Brownlow Street in the parish of St. Giles in the fields'. 1751

HARDING, Henry—(WCM) In Princess Street, No 4 Barbican, loses his apprentice, Robert NEWMAN. 1777

HARDY, John—(WCM) 8 Bridgwater Square, Barbican. 1771

HARDY, Thomas—(WCM) 14 Rosamund St, Clerkenwell. 1802

HARPER, Thomas—(WCM) 16 Monmouth Street. 1781

HARRISON, George—(WCM) Loses apprentice Edward CHAPMAN (age 17). 1762

HASTINGS, John—Age 20, apprenticed to William PLATT (WCM) ran away. 1755

HAWES, Joseph—(WCM) 10 Lower Coleman Street in Bunhill Row, 1795

HEATH, John—(SWCM) Leather Lane, loses apprentice George BLANSHARD (age 15). 1751

HIENS, Robert—(WDM) at the 'Lamb & Dial', New Street, Covent Garden, 'makes and sells all sorts of enamelled dial plates for clocks and watches'. 1752

HIGGINS, Berenger—(CM) 'died at his home in the Old Bailey: was a Cap Maker for watches, but by his ingenuity he found out the art of making porcelain'. 1748

HILL—(WE).Fleet Street. 1730

HILL, Thomas—(WCM) 80 Aldersgate Street. 1777

HILLIER, James—(WGM) 11 Church Street, Spitalfields. Early 19th century

HINNOTT, Samuel—(?WCM) Pelham Street. 1700

HINTON, John—(WG) Little Carter Lane, loses apprentice John GIBBS (age 19). 1755

HISLOP, John—(WCM) Rawstone Street, Islington. With his partner Richard HOLT have absconded after forging Hall Marks and Duty Marks on cases. 1792

HODDLE, John—('eminent' WE) Cock Lane, Smithfield, 'died'. 1751

HOLDER, William—(WE) Red Lion Street, Clerkenwell. 1767

HOLDRED, Theophilus—(SWCM) 'near St. Martins Lane, in Castle Street, in Long Acre'. 1761

HOWARD, William—(WCM) Show Street in the City of Coventry. 1805

HUCKLE—('eminent' WG) Noble Street, near Foster Lane, Cheapside, 'died'. 1765

HUMPHREYS—(WGM) Goulston (?) Square. Early 19th century

HYDE, John—(WCC) 36 Allen Street in Goswell Street. 1794

JONES, William—(WCM) 18 Hosier Lane. 1777

KNIGHT, James—(WG)&(WC) Moves from Islington to Ludgate Hill; hopes to have patronage of former customers that deal in watches etc. 1755

LAWRENCE, Thomas—(WCM) Francis Court, Berkeley Street, Clerkenwell. 1762

LILLEY—(WE) Duck Lane, 'was killed'. 1765

LINDSEED, John—(WG) 'of Charterhouse Square in Long Lane, in West Smithfield'. 1761

LINSEY, William—(WCM) 2 Bridgewater Street. 1794

LITTLEBURY—(WCM) Rosemary Lane, 'died'. 1763

LOVE, John—(WCM) In Blackfryars, Glass House Yard, loses his apprentice James PITTANT.

MARR, John—(PM) Brook St, Holborn. Undated. (1806?)

MARSHALL, John—'Maker of Optic Glasses to his Majesty, Inventor of the Magic Night Watch to show the Hours of the Night in a Dark Chamber'. 1722

MARTIN, Elizabeth—(WG) Little Britain, loses apprentice, John PLATT. 1762

MATHEY, Widow & Son—(SWCMs) Queen Street, Seven Dials. 1762

MAYER, Lewis—(WG&WCC) 9 Lower Coleman Street in Bunhill Row. 1800

MEADHURST, William—(WCM) Blue Anchor Alley, Bunhill Row. 1753

MERCIER—(SWCM) Greek Street, Soho. Loses his apprentice Charles FAULCON (age 16). 1753

MILLER, Peter—(WCM) At Mr Bowes (cabinet maker), 45 Old Compton Street. 1777

MILWARD, William—(WCM) Fleet Street. 1729

MINCE, Jonas—(WCM) 8 Norman Street in Old Street. 1794

MOORLAND—(WCM) 'formerly in St. Ann's, Soho Square, died July 29th aged 85'. 1788

NEVILL, John—(WCM) 14 Cold Bath Square. 1786

NEWMAN, Robert—Apprentice to Henry HARDING (WCM) 'ran away'. 1777

OADES—(PM) Great Sutton Street. Early 19th century

OVERY—(TWCM) Union Court, Holborn, died 11 May, 1767 aged 92

OVETT, James—(WCF) 'of Great Arthur Street, in Goswell Street'. 1771

PALMER, Richard—(S&GWCM) Red Lion Street, Clerkenwell. 1771

PARKER, Thomas—(WCM) Union Court, Holborn in 1769. 1791

WCM = Watch Case Maker
SWCM = Shagreen Watch Case Maker
WG = Watch Gilder
WP = Watch Piercer
WPM = Watch Pillar Maker
WGM = Watch Glass Maker or Grinder
WC = Watch Chaser
CM = Watch Cap Maker
WE = Watch Engraver
WDM = Watch Dial Maker
TWCM = Tortoiseshell Watch Case Maker
S & GWCM = Silver and Gold Watch Case Maker
WCJF = Watch Case Joint Finisher
SWCMSL = Shagreen Watch Case Maker and Springer and
   Liner
C & P = Coverer and Pinner
PM = Pendant Maker
WCC = Watch Case Coverer
WCF = Watch Case Finisher
EDPP = Enamel Dial Plate Painter

PAYNE, Richard—(WCM) Carthusian Street, Charter-house Square loses his apprentice William FRENCH. 1747

PAYNE, Richard—(WCM) Goswell Street. 1752

PENN, Richard—(WG) Late of London. 1743 ·

PENNY, Jnº—(WCM) 1 Crown Court, Aldersgate Street (no date)

PERRY, Thomas—(WCM) Shoe Lane. 1765

PETERSON, Frederick—Enameller decᵈ sale of effects . . . tops of snuff boxes and watches. 1731

PHILLIPS, William—(WCM) 36 Haydon Yard in the Minories. 1802

PHILPOT—(WCM) Of Snow Fields, Southwark, was drowned on April 19. 1763

PINCHBECK, John—(WC) 'of Field Lane in the parish of St. Andrews in Holborn'. 1737

PIRON, Benjamin—(WCM) Gun Street, Spitalfields. 1752

PITON (PITTANT), James—Apprentice to John LOVE (WCM). 1708

PITT, Caleb—(WE) No address. 1797

PLATT, William—(WCM) New Street, Shoe Lane near Fleet Street, loses his apprentice John HASTINGS (age 20). 1755

PORTER—(PM) Red Lion Street. Early 19th century

POTTER—(WG) Fountain Court, Shoe Lane. 1762

POWELL—(WG) Widegate Street. Early 19th century

POWELL, John—Apprentice to Mr DANIEL (WCM) ran away. 1671

PRETTY, William—(WCM) 16 Cross Key Court in Little Britain. 1794

REILLY, Richard—Apprentice to Edward BRADSHAW (WCM) ran away. 1745

RENOU, James—(WCM) St Ann's, Westminster, insolvent. 1723

RENOU, James—(WCM) Lombard Street. 1725

*RICHARDS—(WCM) Halfmoon Street, Ludgate. 1727

*RICHARDS, William—(WCM) Of Half Moon Court in the parish of St Martins in Ludgate. 1721

ROBINSON, John—(SWCM) 'of Albemarle Street in St. John's Square, Clerkenwell'. 1761

†ROUMIEAU, Adam—(WCM) 'near the Black Lyon Inn in Water Lane in the precinct of White Fryers'. 1715

†ROUMIEU, Adam—(WCM) Watchcase stamped 'A.R.'. 1705

ROWLANDS—(PM) Albemarle Street. Early 19th century

RUSSELL, Isaac—(WCM) 7 Priests Court, Foster Lane. 1791.

SALT, Samuel—(PM) 6 St John's Square. 1781

SHARP—(WC) Arundel Street, married. 1764

SIMMONS, John—(WCM&WC) Salisbury Court, Fleet Street, loses his apprentice Robert WHITE. 1747

SIMONS, John—(WCC) 29 Great Sutton Street in Goswell Street, 1791; and 36 Allen Street in Goswell Street. 1797

SIMS, Joseph—(WG) Clerkenwell Green, loses his apprentice John BURTON. 1752

SINCLAIR—(WGM) 'in a Court leading from Red Lion Street to Cow Cross'. Early 19th century

SMITH—(WG) Little Britain, loses his apprentices Richard GLOVER and John AUSTEN. 1752

SMITH, Samuel—(SWCM) Union Court, Holborn. 1744

SMITH, William—(WE) 'No. 5 in Old Street'. 1781

SONES—(WCM) Lillypot Lane. 1751

STEAD, Joseph—(WG) 'of Star Court in Chancery Lane in the parish of St. Dunstan in the West'. 1724

STEEVES, John—(WC) Fell Street, near Wood Street. 1761

STUBBS, John—(WCM) Great Arthur Street, near Goswell Street. 1765

TERRITT, William—(WE) Late of Bell Yard, Golden Lane, charged with theft. 1767

TERRY—(WCM) Aldersgate Street. 1765

TILLEY, Richard—(WCM) 14 Curtain Road, 1791; 35 Norton Fulgate, 1794; *and* 9 Wilton Walk in Curtain Road. 1797

TOMBS, John—(WG) Fetter Lane. 1762

TURNER, Thomas—Apprentice to Samuel WAKELIN (WCJF) ran away. 1774

Note: probably one and the same man
†*Note:* probably one and the same man

USENER—(WGM) 30 Carey Street, Lincoln's Inn Fields. 1776

WAKELIN, Samuel—see under TURNER, Thomas

WALKER, Richard—(WCM) 56 New Compton Street. 1801

WARD, Thomas—(C&P) Bridgwater Square. Early 19th century

WEBBER—(C&P) Pear Tree Street. Early 19th century

WILLOUGHBY, John—(WCM) 'of Elliotts Court in Little Old Bailey in the parish of St. Sepulchers (sic)'. 1719

WITHILL—(WE) The Borough, died 12 July. 1751

WRIGHT, Jacob—(WGM) Bunhill Row. Early 19th century

WRIGHT, Thomas—(WGM) Bunhill Row. Early 19th century

WYNELL, John—(WCM) 'at the Jessamine Tree near the corner of Cecill Street in the Strand, in the parish of St. Clement Danes'. 1710

IV: WATCH PILLARS— A PROGRESSION OF STYLES

Spatial considerations alone must have precluded the variety of designs of watch movement pillars ever approaching that of, say, watch cocks; yet a number of types are well recognised and commonly encountered. To offset that, there are also an as-yet-unrecorded number of 'mavericks', versions that may have existed only in one or two examples, and these represent an area of mystery that is unlikely ever to be fathomed completely. The selection shown here — and that is all that it is — is intended to include most of the more common varieties, together with a few of the more exotic ones. It was usual also to decorate the potence housing the fusee stop-work, probably since, like the pillars, it had to be planted on the edge of the movement and was thus highly visible. Where it has been adjacent to a pillar, it has also been included in the illustrations, since its appearance should at least be compatible with that of its neighbour. Finally, for each movement concerned, the maker and his location are given, to show that — at least in this area of art on the watch movement — provincial and London craftsmen were equally innovative.

In general, it seems not to have occurred to watchmakers to equip their movements with ornamental pillars until towards the middle of the seventeenth century, and perhaps it was the puritan streak, which prevailed throughout the country, that had earlier precluded anything but a plain round baluster, simply a post and nothing more. Edward East, however, was one of the first to adopt the elegant tapering pilaster (1), much used sub-sequently by other makers and either divided, as in this example, or solid, and with or without the engraved 'drapes' that hang around the shoulders. Some authorities regard this as an early depiction of the style known as 'Egyptian' (see [9] below), but this is simply a matter of opinion.

At about the same time — that is, c1650 — openwork patterns started to appear, such as that on a movement by John Knibb, of Oxford (2). Examples (3) and (4) are taken from two movements by the same maker, Thomas Taylor, whose London premises were in Holborn, showing that there was still no common denominator in this particular feature. It was not until around 1690 that the celebrated 'tulip' pattern (5) emerged, in this instance on a watch by Richard Howe of Dorchester. The crested tulip (6), from a movement by Thomas Windmills, is quite a rarity on movements, although the term is often used to describe a hybrid with characteristics derived from both tulip and Egyptian types — see (10) below.

It is perhaps worth a brief diversion, to note that the great Thomas Tompion, on his early movements, used a variety of pillar designs including openwork versions akin to (2) above, as well as a very slender and elongated hybrid, also part-tulip and part-Egyptian. The true crested Egyptian (7) is also rather a rarity, and this example comes from Tompion's movement numbered 2268, c1700. The London maker, Simon Descharmes, was French by birth, and perhaps this influenced his use of the attractive pillar at (8), the movement dating from c1710. This is followed by an instance of the authentic Egyptian pillar (9) from a watch by John Pepys, who was Master of the Clockmakers' Company in 1707, remaining active at least until 1720.

Mention has already been made of a quite commonly encountered hybrid pillar, contrived from the curved outline of the tulip combined with the vertical 'dot and dash' division of the Egyptian style, surmounted by a pierced cresting and sometimes standing on a similar plinth; a particularly complicated example of this (10) comes from a watch by the unfortunate Edward Bodenham. Apprenticed to the eminent Brounker Watts in 1709, he was admitted to the Freedom of the Clockmakers' Company in 1719, went bankrupt in 1725 and ten years later was transported for theft, never to be heard of again. This particular movement is as beautiful an example of everything epitomised by the 'golden era' as could possibly be desired—and it is at least possible that this predilection for the finest decoration on his work brought about Bodenham's downfall, since it must have added considerably to the costs involved.

The pillars described so far have all been taken from watches that were simple timekeepers; when dealing with complicated watches, some changes are inevitable. The additional mechanism needed for a watch that strikes or repeats the time on a bell, or offers an alarm facility, invariably took up more space, not only between the plates of the main frame, but also behind the dial, the latter resulting in a very wide band around the edge of the dial-plate, within which the extra motion work could be deployed. Pillars on such watches are usually much less ornamental than was customary, the most that could be expected being the rather bulbous baluster form (11) taken from a five-minute repeating watch by John Bushman, c1720. Originally Johannes Buschmann, this maker was a High German, born about 1661, who settled in London and became a Brother of the Clockmakers' Company in 1692, rising to be a member of its Court of Assistants in 1720. He was still at work in 1725.

There are only one or two makers who can be associated with a special design of pillar that was not used by others, and one such is John Ellicott. The rather ornate style (12) that he favoured comes from movement number 2598, which can be dated c1745. The curious thing is that this type of pillar is to be found on an occasional Continental watch, and there are probably those who would regard this as placing a question mark against the origin of some of this maker's work. In this context, it has to be admitted that many Ellicott watchcases seem to have come from Switzerland.

The eighteenth century produced some imaginative pillar designs, although few of them seem to have become popular in the way that the tulip and Egyptian versions did. Four unusual examples are shown here, the first (13) from a movement by Francis Clark, whose dates are

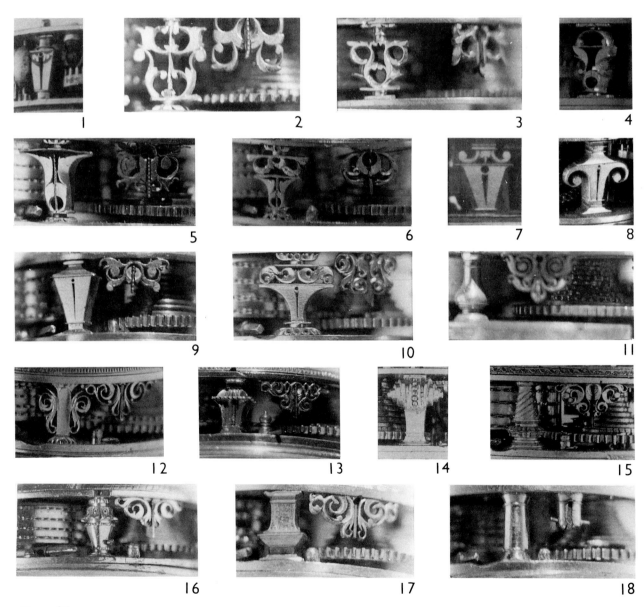

PLATE 84

· *132* ·

given as 1723–9, and who, like Bodenham, became insolvent. The stop-work potence on this specimen, as well as the nicely turned end on the foot of the dial-plate to be seen projecting upwards between these two larger features, all bespeak quality and, therefore, cost. The next example comes from a watch, surprisingly, by a very eminent London maker, Daniel Delander, who died in 1733. This one (14) was probably one of his later products, perhaps c1730; but it is unusual to find the London trade going in for anything so exotic. Our third instance of the unorthodox (15) comes from the work of John Stevenson, a Stafford maker who was active up to about the middle of the century, although this example probably dates c1725. If one had to devise a name for this style, it could only be 'helter-skelter'; and here again, the stop-work potence is well executed. The final example in this short selection of curiosities (16) resembles — if indeed it can be said to resemble anything — what auctioneers call 'a standing cup and cover', the former plain and the latter fairly ornate. The watchmaker concerned was John Newman, emanating from Norwich, and active c1745.

The only decorative pillar from the latter part of the eighteenth century to become really popular is seen in the penultimate illustration. Usually called 'square baluster', the proportions and profile of the mouldings vary considerably between one specimen and another, but the general impression remains the same. This example (17) comes from a movement by Henry Betterton, a London maker working c1780; and it is noticeable that the stop-work potence is visually more interesting than its partner, to which it now bears no relationship whatsoever.

At the end, this account has turned full circle, back to the plain round turned baluster pillar, which was to become the norm throughout the nineteenth century. This particular example comes from a watch by Archibald Coats, of Wigan, and dates c1790; and, as if to reinforce the functional simplicity, it is only necessary to observe the stop-work potence. This is just another pillar, cut in half.

V: A CATALOGUE OF WATCH COCK IMAGERY

1 AGRICULTURE

One of the rarest and most pictorially decorative of all watch cocks, the so-called 'farmyard cock' contains the whole farming scene within the compass of its table, with cattle, pigs, the wellhead, the farmhouse with its smoking chimney and the farmer with his scythe and smoking pipe, even the gate and the garden path. For very many years this cock had never been identified upon a watch

movement and, because one of the elements in it appears to be a Dutch barn, it was always believed that such cocks came from Dutch watches. Eventually, however, a complete specimen was located on an English provincial watch of late eighteenth-century provenance. In 1955, five of these rare cocks were assembled for comparison, from as many different sources — collectors and museums — and it became clear from this, that four of them had, without any doubt, originated from the same workshop: the constituent elements were the same, and differences, such as existed, could be put down to hand-working. The fifth, though, possessed subtle but noticeable differences; the farmer himself was absent, and there were chickens and ducks in evidence, while the surroundings, in terms of foliage and wild birds, were much more prominent. Technically, the major elements were engraved on a shaped platform, but not also embellished with piercing. It seems possible that this example originated from a different source.

In the early nineteenth century an entirely different style of watch cock has some simple engraving of farming elements — a sheaf of corn and a sickle and rake — engraved on the table.

2 ANIMALS

Curiously, domestic animals seem conspicuous by their absence. The present widespread habit of keeping pets had not occurred during the lifetime of the decorated watch cock and, although cats have been domesticated since the time of the ancient Egyptians, the regulating bodies, both for these animals and for dogs, did not appear in England until the late nineteenth century, the National Cat Club in 1887 and the Kennel Club in 1873. Farm animals, apart from their appearance on the 'farmyard cock' (see *Agriculture* above) are rare. There is one splendid bovine example, the animal with long curving horns standing immediately below the centre of the cock table and occupying all the available space there. Stylistically, this cock belongs to the early nineteenth century, and it seems more than likely that it is illustrating a popular event of that time. The Craven Heifer was the most famous cow of its era. Born in 1807, it reached the extraordinary weight of 312 stones (1,980 kg) — very nearly two tons — and was walked all the way from Wakefield, in Yorkshire, to London, being displayed along the route. It was eventually to become the prize in a cockfight.

Wild animals, in recognisable forms, seem again to become more prominent during the first part of the last century, when the concept of the zoo took hold, and became fashionable. Although the first English menagerie was started by Henry I at Woodstock, in Oxfordshire, and later transferred to the Tower of London, it was not until it became the nucleus of the collection of the Royal Zoological Society in Regents Park, in central London, that it fired the imagination of the public. That was in 1829. On watch cocks, caged lions are by no means uncommon; the representation can be above or below the table centre, and the accompanying decoration is variable, suggesting a number of sources for this design rather than a single workshop. Squirrels and rabbits, again mainly on provincially made watches, probably reflected familiar enough images to their country owners. Grotesque animals, that cannot be clearly identified as belonging to any recognised species, appear very commonly in cocks throughout the first half of the eighteenth century, and constitute one of the elements of the imaginatively categorised 'inhabited foliage' (qv). Generally, only the creature's head, often with mouth open and tongue writhing, is visible, flowing from its swirling foliate surroundings, and sometimes almost indistinguishable from them.

3 ARABESQUES

'Intricate and fanciful surface decoration based on rhythmic linear patterns of scrolling and interlacing foliage, tendrils, etc usually covering the entire surface with a network of fine ornament . . .' (*The Penguin Dictionary of Decorative Arts,* 1979).

Probably derived from Saracenic ornament on objects decorated by Moslem craftsmen in Europe, for present purposes this divides easily into the styles usually designated as 'strapwork' and 'foliated' (qv).

On watch cocks, strapwork is virtually unknown entirely on its own; as an element that can combine easily, albeit discreetly, with foliated arrangements, however, it is relatively common from the end of the seventeenth century until c1720. Foliage, on the other hand, makes the perfect decorative foil for so many of the motifs employed to decorate watch cocks, and appears — in developing and subsequently degenerating forms — throughout the whole of the period covered by this book.

4 ASTROLOGY AND ASTRONOMY

The stars and planets have held an enormous fascination for human beings almost since the beginning of time. Natural enough, then, that they should appear not too infrequently on timekeepers. The sun, on its own, can often be found as the prominent motif on the cock table, sometimes occupying the rare, and technically difficult, centre spot where it tends to conflict with the plug inserted there, which carries on its underside the hole for the balance staff pivot. More usually, it is sited below centre. The theme is better illustrated by the arrangement of sun, moon and five or six stars, set into a shield-shaped reserve and against a matted background. It might have been expected that Halley's Comet would feature somewhere in such a context but, unfortunately, the fashion for topical watch cock decoration had hardly appeared in 1759 — the first reappearance of the phenomenon after its initial sighting by Halley in 1682 — and had virtually died out on the next occasion, in the mid 1830s.

Astrology, with its zodiacal connotations, is an exceedingly rare motif, which is surprising in view of its historic popularity. It may be that it is difficult to identify; it verges upon those areas of secretive mysticism with religious overtones, such as freemasonry, whose symbolism is not generally understood by the uninitiated. A single cock is illustrated that seems likely to fall within the astrological ethos, but one cannot be certain.

5 BIRDS, MYTHICAL AND OTHERWISE

Chippendale employed that remarkable creature, the ho-ho bird, the Japanese symbol of good luck, to enrich the decoration of his giltwood mirrors; and contemporary watch cocks often use the same motif, but rarely so effectively. It is probably a matter of scale. Even so, the tall, skinny birds seem to integrate more easily into the decor if only because they can be manipulated; this is not nearly so simple with birds like the owl and the parrot. Swans add their elegance, on occasion, to later watch cocks, but they are not commonly found.

6 COMMEMORATIVES

The fashion for producing commemorative articles to perpetuate people and events that fire the public imagination — battles, coronations, literary and scientific figures and suchlike — has its equal among the themes employed in the decoration of watch cocks. The Battle of Trafalgar — as well as Nelson, on his own — were probably the most popular subjects in this category. In one representation of this theme, the words 'Trafalgar', 'Nelson' and 'Brontë' appear. This immortalises his creation as Duke of Brontë by King Ferdinand I of Naples, in 1799. The case of this watch, by a Coventry maker, bears the hallmark for 1805, the year of the battle, showing that no time was lost in producing such novelties. Another similar representation has been seen on a Sheffieldmade movement, but with slightly different detail.

a

b

c

PLATES 85a,b,c: Watches commemorating Lord Nelson tend to be more elaborate even if, as in the first example, the related decoration was confined to the watch cock. This rather crude specimen, emanating from a Chesterfield maker, presumably bases the outline of its table on the Admiral's cocked hat. The Coventry-made watch features the words 'Trafalgar', 'Nelson' and 'Brontë' in its surrounding ornament; and the final watch, apparently anonymous and said to have been removed from Lord Nelson's body, commemorates the Battle of the Nile. The character of this watch suggests that it is not of English manufacture.

Another, and much rarer version, commemorates an event in the previous year, the Battle of Aboukir Bay, with the cock table bearing the inscription 'Admiral Nelson, Port of the Nile, August 1, 1798', and also incorporating into its pierced decoration the initials 'H.N.'. The movement of this watch is illustrated in Plate 85c. It forms part of a collection of Nelson relics held at an English school, and is said to have been taken from the Admiral's body immediately after his death. Nevertheless, its authenticity must be suspect, for the following reasons. First, the quality of the object does not measure up to the fame of its alleged owner — the workmanship is indifferent, as these things go, and it may not even be

English, to judge from its general appearance; additionally, it is unsigned. Next, it lacks a case, yet it is unthinkable that anybody would scrap the case of such a watch, were its alleged antecedents genuine. It is equally unbelievable that this famous man was carrying an uncased watch movement in his pocket when he was killed.

There does, however, exist a watch, the ownership of which is attributed to Nelson, and which is wholly credible, and that used to be in the United Services Museum when it was in the Banqueting Hall in Whitehall. When last heard of, this watch was in a display case at Chequers, the Prime Minister's official country home. One of Josiah Emery's excessively accurate lever watches, it is just such as Nelson might have been expected to own, aside from its well-documented provenance.

The more usual commemorative cock simply takes the form of a named portrait of some major personality. Wellington, Benjamin Franklin and Robert Burns are the most common in this very rare category. Like all objects that are essentially novelties, they go out of fashion and are discarded. Where complete examples have survived, they seem always to be on North-Country watches, and the practice does not ever seem to have found favour in the metropolis.

PLATE 86: The usual 'commemorative' watch simply has a named portrait on its watch cock, as on this Midlands movement, of no other interest apart from its dedication to the Duke of Wellington.

7 FISH, MYTHICAL

Fish leaping out of, and through, water is such an obviously decorative idea that its use on watch cocks seems inevitable. The fish, however, tend to be depicted in somewhat unsuitable environments, like thick jungle, as well as immoderately foreshortened, so that the tail gets lost in the undergrowth. It is fair to say that these creatures are recognisable as fish but, like so much of the animate motifs used in this kind of ornament, they belong to no readily identifiable species. There is also a quality of the caricature about many of them; the head, the only clearly discernible part, appears bloated to emphasise the character of the creature.

8 FLOWER ARRANGEMENTS

This is a comparatively rare motif, *per se,* although containers for flowers — baskets, vases and the like — are common enough. The example illustrated, again from a late period, is perhaps more properly described as a potted plant. There spills from the decorated pot some half a dozen large blooms, which are deployed strategically around the centre of the cock table, interspersed with an equal number of beautifully portrayed stems of leaves. A coarser and much less sophisticated version of this theme depicts three miserable little blooms drooping over the edge of the flower pot, while four others, equally small, are sited equidistantly around the rim of the cock table, the intervening space being so inadequately filled as to merit the whole plant being dismissed as 'leggy'.

9 FOLIAGE (SEE ALSO ARABESQUES)

The verb used to describe cocks with foliage decoration is 'foliated' and it is surely the commonest theme in use on watch cocks. Originally employed for its own sake, it soon became customary to combine it with often somewhat obscure forms of animals and birds, when it came to be described as 'inhabited foliage'. The origin of this term can almost certainly be attributed to the late Philip Coole who 'invented' it when cataloguing watches for Sotheby's, the auctioneers.

10 FUNCTIONALISMS

There are two principal instances where the function of the watch cock is allowed to supervene, thus influencing, if nothing more, the decoration of this component.

INTEGRAL REGULATORS The performance of the watch as a timekeeper is 'tuned' by means of the balance spring, the effective length of which can be varied by a regulatory system built into the back of the movement. The indicator, by which the amount of any adjustment can be measured, can take several forms; the small silver dial, set into the slide plate, which can be turned in either direction, is just one. Another, especially in later periods, has the regulatory system mounted on the cock table, with the 'index' — the arm, generally of polished steel, which can be moved to left or right to measure the adjustment against an engraved scale on the table — running from 'F' (fast) at one end, to 'S' (slow) at the other.

In most cases the regulator on the cock table is a simple device and plain for all to see. Very rarely indeed, an attempt is made to disguise it by causing the entire cock table to rotate with the index, which reads against a discreet scale on the neck of the cock. In this form, there is practically no interference with the decoration of the table, since the scale is not located thereon.

RISING CENTRES   In rare instances the central area of the cock table, which houses the pivot hole for the back pivot of the balance staff, or axle, has been deliberately raised well proud of the cock table surface, to form a kind of central boss. The effect of this, mechanically, is marginally to lengthen the staff; and it may be that, with proper contouring of the interior of this boss, the locating of the pivot hole when assembling the movement becomes easier. In any event, the platform thus provided on the cock table was carefully integrated into the general scheme of decoration.

11 GLAZED COCK TABLES

A pleasant fancy, employed at different times during the eighteenth century, was to place a glass over the suitably recessed decoration of the cock table: this glass was usually held in place with rim screws. Although generally confined to provincial watches, there is at least one known example by Ellicott and another by Will Kipling. A companion feature, often present in such watches, is a glass- and silver-mounted cap around the rim of the movement to exclude dust, while the embellishment of the Ellicott movement is yet further enhanced with the use of a garnet endstone in a silver setting at the centre of the cock table, and a slide plate fashioned in silver.

Sometimes blue glass seems to have been used in cock tables, but these are mainly found on foreign watches, notably Polish.

12 GROTESQUES

'A fanciful type of decoration composed of small, loosely-connected motifs, not unlike Arabesques but including human figures, monkeys and sphinxes, etc.' (*The Penguin Dictionary of Decorative Arts,* 1979).

Watch cock decoration employed elements of these, arabesques, strapwork and other well-defined classical styles indiscriminately, both separately and in combination with one another. Grotesques are based on wall decorations found in ancient Roman buildings that came to light during the Renaissance, one such being Nero's Golden House, on the Esquiline. Such decorations had been buried for centuries in subterranean ruins popularly known in Italy as 'grotte', hence the term used to describe them.

13 HERALDRY

This is very rare in watch cock decoration, although there is at least one well-established version. For some yet-to-be-discovered reason there is one variety of late seventeenth-century watch, the so-called 'wandering hour' watch (qv under dials) that seems to have attracted, at the time, a royal connotation. Consequently, such watches, in the majority of cases, display the royal arms on the cock table or, less often, in the centre of the dial. Associated with this, too, there will often be found an enamelled miniature of one of the then-current royal family.

The design of watch cocks displaying the royal arms is not so consistent that it is possible to state that all such components originated from the same workshop. For instance, sometimes there is only a single motto — *Semper Eadem* (always the same) — flanking St George and the Dragon. In other examples, this motto is scrolled above a mask on the neck, and immediately above that, the arms are surrounded by the Garter, which itself contains the other familiar motto *Honi Soit qui Mal y Pense.* That example also shows the supporters — the lion and the unicorn — with a crown surmounting the whole. It is a most impressive depiction, and beautifully executed.

The arms themselves are worth examination, since the armorial detail is useful as an aid to dating — royal heraldry has the advantage of being well-documented and scrupulously updated as reign succeeded reign, or the circumstances of the reigning house ordained. In most cases, the arms shown were those in use during the period 1707–14, although 'wandering hour' watches, on which they so often appear, are usually regarded as up to ten years earlier.

Another, later, style of watch cock shows the lion and

the unicorn flanking a crown, which is located immediately above the table centre; below is the motto *Dieu et Mon Droit,* this surmounting the cypher 'GR'. Again, the precise significance of this symbolism is not yet understood. (See also under *Mottoes.*)

14 INSECTS

This is an uncommon motif in watch cock decoration but, where it does occur, there are no doubts of its identity. Illustrated is a cock depicting a spider's web, complete with spider and captive fly, as well as a predatory-looking bird that, seemingly, will eventually eat everything in sight. There is a kind of nursery-rhyme flavour about this cock, and it must have had some contemporary significance. It is even reminiscent of that old poem which starts, '"Will you come into my parlour?" said the spider to the fly', but Mary Howitt who wrote it flourished rather too late in the day — 1799–1888 — to have inspired this depiction.

15 MASKS, GROTESQUE AND OTHERWISE

This is one of the earliest motifs to emerge from the jungle of foliage that, initially, comprised the entire decoration on watch cocks. Masks always seem to occupy the same area — on the table, immediately below centre, and often extending on to the neck — and when, rarely, one is found above centre, it is usually the head of a *putto.* Traditionally, the mask was supposed to represent Father Time — but, if so, he is a different old gentleman from the views of him seen on other artifacts. Far from kindly, he is often showing a mouth full of large teeth in a threatening display; and, as the decades pass, this gets more and more aggressive. He also tends to become multinational: some portrayals have a Chinese slant to them, others Red Indian. The degeneration of the mask heralded the beginning of the decline in watch cock decoration, *per se.*

However, there were some masks, occupying the same position on the cock, that were of an entirely different nature. More often than not these are clearly children's heads, not the stylised heads of the *putti* but something more akin to real girls and boys. As such they can be wholly delightful minutiae and well worth careful consideration.

16 MASONIC SYMBOLISM

This is as difficult an area of watch cock decoration as monograms, and for some of the same reasons. In both cases, the elements of secrecy and private knowledge play

a large part. Many years ago the late Philip Coole, examining a tray of watch cocks that comprised part of the large collection formed by the late Col A. S. Bates, and now deposited in the British Museum, commented that four of them had masonic significance. The other observers could identify only one, and Coole, being himself a freemason, tantalisingly refused to identify the other three.

Common knowledge has advanced just a little since then. The most obvious masonic symbols are clearly recognised as such — the dividers and set square, the trowel, the sun, the bell, even certain elements, such as the beehive, which are rumoured no longer used. The entrance to the Temple of Solomon, with its unique pillars flanking the grand staircase, is fairly easily recognised even though some depictions of it are of coarse quality. Beyond that, however, it is mostly supposition; and there remains an uncomfortably large proportion of 'mystery' watch cocks, masonic and otherwise, whose true significance still waits to be uncovered.

17 MILITARIA (SEE ALSO SOLDIERY)

The so-called 'trophy of arms' was originally a memorial to a victory. It consisted of spoils taken from an enemy, generally arms and armour, that were then hung on a tree or pillar as a kind of monument. It is a common theme on watch cocks, the interesting aspect being the great variation in the degree of emphasis accorded to it. On some examples, it is so discreet as to be barely discernible unless specifically sought out. In others, it will be the dominating feature. The details of these arrangements of military equipment remain fairly constant save that the use of cannon, perhaps because of the shape, is not as common as might be anticipated; and where they do appear, they tend to dominate the setting. The commonplace components remain a centrally located helmet, flanked by lances, often carrying pennants. Now and again there will be incorporated what appear to be axes, presumably to be used by the farriers and also, occasionally, a shield; and, rarely depicted, an obviously military bass drum (not to be confused with the musical trophy, qv). The last third of the eighteenth century — from c1770 — seems to have been the most popular period for this theme.

18 MONOGRAMS

These seem to divide into concealed and explicit depictions. If one can draw a comparison with the usage on fob seals during the late seventeenth and throughout the eighteenth centuries — a usage where initials are much more common than on watch cocks — the great majority are plain for all to see. Every now and again, however, a 'design' of initials is encountered, which is generally described as a cypher, and which can be so intrinsically complex that it is virtually impossible for the uninitiated to be certain which initials are included and where each stops and starts. It has been said that the purpose of these was to ensure their recognition by those 'in the know', who might often be illiterate and unable to recognise initials for what they truly were, but who were quite capable of memorising and recognising what might, to others, simply appear as a symmetrical pattern of curving lines. Translating this into the context of the watch cock, however, one immediately encounters the problem of random background decoration, which is not present on the fob seal. The effect of this is only further to confuse an already hazy picture, for where does the decoration cease and the cypher start? In consequence, there are inevitably a large number of cases where the very existence of any concealed meaning among the swirling tendrils of the foliated background has to be a matter for conjecture. It can be argued that, if you try hard enough, it is almost always possible to 'see' initials among the mass of attendant jungle; and the probability is that, in many instances, there is indeed a meaningful monogram there, but the people for whom it had significance have long since departed this world. We shall never know for certain.

When, however, it is possible to unscramble from the maze initials that happen to be those of the maker whose name appears on the watch movement, then it is reasonably certain that this is a deliberate ploy on his part; and a number of makers did indulge their conceits in this way. The fact that this device is often found on watches made for the Turkish market offers one plausible explanation, too. The proper English name of the watchmaker had often to be represented on the watch movement in Turkish characters whose authenticity, when re-translated, was found , occasionally, to be spurious. His only means, then, of identifying one of his own movements was to build his initials into the watch decoration where it would not be recognised and challenged by foreigners, yet would preserve the integrity of his work intact. Among the makers who are known to have employed this tactic can be numbered Ralph Gout, the Prior family — John, George and Edward — and George Charle, who seems to have had some kind of business relationship with George Prior.

Finally, like the fob seals, there are plenty of examples where monograms are wholly explicit. These can form such a major part of the overall decoration that their purpose is not in doubt, or they can be a separate feature, engraved upon a reserve set into the cock table. It has been suggested that, in some cases — the less explicit examples, it might be thought — initials relate to the maker of cock and slide plate, these being his only means of identification; yet it would be much simpler to punch them on to the underside of the cock foot. This practice does, in fact, exist but examples are so very rare as to be discounted, suggesting that these craftsmen were not unduly concerned for their work to become recognised. There remains as the only other probable owner of such initials, the owner of the watch. When in doubt, accept this most likely explanation!

19 MOTTOES

Not common at any period, these nevertheless feature from time to time in all of them. Royal armorial cocks (see *Heraldry*) usually include one of the appropriate mottoes — the example illustrated shows *Semper Eadem* flanking a lightly engraved figure of St George and the Dragon — and, at a much later time, *Peace and Plenty* is a favourite maxim. *Ora Labora,* with one word either side of an open prayer book, is the pious exhortation to be found on the table of a pendulum cock of c1700. The most expected of them all — *Tempus Fugit* — seems conspicuous by its absence.

20 MUSIC

Another very popular decorative idea, and one that shares many of the conventions of the trophy of arms with which it is sometimes combined (see *Militaria*), is the musical trophy. In this, the dominant feature is always trumpets, pointing upwards to give the atmosphere of soaring fanfares. To make the impression even more vivid, the page of music itself is occasionally included; the scrolling effect is very useful as a cohesive factor.

Individual musical instruments are sometimes to be found. One example, of what is unquestionably a depiction of a harp, disguises the fore-pillar as a caryatid figure, of somewhat American Indian aspect. The lyre is another instrument to be found from time to time, which is not surprising, since it also is featured in clocks; the French even created a style known as a 'lyre clock', the association being unmistakable.

21 NAMES

The appearance of names on watch cocks is highly unusual; but where they do occur they fall into one of three fairly well-defined categories.

a) *The maker* or, at least, the craftsman who signs himself as such. Very few makers indeed seem ever to have chosen this particular site for their name, which instead is almost invariably engraved directly on to whatever surface of the back plate of the movement may remain exposed after the 'superstructure' has been added. Makers of skeletonised watches (qv) have no choice, of course, as there is no back plate, per se; so their names have to go on the cock or not be seen at all. Among those who have deliberately used the cock table, can be cited Thomas Wright in the Poultry, 'Watchmaker to the King' — George III, that is. No formal record of Appointment has come to light, however, and that is probably because Wright, like Daniel Quare before him, was a Quaker and so would not have been able to take the Oath of Allegiance. Another maker who seems always to have preferred his name on the cock table was J. Banks of Nottingham. He was active around the turn of the seventeenth century, and was probably the John Banks who is known to have received his Freedom in Chester in 1682. In both instances it is reasonable to suppose that the makers themselves must have overseen and approved the embellishment of their watch movements.

b) A *patentee* of some mechanical feature of the watch. Cocks bearing the inscriptions 'Massey's Patent' and 'Savage's Patent', both of which relate to variations of the lever escapement, are recorded but not, be it noted, on watches made by those particular makers themselves. It is clear, therefore, that by the early nineteenth century — the period of these examples — the law relating to patents was being scrupulously observed, which had not always been the case in the previous hundred years.

c) *The owner* — one must assume. Watch cocks do sometimes occur with a name added, usually, to the cock foot. This can be either on a specially provided panel left vacant for it, or on the chamfered outer edge of the foot, which has been specially polished prior to engraving. All sort of arguments have been advanced as to the ownership of such names: there are those who say that they relate to the maker of the cock and slide plate, or the finisher of the movement; but there is no evidence to support any such conclusion. Indeed, it is very unlikely that such craftsmen would have been permitted this degree of ostentation, for cocks like these appear on movements that have been 'signed' in the conventional way, but with, of course, a different name. The only option left, therefore, is the assumption that they belong to the owner. It is also worthy of note that these names have been added to the cock *ab initio,* for the gilding runs over the top of them with no variation in colour. Presumably, then, as some kind of protection against loss or theft — a modern equivalent might be the facility to have the registration number of one's car etched on to all the windows — as well as to aid identification if such a tragedy occurred, it was possible to order this feature at the time the watch itself was commissioned.

22 ODDS AND ECCENTRICITIES

Especially in the later periods, there will always be watch cocks using patterns of decoration that are so rare that only one example may ever be encountered. These do not readily lend themselves to the sort of classification adopted up to this point, and when combined also with some quite unconventional shape, they sometimes almost defy description.

All, therefore, that can be achieved here is to cite some of the rarer examples, culled not only from surviving specimens but also from published illustrations of famous collections going back to the early part of the present century.

Spikes   When the wedge-shaped cock was in its infancy the strong outline of the cock table was, very occasionally indeed, allowed to give way to a border of spikes — for want of a better term.

Inverted wedges   Perhaps to vary the wedge-of-cheese outline that was to become the eventual shape of the watch cock, even after all attempts at decoration had disappeared, an inverted outline was attempted. It cannot be pretended that this was a very happy form, but at least it was different.

Rectangles   Again, perhaps as a relief from the ubiquitous wedge, some late cocks adopted a rectangular table; in extreme cases the foot was also rectangular, thus minimising the mechanical rigidity that was, or should have been, a prerequisite of this component, when in position.

Crowns and crescents   As reflected in watch cock design, these outlines are inversions of one another, or almost so. The crescent seems to have been an extension of the 'ears' of an earlier shape, and indeed, given sufficient examples, it is possible to detect the gradual development of this feature from a point in the second half of the eighteenth century to another, quite late, part of the nineteenth.

Transitionals   Long before the wedge-shaped cock table came into general use, it was being delineated on the circular table that was still in vogue. Examples of this are not uncommon, but rarely recognised for what they were — the shape of things to come.

Mechanical symbolism   A very rare cock indeed — only a single specimen at present recorded — apparently sets out to reflect what is going on immediately beneath itself. It has to be said that it is hardly more than an artist's impression, which cannot be praised for its accuracy. Nevertheless, it does appear to depict the spiral balance spring and six arms — or spokes — of the balance itself. On the cock foot, two wheels seem to be trying, not very successfully, to mesh. Even so, it is a remarkably effective design and cannot have been easy to make.

Fantasies   The outline of the cock table is, on occasion, given over to the motif used to decorate it, presumably to heighten the effect. The phoenix rising from the flames is one example. A cut-out star is sometimes seen, and the foul anchor, also cut out, can be found. There are many others.

23 PATRIOTICS

On an occasional nineteenth-century watch cock can be seen the figure of Britannia, looking much as on contemporary coinage. This is thought to be the only design in which the Union flag is depicted, and then only on the subject's shield.

24 PORTRAITS

This is an omnibus classification, to include all the representations of human faces that commonly occur on watch cocks, apart from classic ornamental devices such as *putti,* and masks (qv); both these categories can, on occasion, be far from human. The more generally occurring examples fall usually into the following classes:

a) *Named portraits* — see *Commemoratives*
b) *Unidentified portraits*   These are reasonably commonly found on the cock table, where they can occupy either of two positions. Below centre, and generally covering the neck as well, the portrait is almost invariably set in profile and within an oval medallion against a matted, or sometimes a hatched or 'brickwork' ground. When, rarely, a portrait head is allowed to be free-standing against the surrounding decoration, it can be remarkably attractive. Some collectors purport to identify such images solely from their appearance, the appropriate king — often George IV — and Nelson being among their favourite choices. It is suggested, however, that this is a practice to be avoided, since it is incapable of proof; the images are so tiny that perhaps 'impressions' might be a better description of them, and this alone makes such attributions susceptible to an unacceptable degree of doubt. The longest dimension of this version is usually 3/8in (9·5mm).

The second position for such images on the table is above centre; when they occupy this site, 'tiny' becomes an understatement. They are minute. This is a much rarer variety than the previous one and, in technical terms, almost always free-standing albeit in a cut-out frame. One-fifth of an inch (5mm) is usually the largest dimension of these miniatures; and not even the most optimistic would attempt to assign any specific identities to them.

Finally, and easily the rarest of all — but possibly because they are not intended to be readily seen — is the 'sideways-on' portrait. Lay the cock at ninety degrees to its natural orientation — that is to say, with the foot on the left and the table on the right — and sometimes, in the width of the neck, there will be found a profile outlined. Because of spatial limitations, the modelling of these leaves much to be desired. However, good examples cannot be mistaken. Again, any attempt at identification can be nothing but highly speculative.

So far, only portrait heads have been considered. The portrait bust — full head and shoulders — can also be encountered and, at its best, has a classical flavour that is very appealing. One seen recently on a cock of date c1720 depicted a female, décolleté, but with just the topmost drapes of her low-cut dress showing, these flowing from a mid-breast medallion; the lady also had some sort of headgear, which could have been either a 'pill-box' hat or possibly a hairband. Portrait busts are extraordinarily rare, even so, but may appear either above or below the centre of the cock table.

25 PRINCE OF WALES'S PLUMES

In bygone days it seems to have been commonplace for crafts to make whatever personal use of royal insignia could prove most profitable; permission seems never to have been sought, or demanded. There are many thousands of watch papers — those printed wafers placed between the inner and outer cases of pair-cased watches, to ensure a tight fit — on which the royal arms is shown in association with a watchmaker having no pretensions whatsoever to any connection with the reigning house. This state of affairs persisted, so it would seem, until as late as 1883, when Section 106 of the Patents, Designs and Trade Marks Act (46 and 47 Victoria Cap. 57) imposed a fine not exceeding £20 on the summary conviction of anyone for using the royal arms without authority.

So with the Prince of Wales's Plumes — they are often to be found on watch cocks, usually in later rather than earlier periods, and in various locations on the cock. Quite often, although their identity is beyond question, they are so insignificant — because of small size, or inferior workmanship — as to contribute nothing whatever to the overall effect. At their best, they make an attractive subsidiary feature; they cannot stand on their own.

26 SCALLOPS AND SNAILS

The scallop shell has been a favourite ornament since classical times and on many classes of artifacts, including ceramics, silver and furniture. The rare mezzotint portrait of John Ellicott, George III's watchmaker, shows his arm resting on the corner of a table whose cabriole leg has, at its knee, one of the finest carved scallop shells anyone could hope to find. Similarly with watch cocks, the scallop shell can, at its best, provide a focus of attention on an otherwise not specially notable specimen. Like the mask, the scallop was early to emerge from the jungle, and at least one example exists where the artist has tried — not very convincingly — to combine the two together or, at least, that is the impression given.

The snail, generally in its shell, is a later development. Even the term 'snail' is one of convenience, since the spiral whorls are usually all that can be seen of this gastropod mollusc, making finer identification impossible. Even at its best, it is not capable of any great visual impact.

27 SKELETONS

This category is not concerned with the representation of the human or animal frame in its most primordial state, but with the so-called 'skeletonised' watch movements. In these, the mechanism has been deliberately stripped down to the barest possible essentials, presumably to facilitate observation of the machine in action. To this end, one of the main members of the frame — the back or potence plate — is cut away to such an extent that, in extreme cases, it virtually disappears and all the pivots of the gearing that it would normally carry are, instead, planted in brackets springing from the remaining one, which is usually called the pillar plate.

The effect of this is to reduce the space for decoration to a minimum, and the most that can be hoped for is some small stylised treatment of the cocks and bridges that replace the back plate. Even the maker's name has to take second place to the achievement of this rare, but dramatic, effect, and is usually relegated to a place on the cock table, the only flat space left available. It is said that most skeletonised watch movements are of Swiss origin, but even so, they form a well-recognised element in the later eighteenth-century English watchmaking scene.

28 SNAKES AND SERPENTS

The immediate impression conjured up by snakes is one of writhing, entwining creatures — and so they invariably appear in watch cock decoration, even if there is only one of them! Usually seen to best advantage on later cocks — late eighteenth- and early nineteenth-century examples are commonest — they are frequently isolated on a matt ground around and above the neck, this surface often shaped into a reserve to give it impact. However, the modelling of the reptiles, on such a small scale, quite often leaves much to be desired; sometimes they appear as little better than earthworms wearing a snake's head mask.

The other common form of serpentine decoration is the self-consuming snake, which appears to be swallow-ing its own tail. The resulting circular effect makes an excellent framing device for other motifs.

29 SOLDIERY (SEE ALSO MILITARIA)

It is very rare indeed to find a representation of a contemporary uniformed soldier on a watch cock, but they do exist. The one illustrated is as good an example as is to be seen. An infantryman, long-barrelled musket over his shoulder and caught in mid-pace, the plumed headgear and essential lines of the uniform have been well captured, considering the scale. The entire figure, from the tip of the plume to the sole of the boot, is exactly ½in (12·5mm).

Classical soldiery, on the other hand, is not all that uncommon. Usually, this motif takes the form of a helmeted head only, the general impression leaning more, perhaps, towards the Shakespearian stage costume than the genuine article. The impact, however, can be quite striking.

30 SYMMETRICAL GEOMETRY

In terms of sheer industry per square millimetre of surface area, those cocks that can be classified under this heading must rate among the most complicated of all. One of the commonest is that type which displays a star — generally six-pointed — as its central feature. Others have complex patterns of pierced and engraved decoration such that, in most cases, it would be difficult, if not impossible, to find a universally understood term to describe them. There does appear to be one well-defined type that might have been inspired by the high-powered magnification of snowflakes. Others seem to reflect wave patterns and swirls; others again may have a basis in the possible variations of a spoked wheel. Most, perhaps, are simply patterns of minute holes, with usually not even peripheral ornament to hold them together. None of these forms of decoration can be immediately related to other classes of artifacts, yet clearly they enjoyed enormous popularity and they appeared constantly during the last quarter of the eighteenth, and the early part of the nineteenth centuries.

31 TEMPLES AND TOMBS

Part of the idyllic scene, so often regenerated in watch cock decoration, is the small classical temple — or is it really a folly? Usually represented in the most simplistic manner — columns surmounted by a half-round cupola — the temple occurs most often below the centre of the cock table and rarely enjoys sufficient separation from its

COLOUR PLATE 15: In the latter half of the eighteenth and first half of the nineteenth centuries, painted watch dials offered as great an opportunity for naive art as did underpainted horn watchcases. In this selection, farming scenes and country pursuits vie with the Industrial Revolution, in the form of an early railway train, for the admiration of the viewer.

surroundings to afford it any real 'personality'.

The tomb is one of those speculative identifications for which only the evidence of one's eyes exists. In one example shown, an open book — the Bible, perhaps? — surmounts a pair of closed doors, at the top of a grand staircase flanked by columns. A mausoleum, surely? Or are the 'doors' merely the base of a lectern? The only certainty is that this is symbolism of some kind, and eventually it will be revealed.

32 Urns, Vases, Baskets and Cornucopiae

Properly speaking, an urn has to be wide-mouthed, with a cover, and of round or ovoid form, with two handles and a foot. It was used for the ashes of the dead. If anything can be so-described, such elements were the essential paraphernalia of watch cock decoration. When nothing else presents itself, it is so easy to site one of these on the neck of a cock, allowing all the other decoration to spring from it, incongruous though some of this may be. Urns are found open or covered, free-standing among other decorations or placed in a shaped reserve or on an oval medallion. All these elements are among the most common features on the cock over a long period and, often enough, serve no other purpose than as space-fillers. The cornucopia, or horn of plenty, was associated in classical times with the goddess Ceres.

Colour Plate 16:The magnificent watch garniture presented by Louis XVI to Queen Charlotte, wife of George III. It is easy, from this illustration to believe the report that this object incorporates over three thousand rose-diamonds and some six hundred and fifty brilliants.

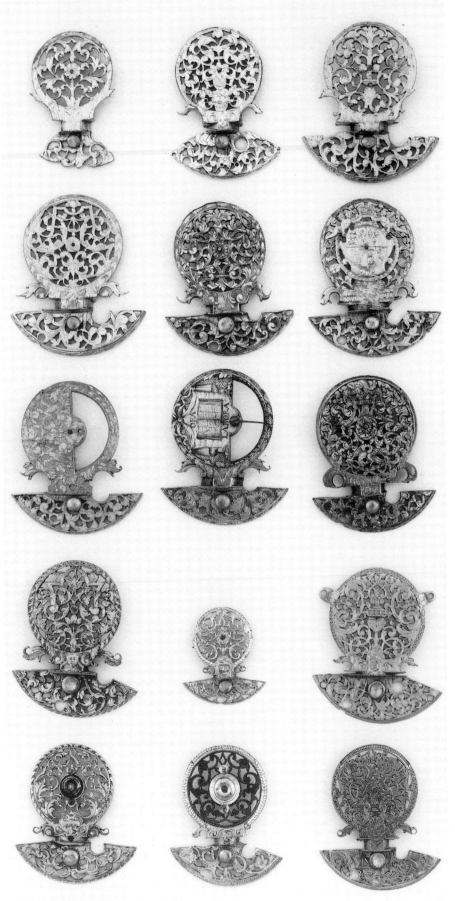

PLATE 87:

TOP ROW: The wavy edge to the foot and noticeable ears of the first example clearly suggest the 1680s, while the widening splay and streamers of the second indicate a decade later. By 1700, the splay of the foot has stretched to its fullest extent, where it was to remain for the next twenty years. There is a charming child's head mask on the second specimen, from a watch by Thomas Windmills.

SECOND ROW: Different designs of streamers, sometimes called wings, and otherwise conventional period decoration save for the royal arms on the third example, with the motto 'Semper Eadem' flanking a St George and the Dragon, faintly cut and only just detectable in the original. This version of the arms was used during the period 1707–14.

THIRD ROW: Two pendulum cocks, one inscribed 'Ora Labora' flanking a depiction of a prayer book. A tiny head of a child nestles among the birds and foliage on the other. The third has a predatory bird at the top of the table, presiding over the conventional foliate decor while, below centre, his mate preens. The streamers include dogs' heads, on the first pendulum cock.

FOURTH ROW: These three cocks show the gradual narrowing of the foot, usually from the right-hand side, which post-dates c1720. There is also a noticeable size difference, and the middle specimen must have been taken from a lady's watch. The right-hand example has the cranked lugs for extra rigidity favoured by, among other makers, Daniel Quare, for his most accurate watches. All three cocks have children's heads in the conventional 'mask' position.

BOTTOM ROW: The central cock has a table centre of blued-steel fitted into the gilt bezel, and a rather primitive and large bearing for the balance pivot; the more usual version of this last feature can be seen in the first example. All three cocks have masks at the neck, the last with 'hair' which resembles the ribs of a cockleshell — another conventional motif for this position. Perhaps the decorator changed his mind!

PLATE 88:

TOP AND SECOND ROWS: An endless variety of depictions of faces occupied the 'mask' position on the neck of the cock, as these examples show. The first cock in each row incorporates the heads of grotesque creatures, nicely executed in the first and perfunctory in the second.

THIRD ROW: These three cocks represent a class that occurs in enormous numbers on mid-eighteenth-century watches, any differences being wholly attributable to hand-working. The late Colonel A. S. Bates who formed the largest collection in England of these attractive objects, reckoned to have amassed more than forty specimens in which differences were almost negligible, and this he regarded as evidence for the existence of pattern books at that period, even though none seems to have survived.

FOURTH ROW: The first cock incorporates a nice classical helmeted head and also possesses a feature commonly found, in the shape of a small chamfered area springing from the edge of the cock foot and often, as in this case, having different decoration. This was needed to provide clearance for the tail of the cap spring screw, on watch movements supplied with dust caps. The second and third cocks, although they do not show up in the picture, both possess raised bosses in the table centres, these standing proud of the surrounding surface by as much as $1/16$in (1·5mm).

BOTTOM ROW: All three cocks are of the type familiarly known as 'lace-edged'. This pierced ornament can extend around the edges of both foot and table, as in the first example — in which case, it would certainly also extend along the edge of the slide plate — or it can be confined simply to the table edge, as in the other examples. The foot is found either pierced or solid, and will occasionally be used as the site for a name, as in the third example. As this type of cock is wholly restricted to a handful of years around 1760, it seems likely that the number '1759' included in this last, is actually the date of it, rather than the serial number of the watch.

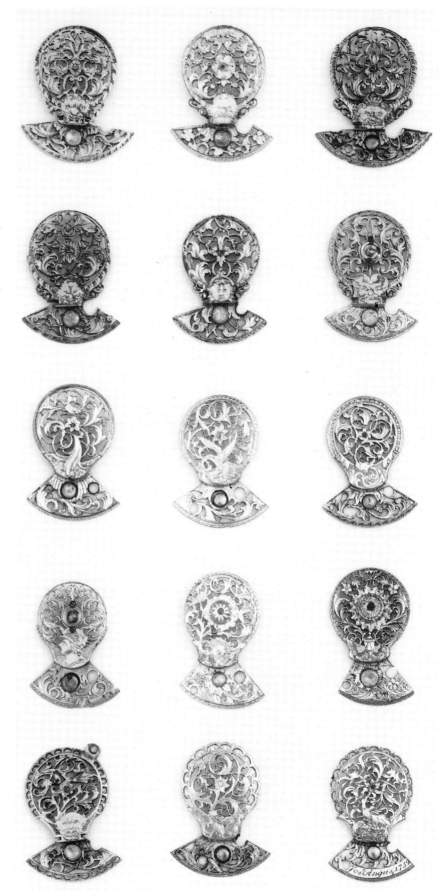

PLATE 89:

TOP ROW: Engraved portrait heads usually feature on oval reserves; occasionally, as in the first example, they are free-standing. The association of a crown and military symbolism, in the third example, might suggest that the portrait represents the King, possibly George IV.

SECOND ROW: Portraits sited at the top of the table are usually of little significance. Next to it, the squirrel and predatory bird are far better depicted. The shaped reserve with matt ground on the last cock contains rather crude representations of marine life, including sea monsters and shells.

THIRD ROW: In a reserve of the same character as the previous example, swims a swan. Caged lions can be above or below centre. The last cock shows the head of some imaginary creature, of fearsome mien.

FOURTH ROW: Three examples of military symbolism including one with two separate trophies of arms, above and below the table centre. The last cock has quite a good version of the Prince of Wales's Plumes with, below centre, an unusual musical trophy of a lyre with two clarinets, possibly reflecting a military band.

BOTTOM ROW: Four masks, different though they are, give only a slight impression of the enormous range of versions of this motif.

PLATE 90: Some examples of the more out-of-the-way motifs that enlivened watch cocks at the end of the eighteenth century and during the first two or three decades that followed.

TOP ROW: A design based on the large and ornate wheels of a state coach, is followed by one incorporating a harp with human fore-pillar. Next comes an infantryman marching with rifle at the slope, and then a strange complex of royal symbolism which includes the cypher 'GR' and motto 'Dieu et mon Droit'.

SECOND ROW: The explosion of flowers seen on some early dials is recollected in the well-conceived design of the first example; next, the Craven Heifer with, above, an entwined monogram 'IH', and, finally, two farmyard scenes, probably by the same hand, despite obvious differences in content.

THIRD ROW: Two commemorative cocks bearing inscribed portraits, of Burns and Franklin; a cock that is probably designed to imitate the spiral balance spring sited immediately beneath it; and a nursery rhyme version, with spider's web, fly and predatory bird.

FOURTH ROW: The first two cocks have masonic connotations, featuring prominently the tools of the craft — set square, protractor, dividers and so on. The succeeding two cocks might also seem to have some inherent meaning, although it is not clear what it might be.

BOTTOM ROW: A beautiful Sun-face on the first cock makes it worthy of note; the remaining three all have astronomical or astrological symbolism. On the second cock, the planet signs running clockwise from 'GS' — whatever that might mean — represent Venus, Saturn, perhaps the Moon although the more usual version is a crescent, Mars, Jupiter and Mercury, with the Sun at the centre. The last two cocks have shaped reserves, one like a shield, upon which astronomical bodies stand out from a matted ground. The first of these also features a bird surmounting a cornucopia.

PLATE 91:

TOP ROW: Variants of the central star motif found frequently upon cocks dating from the end of the eighteenth century and later. Usually six-pointed, the fourth example has eight points. The almost filigree effect of the second example is especially attractive.

SECOND ROW: Yet another example of the star motif is followed by one perhaps inspired by leaves blowing in the wind; the curlicues of the third are uncommon, and the last is probably the most interesting of them all, as an attempt has been made — surprisingly successfully — to impart some three-dimensional modelling to the simplicity of two leaf fronds. Although this hardly shows up in a photograph, it is very effective in reality.

THIRD, FOURTH AND BOTTOM ROWS: All these examples are of symmetrical abstract patterns apart from the first, which is a simple 'ring o' roses'. Once again, varieties of this concept are legion, some very coarse, being little more than patterns of holes. Some of the versions illustrated have merit; the spiralling snowflakes at the beginning of the fourth row, and the breaking waves immediately below it, reveal exercise of the artistic imagination.

PLATE 92:

TOP ROW: This demonstrates the scale of commonly encountered watch cocks. The longest dimension of the largest example is exactly 2in (50mm); of the smallest, 7/8in (22mm). The decoration is quite conventional.

SECOND ROW: The first example has a glass over the table, held in place with a retaining screw in the neck. Both this and the one that follows have monograms worked into the table — 'TS' and 'TW' respectively. The last two have monograms above the table centre 'ID' and 'IH', seemingly.

THIRD ROW: Two cocks have been laid on their sides to permit easier recognition of the two mystery faces profiled at their necks; both somewhat resemble ships' figureheads, and this may not be too fanciful a connection. The remaining three cocks each have a name inscribed upon them: the first, 'Wright, Watchmaker to the King', is the usual version to be found on the products of this fine maker, Thomas Wright, who had premises in the Poultry, and held the Royal Warrant of George III. Its two unusual features are its small size, and the straight edge to the foot, this last almost always betokening its original home as the special kind of timepiece used in sedan-chairs. The two following cocks have names inscribed on their feet, viz 'Jas. Stewart' and 'Jas. Diack', neither being recognisably that of a maker.

FOURTH ROW: The first cock has a rotatable table centre to which is attached the index for the balance spring regulator; this registers on a scale around the neck of the cock, which also has two cranked lugs for extra rigidity. The second cock has been gilded but remains totally plain; its shape proclaims the turn of the eighteenth century. The last two cocks include in their decoration the Prince of Wales's Plumes and a patera, and in the second, a splendid mollusc.

BOTTOM ROW: A great many cocks with the conventional round table seem to have contrived to predict, within their decoration, the shape of things to come; these four all incorporate wedge-shaped designs stretching up from the neck, so that, were the table to be cut back to those outlines, the results would be wholly nineteenth century in appearance. Apart from this, motifs include a spiralling snake on the second specimen, and a crown on the last.

PLATE 93: In the nineteenth century, attention turned to the possibility of changing the outline of the cock, and all sorts of exotic shapes appeared. There is no particular reason why the table has to be round other than to provide the maximum protection for the balance wheel immediately beneath it; and although it might seem obvious that the rigidity of this component depended largely upon a substantial anchorage through the foot, even this part was not immune from change.

TOP ROW: The two examples in the middle have integral regulators to act on the balance spring; at either end, unusual outlines.

SECOND ROW: The fourth example shows how fashions spread. It was not originally made in this shape, and has been cut down from a cock with a conventional round table; this is immediately clear even from a casual examination of the uneven edge, with its absence of gilding.

THIRD ROW: The squirrel reappears as a motif on the first example, but the phoenix on the third is quite new. The fourth specimen might possibly have been taken from a skeletonised movement, qv.

FOURTH ROW: The move towards the wedge-shaped cock is becoming apparent. Piercing on the first example is a pleasant throwback to better times; the second has agricultural implications, with its rake and sickle protruding from behind a stook of sheaves. The third is from a Liverpool-made watch — 'PATENT' on the foot of this style of cock almost always refers to one of the types of lever watches being made there in the early part of the last century — and the last probably comes from the same area, the lion being particularly jolly.

BOTTOM ROW: Another Liverpool cock has a somewhat effete stork holding a ribbon inscribed 'Peace and Plenty' which, as everybody knows, is normally held to be 'the Reward of Temperance'. With the true wedge shape now more than ever in evidence, the next example has a rare portrayal of Britannia — or could it be Boadicea? — with marine creatures on the foot. The last two specimens exhibit machine engraving of a stylised form which, complex though it appears, is surprisingly repellent in comparison with what has gone before.

Summarised Bibliography

Most sources quoted are identified in the text but, for ease of reference, those that have been found more generally useful are listed below.

BAILLIE, G. H. *Watches: their History, Decoration and Mechanism* (1929)

BAILLIE, G. H., ILBERT, C. A. and CLUTTON, C. *Britten's Old Clocks and Watches and their Makers* (9th edition revised by Clutton, 1982)

BASSERMANN-JORDAN, E. VON and BERTELE, H. VON. *Uhren* (1961)

BENJAMIN, Susan. *English Enamel Boxes* (1984)

BENEZIT, E. *Dictionnaire des Peintres, Sculpteurs, Dessinateurs et Graveurs* (1976)

BREWSTER, David. (Conducted by) *The Edinburgh Encyclopaedia* (1816)

BRITTEN, F. J. *Old Clocks and Watches and their Makers* (6th edition, 1932)

BRITTEN, F. J. *Watch and Clockmakers' Handbook, Dictionary and Guide* (10th edition 1902)

BROMLEY, John, *The Clockmakers' Library* (1977)

BRUSA, Giuseppe. *L'Arte dell' Orologeria in Europa* (1978)

Bryan's Dictionary of Painters and Engravers (1964)

BUTTERS, Laurence. (Revised by) *Fairbairn's Crests of the Families of Great Britain and Ireland* (1986)

CAMERER CUSS, T. A. *The Camerer Cuss Book of Antique Watches* (1976)

CAMPBELL, R. *The London Tradesman* (1747)

CARDINAL, Catherine. *La Montre des Origines au XIXe siècle* (1986)

CHAMBERLAIN, Paul. *It's about Time* (1941)

CLUTTON, C. and DANIELS, G. *The Clockmakers' Company Collection* (1975)

CLUTTON, Cecil and DANIELS, George. *Watches: a complete history of the technical and decorative development of the Watch* (1979)

COLLINS, A. J. *The Jewels and Plate of Queen Elizabeth I: The Inventory of 1574* (1955)

COLLYER, J. *The Parents' and Guardians' Directory and the Youth's Guide in the Choice of a Profession or Trade* (1761)

DIDEROT et D'ALAMBERT *La Grande Encyclopaedie* (1751–72)

FLEMING, John and HONOUR, Hugh. *The Penguin Dictionary of Decorative Arts* (1979)

FOX-DAVIES, A. C. *Armorial Families* (1902)

GÉLIS, Edouard. *L'Horlogerie Ancienne* (1949)

HAYWARD, J. F. *English Watches* (1956)

HUGHES, Thurle and Bernard. *English Painted Enamels* (1967)

JONES, Owen. *The Grammar of Ornament* (1910)

KEARSLEY, G. (Printed for) *The English Encyclopaedia* (1802)

LEITER, Alfred and HELFRICH-DÖRNER, Dr. *Die Uhr* (1967)

LOOMES, Brian. *The Early Clockmakers of Great Britain* (1981)

MARTIN, Thomas. *The Circle of the Mechanical Arts* (1813)

OSBORNE, Harold (Ed by) *The Oxford Companion to the Decorative Arts* (1975)

OWEN, W. (Printed for) *A New and Complete Dictionary of Arts and Sciences* (1754)

PAPWORTH, J. W. and MORANT, A. S. *An Alphabetical Dictionary of Coats of Arms . . . Ordinary of British Armorials* (1874)

PIPPA, Luigi. *Masterpieces of Watchmaking* (1966)

REES, Abraham. *The Cyclopaedia: or Universal Dictionary of Arts, Sciences and Literature* (1805–18)

SPELTZ, Alexander. (Revised by R. P. Spiers) *The Styles of Ornament* (1910)

STALKER, John and PARKER, George. *A Treatise of Japaning and Varnishing* (1688)

TAIT, Hugh. *Clocks and Watches* [in the British Museum] (1983)

WARD, James. *Elementary Principles of Ornament* (1890)

WEISS, Leonard. *Watch-Making in England: 1760–1820* (1982)

WILLSBERGER, Johann. *Zauberhafte Gehäuse der Zeit* (1974)

Extensive use has also been made of long runs of catalogues of specialist sales conducted by the principal London auctioneers, as well as those of relevant exhibitions mounted by national and other museums in England, especially including 'Rococo — Art and Design in Hogarth's England', which was shown at the Victoria & Albert Museum in 1984.

Index